D0559299

The Modern Presidency & Civil Rights

NUMBER THREE
Presidential Rhetoric Series

Martin J. Medhurst, General Editor

In association with
The Center for Presidential Studies,
George Bush School
of Government and Public Service

The Modern Presidency & Civil Rights

Rhetoric on Race from Roosevelt to Nixon

GARTH E. PAULEY

Texas A&M University Press
College Station

PROPERTY OF THE LIBRARY
YORK COUNTY COMMUNITY COLLEGE
112 COLLEGE DRIVE
WELLS, MAINE 04090
(207) 646-9282

Copyright © 2001 by the Program in Presidential Rhetoric
Manufactured in the United States of America
All rights reserved
First edition

The paper used in this book meets the minimum requirements
of the American National Standard for Permanence
of Paper for Printed Library Materials, z39.48-1984.
Binding materials have been chosen for durability.

∞

Library of Congress Cataloging-in-Publication Data

Pauley, Garth E., 1971–
　　The modern presidency and civil rights : rhetoric on race from
　Roosevelt to Nixon / Garth E. Pauley.
　　　　p.　cm.—(Presidential rhetoric series ; no. 3)
　　Includes bibliographical references and index.
　　ISBN 1-58544-107-4 (alk. paper)
　　　1. Presidents—United States—Racial attitudes.　2. Presidents—
　United States—Language.　3. Rhetoric—Political aspects—United
　States.　4. Political oratory—United States—History—20th century.
　5. Communication in politics—United States—History—20th century.
　6. United States—Race relations—Political aspects.　7. Afro-Americans—
　Civil rights—History—20th century.　8. United States—Politics and
　government—1945–1989.　9. Political culture—United States—History—
　20th century.　I. Title　II. Series.
　E176.1.P3946　2001
　323.1'73'0904—dc21　　　　　　　　　　　　　00-010637

Contents

Acknowledgments

An earlier version of chapter two appeared as "Harry Truman and the NAACP: A Case Study in Presidential Persuasion on Civil Rights," *Rhetoric and Public Affairs* 2 (1999): 211–41, copyright 1999 by Michigan State University Press; used by permission. An earlier version of chapter five appeared as "Rhetoric and Timeliness: An Analysis of Lyndon B. Johnson's Voting Rights Address," *Western Journal of Communication* 62 (1998): 26–53, copyright 1998 by the Western States Communication Association; used by permission.

Although I cannot possibly thank all the individuals who helped me with this book, a number deserve special mention.

First, I thank the members of my doctoral committee at the Pennsylvania State University, where this book took its initial form as a Ph.D. dissertation. Friendly encouragement and pointed intellectual prodding from Stephen Browne, Richard Gregg, and Jeffrey Walker helped make this project meaningful and enjoyable. My advisor, Thomas Benson, has been an extraordinary editor, teacher, mentor, and friend. His example of intellectual curiosity and generosity serves as a model for my scholarly life.

Second, I thank the archivists and organizations that help preserve the nation's presidential history. The Harry S. Truman Library Institute provided a grant that allowed me to conduct research at the Truman Library during the summer of 1998. Their generous support helped me refine my analysis of President Truman's civil rights rhetoric. The staff of the Franklin D. Roosevelt Library, the Harry S. Truman Library, the Dwight D. Eisenhower Library, the John F. Kennedy Library, and the Lyndon B. Johnson Library lent me their skills and knowledge. Archivists Dennis Bilger, Barbara Constable, and Allen Fisher were especially patient, generous, and cheerful.

Finally, I thank Kathi Groenendyk—to whom this book is dedicated. Kathi deserves more praise and adoration than she receives for the intellectual counsel and editorial services she has provided throughout my scholarly endeavors. Moreover, her emotional support kept me sane—usually—during the research and writing of this book.

**The Modern
Presidency
& Civil Rights**

PROPERTY OF THE LIBRARY
YORK COUNTY COMMUNITY COLLEGE
112 COLLEGE DRIVE
WELLS, MAINE 04090
(207) 646-9282

CHAPTER ONE

Presidents, Race, and Rhetoric

Near the height of the civil rights controversy during the Kennedy administration, Louis Martin—an African American aide JFK asked to read the pulse of the black community—drafted a memorandum that emphasized the importance of the American presidency in the civil rights struggle: "Traditionally most of the agitation of Negroes over abuses of their civil rights have been directed toward the White House. Since the time of Lincoln, Negroes have looked to the White House for hope and redress of their grievances."[1] Historians, too, have noted that the drive for civil rights now centers largely on the presidency and that where presidential involvement was once brief and intermittent, it is now direct, inevitable, and enduring.[2] James MacGregor Burns calls the modern presidency "the most effective single protector of individual liberty in our governmental system" and claims that presidential protection of civil rights has become institutional rather than personal.[3] Presidential scholar Richard Longaker notes that the modern American presidency has been forced into the field of civil rights primarily because of the influence of the Cold War, the political power of minorities, and the limits on the other branches of government.[4] The nation's intensified commitment to democratic ideals in the wake of World War II also has expanded presidential involvement in civil rights matters. As a result of circumstances, prior presidential action, and citizen demands, modern presidents inevitably confront civil rights issues during their tenure in the White House.

Modern American presidents also inevitably face demands that they speak publicly about the nation's racial problems. This book is an inquiry into that unique kind of presidential action on racial issues—modern presidents' communicative and symbolic involvement in civil rights matters. A significant

3

dimension of the presidency's involvement in civil rights is public discourse: presidential rhetoric on racial matters has the potential to educate the American public, to effect legislative change, and to inspire the African American community to continue its activism. While civil rights protesters have urged presidents to act, many also have accentuated the importance of a rhetorical commitment to their cause. For example, many civil rights activists lauded Harry Truman very early in his administration, in spite of little executive action, because of his strong public discourse. Truman's vocal support for civil rights was a noticeable contrast to Franklin Roosevelt, who had said very little about racial issues. Noticing President Truman's departure from Roosevelt's relative silence, the *Kansas City Call,* an African American newspaper, claimed, "Since the Missourian has been in the White House, there has been no occasion for Negroes to sigh, 'If only the president would speak out!'"[5] Civil rights advocates did lament, however, that Truman's successor did not speak out with force: they demanded that Dwight Eisenhower make a public statement in support of the 1954 Supreme Court decision in *Brown v. Board of Education.* Although President Eisenhower helped ensure passage of two civil rights laws during his administration, many African Americans condemned him because he failed to make a strong rhetorical commitment.

Eisenhower's successor, John F. Kennedy, was berated by many African Americans for equivocating in his public rhetoric on civil rights: His strong public statement on June 11, 1963, was a turning point in his relationship with civil rights supporters. Many blacks worried that southerner Lyndon Johnson would slow civil rights progress upon assuming the presidency; his legislative performance soon calmed most fears. So, too, did his forceful public discourse. When, on March 15, 1965, Johnson proclaimed, "We shall overcome"—the anthem of the civil rights movement—National Association for the Advancement of Colored People (NAACP) executive secretary Roy Wilkins claimed, "I had waited all my life to hear a president of the United States talk that way."[6]

More recently, public discourse became the centerpiece of the presidential civil rights agenda. The President's Initiative on Race and Reconciliation—which Bill Clinton introduced in June, 1997, to improve race relations through "thoughtful study, constructive dialogue, and positive action"—emphasized creating and sustaining a conversation about race relations. Clinton's own public communication, including his commencement address at the University of California at San Diego and his speech in Arkansas on the fortieth anniversary of the integration of Little Rock's Central High School, was an important part of his race initiative. In his June 14, 1997, speech in San Diego, Clinton promised "to lead the American people in a great and unprecedented conversation about race." The president also aimed to get citizens talking to each other about racial issues through a series of town hall meetings and local dialogues and hoped to educate the public through regular reports from his Advisory Board on Race Relations, headed by distinguished historian John Hope Franklin. Neither Franklin nor Clinton argued that talk alone will fully resolve America's racial difficulties, but the White House did claim that the "discussion alone could have long-lasting value."[7]

Yet many of the president's critics charged that his race initiative was "nothing but talk," which many of the initiative's critics argue is unhelpful for solving the nation's racial problems.[8] For example, Gerald Reynolds, president of the conservative Center for New Black Leadership, and former House speaker Newt Gingrich argued that a national dialogue is not what is needed now.[9] Harvard historian Stephan Thernstrom suggested that a public discussion could make race relations worse and that the nation might be better off if it took a break from the divisive issue of race: "Having a dialogue on race may be exactly the wrong way to go about it." Some civil rights leaders, too, expressed reservations about the race initiative's focus on public discussion, worrying that Clinton's plan would be merely "an exercise in feel-good rhetoric, with no action."[10] In contrast, Georgetown University professor of government Stephen Wayne claimed that the president can function as a public educator by trying to change biases and attitudes—a role important apart from any connection to public policy.[11]

The discourse surrounding Clinton's race initiative exhibits a set of critical *topoi,* or topics for criticizing public discourse, that have been a feature of nearly every public discussion about presidential leadership on racial issues: a disjunction between rhetoric and action, a dispute about the value of talk itself, a debate about the timing of presidential discourse, and a disagreement about the saliency of civil rights as a problem. Throughout the modern presidency, critics have decried chief executives for failing to back up their words with deeds but also for failing to complement their actions with strong, supportive rhetoric. Some critics of presidential leadership on civil rights have questioned whether discourse can make a difference at all, even when connected to policy, while advocates of strong presidential leadership argue that discourse makes all the difference in the world. Civil rights advocates have regularly berated presidents for speaking too late, while those resistant to civil rights reform have frequently condemned them for acting prematurely. In the modern era, the public expects the president to act to solve social problems, but the public does not perceive all troubling conditions as social problems. It is precisely at those moments when troubling social conditions are not perceived as public problems that rhetorical leadership can make a significant difference, but it is also at those moments when the public might react most strongly against a president's definition of a problem. The challenge of rhetorical leadership on civil rights for the modern presidency can be stated simply as a question, yet it is a complicated and difficult question to answer: What are the purposes and possibilities of presidential discourse on racial matters?

This book is an inquiry into that general question, focusing specifically on four significant speeches on civil rights by modern American presidents. Its perspective is both historical and critical. The study is grounded in the assumption that the analysis of multiple instances of presidential speech may yield insights into the history of presidents' rhetorical management of civil rights issues and into the general nature of presidential civil rights rhetoric. In other words, I hope to inform the reader of an unfolding presidential discourse on race in the modern era and to indicate the promise and limitations of presidential talk with regard to civil rights. The modern civil rights movement had its genesis during the presidency of Franklin Roosevelt and declined during Richard Nixon's presidency: never was the expectation that a president should speak out on civil rights so urgent as it was during the era between the Roosevelt and Nixon administrations. Each of the four intervening presidents delivered an address on civil rights that is historically and rhetorically significant. Thus, we will examine in detail four significant episodes of American presidential civil rights discourse: Harry S. Truman's June 29, 1947, address to the National Association for the Advancement of Colored People; Dwight D. Eisenhower's September 24, 1957, national address following the integration crisis at Little Rock, Arkansas; John F. Kennedy's June 11, 1963, speech that labeled civil rights as primarily a moral issue; and Lyndon B. Johnson's voting rights message of March 15, 1965. My analysis of these four presidential messages will be undergirded and guided by several conceptual and analytical assumptions about the presidency, civil rights, and rhetoric. In the remainder of this chapter I will first discuss the scholarship on presidential rhetoric, aiming to illuminate the nature of the presidency as a largely rhetorical office and the power of the president to effect change through discourse—especially on civil rights issues. Then, I will outline the analytical perspective of the book—rhetorical criticism—and my specific method for the analysis of presidents' civil rights rhetoric. Finally, after explaining the key assumptions guiding the study, I will discuss the historical precedents for presidential speech on civil rights in the modern era—

focusing on Franklin D. Roosevelt. That is, to better understand presidents' civil rights discourse, we need a historical framework for critical judgment in addition to a conceptual and analytical one.

Presidential Rhetoric

A study of presidents' civil rights discourse is grounded in the general assumption that presidential rhetoric matters. Of central concern to many political scientists, historians, and rhetoricians is how and to what extent presidential rhetoric matters. While the earliest scholarship on the modern presidency considered mainly how presidential public address related to the roles and institutional and doctrinal powers of the presidency, this review will show how the scholarship has moved on to evaluate what kind of leadership public discourse affords presidents, how rhetoric influences policy, how rhetoric affects the polity itself—including the processes of governance and the doctrinal powers and roles of the government—and how rhetoric shapes political meanings and interpretations.

Until 1960, scholars of the presidency focused primarily on the powers and roles of the office. One landmark study in this vein is Edward Corwin's *The President: Office and Powers,* which examines the constitutional and statutory powers of the presidency and warns against the "dangerously *personalized*" nature of presidential power in the modern era.[12] Another is Clinton Rossiter's *The American Presidency,* which explores the powers and limits of the office by examining "the major roles [the president] plays in the sprawling drama of American government": chief of state, chief executive, commander in chief, chief diplomat, chief legislator, chief of party, voice of the people, protector of the peace, manager of prosperity, and world leader. The role most closely related to a study of president's civil rights discourse (or presidential rhetoric in general) is that of the voice of the people. Rossiter sees public speech as one of the presidency's great powers: "The President is the American people's one authentic trumpet, and he has no higher duty than to give a clear and certain sound." Rossiter also conceives of the office as a "bully pulpit," claiming that the president "serves as a moral spokesman for all." The grounds for rhetorical leadership—moral or otherwise—in Rossiter's formulation is, however, unclear. At times he suggests that presidents should speak the "General Will" or "real sentiment of the people," but he also argues that presidents must speak the popular sentiment before it is apparent and sometimes speak in defiance of loudly voiced contrary opinion. Furthermore, he suggests that compelling presidential discourse might be grounded in "the language of Christian morality and the American tradition."[13] In short, Rossiter implies that the power of public speech is a significant kind of presidential leadership, but his book is undeveloped with regard to how that form of leadership might work. Yet Rossiter's work suggests important questions about presidential leadership and persuasion: Is effective popular leadership merely reflective of public sentiment, or is it constitutive of public sentiment? Or, might rhetorical leadership work through some combination of the two? Both Corwin's and Rossiter's works also implore scholars to ask a question that has guided inquiry into the "rhetorical presidency": Is there a constitutional or doctrinal authorization for presidents' rhetorical leadership?

Both scholars' orientations to studying the presidency also suggest questions specific to the study of presidents' rhetorical leadership on civil rights. Is presidential discourse on civil rights merely a response to mixed public sentiment and political calculations? If so, is this a problem for the presidency and the polity? Many Americans have looked to the president to speak out on civil rights issues, but are there good constitutional or doctrinal reasons for the president to endorse publicly Supreme Court decisions, to advocate civil rights bills, or to serve as a public educator on race relations? Should presidents use the "bully pulpit" to speak out about racial problems; or should they let Supreme Court opinions do the work of defending popular rights; let presidential messages to the Congress and congressional deliberation do the work of legislative advocacy; and let community organizations, interest groups, schools, churches, and families do the work of public education?

While Corwin and Rossiter provide insight into the roles and powers of the presidency, Richard Neustadt claims in his 1960 book, *Presidential Power,* that their work seems ill-equipped to explain many dimensions of actual presidential leadership either because they neglect or merely decry a central component of the modern presidency, personal and dynamic leadership. And this kind of leadership is accomplished through persuasion—bureaucratic negotiations to induce others on Capitol Hill to go along with the president's plans. Neustadt's thesis—capsulized in his famous dictum, "Presidential power is the power to persuade"—is that the presidential roles and powers discussed by Corwin and Rossiter function less as powers than as sources of influence or bargaining chips in the process of leadership.[14] Recent scholars of the presidency have criticized Neustadt for equating persuasion with bargaining and for failing to analyze presidents' popular appeals as a component of presidential power.[15] Strategic use of the bully pulpit has become a prominent theme of Neustadt's more recent work, thereby placating some of his critics, but a close look at his work shows that even his original formulation considers presidents' popular discourse. Neustadt's discussion of public prestige in *Presidential Power* analyzes the presidential role of "teacher to the public." His view of rhetoric is limited, however; he treats it only as a kind of leverage for bargaining on Capitol Hill. Neustadt claims there are four primary features of presidential teaching: first, his pupils are largely inattentive; second, they are attentive only when the issues he interprets are already on their minds for reasons independent of his discourse; third, he teaches less by telling than by acting within the context the public has in mind; and fourth, his previous words and actions will influence that context.[16] This conception of the president as public educator can inform studies of presidential discourse on civil rights—an issue both protesters and presidents have claimed is one requiring public education. Yet a rhetorical approach toward presidential civil rights discourse will challenge Neustadt's assumption that the only meaningful form of public discourse is policy-oriented speech that aids in bureaucratic bargaining and his assumption that public discourse is ancillary to action. Presidential rhetoric in the form of public teaching itself can serve an important function in the polity, and it is a special type of action—symbolic action.

Like Neustadt, political scientist George Edwards has focused his inquiry into presidential discourse on speeches aimed at enhancing influence in Washington, primarily with the Congress. Edwards's book *The Public Presidency*, though, views presidents' popular speeches as persuasion rather than as instruction; presidents' public discourse does not function merely to enhance their prestige, but rather it can persuade the public—which in turn can urge Congress to act. Edwards also emphasizes the power of political language to influence people's understanding of issues and thereby the policy-making process itself: "Language is not only a vehicle for expressing ideas. Words also can shape people's ideas by affecting what is expressed and how it is remembered, by evoking emotions, and by classifying objection of attention into categories that influence how they will be evaluated and what information will be relevant to them."[17] For inquiry into presidential persuasion on civil rights, it might seem that Edwards would counsel close study of the kind of language that presidents use to define civil rights and its influence on public understandings and deliberation of racial issues. But, while Edwards recognizes the importance of presidents' public discourse to leadership, especially the power of definition, he does not attend closely to the very stock-in-trade of presidential persuasion:

words, language, symbols, and arguments. As a social scientist, he focuses instead on analyzing public opinion: in fact, in a later essay, Edwards outlines a narrow method of gauging the effects of presidential discourse through the analysis of public opinion.[18] While it is important to heed Edwards's warning against assuming *a priori* that presidential rhetoric influences public opinion, it is equally important to understand that public opinion cannot be reduced to public opinion polls and that aggregate public opinion, the focus of his inquiry, is not necessarily the kind of opinion that presidents aim to influence. Students of presidential rhetoric also should keep in mind that there are reasons apart from its effect on public opinion for studying presidents' public messages. With regard to the study of presidential civil rights messages, this includes the impact of presidents' speeches on subsequent administrations and the impact of their words on presidents themselves. These too, though, are impossible to gauge with the scientific accuracy that Edwards seems to demand, but such is not the rhetorical critic's task.

Like Edwards, Samuel Kernell has investigated presidential strategies of public persuasion aimed at influencing Congress; like Neustadt, Kernell has examined presidential bargaining in Washington. Indeed, Kernell claims that by "going public"—speaking around the country to gain support for their agendas—presidents have fundamentally changed the political bargaining process. For a variety of reasons, the walls that had long insulated political bargaining from public scrutiny have broken down; as a consequence, presidents can improve their bargaining positions on Capitol Hill by taking their cases to the people. But, Kernell warns, going public can damage the White House's position—both when the president is an ineffective persuader and when public advocacy offends the members of Congress whom the president must ultimately influence. Furthermore, going public can subvert the logic of bargaining as a political strategy, because it does not extend political benefits to legislators for compliance but can impose costs of noncompliance. In addition, Kernell argues, "Going public is more akin to force than to bargaining . . . it makes subsequent compromise with other politicians more difficult."[19] Kernell's warnings about the potentially negative effects of going public can inform studies of presidential rhetoric: his claims should prompt rhetorical critics to consider how presidential discourse might influence the configuration of events that makes persuasion possible and how presidential discourse might affect the polity itself in the long run. With regard to civil rights discourse, one should consider, for example, how presidential rhetoric advocating a piece of civil rights legislation might ultimately constrain policy options by precluding certain kinds of bargaining with Congress during the policy development and deliberation stages.

That presidents' public addresses might disrupt bargaining and deliberation is a key concern for critics of "the rhetorical presidency," one of the most influential analytical constructs in recent studies of presidential rhetoric. Jeffrey Tulis's *The Rhetorical Presidency,* for example, argues that presidential appeals to the public "over the heads" of Congress often force presidents to speak in contradictory ways to different audiences—the public and the Congress—and often substitute emotional appeals and empty symbolism for serious deliberation.[20] Tulis and his coauthors have other complaints, though, against regular presidential popular appeals. Most important, they argue that the dramatic increase in discourse aimed at persuading the public is a radical change in doctrine from what the founders had in mind for the office of the presidency and governance in general, as expressed in the Constitution. Tulis claims that using popular rhetoric as a principal tool of governance violates the founding principle that the president should be independent from popular opinion and disrupts the proper functioning of the separation of powers. This change in doctrine, Tulis argues, represents a "second constitution," which is fundamentally "opposed to the founder's [sic] understanding of the political system." Moreover, he claims that the surfeit of presidential rhetoric has led to a greater mutability of policy because complex policy arrangements are packaged and defended as wholes, and to a decay in political discourse because political discussion has become a competition to please or manipulate the public.[21] In addition, Ceasar et al. claim that popular appeals over Congress's heads regularly raise public expectations beyond what can be accomplished by appealing to the public emotions, that this kind of presidential discourse too often relies on "inspirational" or crisis rhetoric to deal with normal problems, and that the rhetorical presidency has created a widespread public perception that "speaking *is* governing."[22]

Although the critics of the rhetorical presidency point to areas of legitimate concern about presidents' popular rhetoric, there are several problems with their claims.[23] First, they often use the term "rhetoric" to mean only demagoguery, or emotional appeals aimed at an ignorant audience. Second, they focus almost exclusively on policy-oriented rhetoric and treat rhetoric as ancillary to action. Third, their criticism that an excess of presidential speech makes it difficult to distinguish between real and spurious crises assumes that it is easy to distinguish between real and spurious crises: in other words, they treat political crisis as a purely metaphysical issue rather than as an interpretive issue too.

Nonetheless, these scholars rightly urge critics of presidential rhetoric to consider the constitutional implications of political communication and the potential long-term implications of that discourse; their orientation suggests close examination of historical, cultural, and political circumstances while avoiding any tendency to judge political discourse using a purely short-term, instrumental standard. With respect to presidential civil rights rhetoric, specifically, Tulis's warning about packaging and defending policy arrangements as wholes could provide the grounds for a critique of Clinton's recent "President's Initiative on Race." A critical orientation informed by Tulis and others also would consider how presidential civil rights rhetoric influences civil rights legislation, examine how presidential civil rights rhetoric might be perceived as governance, and—to extend their perspective—ask whether, in regard to racial issues, speech is an important kind of governance.

Roderick Hart's book *The Sound of Leadership* focuses on the relationship between speech and governance, and—in a slightly exaggerated version of Ceasar, Thurow, Tulis, and Bessette's claim—he argues that "public speech no longer attends the process of governance—it *is* governance." Hart details the frequency of presidential speech making, concluding that, given the increase in presidential address to the public, "modern presidents now view their opportunities to speak to the American people as their greatest political assets" and that the American people "have been led to believe if a president can speak in public he can lead in private *and* that he is unable to do the latter unless he can do the former." These dimensions of presidential leadership in the modern era, Hart suggests, divert attention away from other aspects of leadership— such as careful policy formulation, deliberate decision-making, and congressional savvy—and fool the public into thinking that all real governing occurs in public. Like the scholars of the rhetorical presidency, Hart argues that many Americans think that governance occurs only when the president talks, but he claims further that U.S. presidents have come to think that too. The public, the press, and the president act as if speech is its own accomplishment, and because of the pronounced rhetorical dimensions of their office, "many presidents come to feel that *to have spoken about a matter is to have done something about that matter*."[24]

If Hart is right, the problems for the polity could be severe: modern presidents would neglect other kinds of action, such as issuing executive orders or proposing legislation, in order to solve social problems, and the public would wrongly feel that the government is doing something to solve those problems since there is so much talk. And Hart suggests that if the public feels that political needs are being fulfilled by rhetorical abstractions (for example, the Great Society, the President's Initiative on Race), then they might not deal with problems or try to effect change in their local communities.[25] Inquiries into presidential communication, then, should consider the conditions under which rhetoric might displace certain kinds of action. For example, already critics of Bill Clinton's race initiative have charged that it is merely rhetorical; but, the president's packaging could give a discretionary issue like civil rights a saliency that would make political inaction an embarrassment to the White House. Finally, scholars of presidential rhetoric should not discount the symbolic force of rhetoric itself, especially on issues like race. Hart notes that presidents have talked a lot about civil rights in spite of little legislative action. Although I do not mean to suggest that presidential rhetoric is a wholly adequate substitute for political action on social problems like civil rights, it can sustain people through difficult times, shift the moral balance, and effect some change in American culture. Close attention to presidential civil rights rhetoric can reveal the language and ideas that might aid in compelling the citizenry to overcome the legacy and problems of racism in the United States.

Communication scholar Theodore Windt, however, emphasizes that "the primary purpose of presidential rhetoric is not to educate, but to assist in governing."[26] Although it is important to remember that a president's central goal usually is to gain or maintain public support for policies, Windt neglects the importance of education in governing, as a tool for both gaining policy support and influencing attitudes and beliefs apart from any connection to a specific policy initiative. But Windt—like Tulis—does argue that presidential rhetoric does more than arouse public opinion in order to get certain initiatives on the legislative agenda; it creates the framework within which political thought and action proceed. Presidential rhetoric often sets the terms and structures the language of subsequent political discussion, thereby influencing the very meaning of policies and events.[27] Tulis, however, claims that only popular address by the president structures subsequent "sober" policy deliberation by altering the terms of discussion.[28] As such, he assumes that it is possible to have some kind of political discourse that will not have this effect; in point of fact, any kind of political language—including the vocabulary of a written presidential message, the terminology of legislative proposals, and the partisan idioms of "sober" deliberation—influences the meaning of policy. In contrast to Tulis, Windt recognizes that any political rhetoric will influence political deliberation, thought, and action but chooses to focus his attention on the political rhetor with the most significant influence: the president. One aspect of presidential rhetoric that Windt features in *Presidents and Protesters* is the power to define certain situations as crises. He not only underscores the president's symbolic power to designate an event as politically meaningful, as does Tulis, but also emphasizes that "crises are primarily rhetorical." Unlike Tulis, Windt does not attempt to uncover how presidential rhetoric might efface the differences between real and spurious crises; he claims, "Rather, presidents' perceptions of situations and the rhetoric they use to describe them mark events as crises."[29] Windt offers an almost purely interpretive instead of metaphysical understanding of situations as political crises. His claims do encourage scholars to concentrate on the public language presidents' use to interpret situations, but Windt fails to provide the grounds for judging whether or not presidential discourse is a reasonable interpretation of empirical events.

This kind of judgment is difficult. Could one, for example, say unequivocally that civil rights represented a crisis during the last year of the Kennedy administration? Brutal racism had existed long before 1963, as had discrimination in public housing and discrimination in public transportation and places of public accommodation—yet these conditions were not always perceived as crises. But while Kennedy's definition of civil rights as a crisis was significant, could one say that his discourse created the crisis? Furthermore, what role does public perception—an important variable Windt neglects—play in the understanding of a situation as a crisis? And which publics do critics consider? Also, cannot other rhetors, including the news media, challenge the president's definition? Finally, whereas Windt suggests that presidential definitions garner widespread public support, I would amend his claim to suggest that public support will be short-lived unless the definition is consonant with existing ideological understandings. Murray Edelman, also a social constructivist, notes that political problems or crises come into existence in our political language as reinforcements of ideologies.[30] Edelman would remind critics to analyze presidential rhetoric on social problems like civil rights closely to explain how political language is grounded in certain ideologies, reinforces some ideological understandings, and challenges others. Such a perspective also would guide a rhetorical critic to consider presidents as placed, socially conditioned subjects and to consider that presidential rhetoric on social problems enters into an already constituted language system. Presidential rhetoric is an important kind of leadership and central to the process of governance, then, not only because it can create public pressure for Congress to act on policy initiatives but also because it shapes the ideologies in which political meanings and interpretations are grounded.

The scholarly literature on presidential leadership and governance, the rhetorical presidency, and presidential rhetoric is helpful for judging presidential rhetoric on civil rights, especially for evaluating the institutional powers of presidential rhetoric, rhetorical leadership, and the relationship between rhetoric and policy. But assessing presidential leadership on civil rights requires analysis of the dynamic contexts of leadership, not merely the historical or institutional roles of the presidency. The rhetorical power of the presidency is derived from history and the institution, but it also depends upon the ability to adapt to changing circumstances. Finally, the rhetorical power of the presidency can help enact meaningful policy but also is an important kind of power in its own right that deserves close analysis from a uniquely rhetorical perspective.

Rhetoric and Public Address

My approach to presidential civil rights discourse is drawn from a rhetorical perspective. A rhetorical perspective is an approach to the study of human communication focused on messages and meanings; it is concerned with the ways in which humans symbolically assign meaning to the world and with the ways in which they attempt to induce others to share those meanings. The critic working from a rhetorical perspective focuses on how people choose what to say in a given situation, how they arrange or order their thoughts, how they select a language or terminology to employ, and how they decide to deliver their message.[31] Rhetorical criticism, then, is the systematic interpretation and evaluation of public messages aimed at inducing shared meanings among people. In other words, rhetorical criticism is a method that analyzes and judges how various persuaders attempt to influence people's thoughts and actions through language. This systematic process involves the close examination of texts, contexts, rhetors, and audiences in order to illuminate and judge the different aspects of rhetorical processes.

Although rhetorical criticism can be applied to a variety of messages, it came into existence as a method for the study of public speaking. A rhetorical approach to public address favors both close analysis of the speech text itself and consideration of the historical situation surrounding the speech. Close analysis of the speech itself involves breaking down its rhetorical elements in order to determine how they function individually and to explain how they interact to shape the speech as a strategic response to the exigencies of its context.[32] Breaking down the elements of a speech will involve mapping its argument, analyzing its structure, examining its language (for example, its metaphors, "god" and "devil" terms), or identifying the values upon which it draws. So, for example, we will elucidate Lyndon B. Johnson's "We Shall Overcome" speech by tracing his use of the language of civil religion throughout the text and by demonstrating how that language helps authorize his argument for voting rights legislation. Explaining how a speech responds to its context means illuminating how the message both emerges from its historical moment and invites a reconstruction of the events about which it speaks. That is, a speech comes into existence as a product of a historical moment and in response to perceived exigencies of that moment, but it also attempts to induce the audience to perceive historical events in particular ways. A speech's context might include a social ideology to which it responds and against which it attempts to mobilize opponents. Such a speech—say, one criticizing white supremacy— might use the language of an opposing ideology, a rhetorical feature that underscores the inseparable relation between text and context. To explain what a rhetorical text might mean or how it functions, we need to understand how the rhetorical features of a speech—its language, argument, structure, and style—interact with its world.

A rhetorical approach to public address also favors close attention to speakers and their audiences. In part, this means attending to what audiences already believe about a speaker, his or her rhetorical intentions, and the process by which a speaker (and his or her speechwriters) crafts messages. But it also means examining the processes by which speakers rhetorically construct their public personae. For most of us, what we know about a public figure like the president is the product of communication. Rhetorical critics are concerned with how ethos, or the image of a speaker constructed though communicative interaction between speaker and audience, influences rhetorical processes. Presidents may convince us through public messages that they are credible, competent, trustworthy, and good-willed, or that they possess none of these qualities. Ethos is not a fixed attribute: it can develop or decline over time. For example, many civil rights activists perceived President John F. Kennedy's early public messages as president to reveal little personal commitment to their cause, but by 1963, many believed that his speeches demonstrated a clear interest (both personal and political) in civil rights. This change in ethos fundamentally altered the context in which Kennedy's persuasive efforts on civil rights were situated. In addition to shaping perceptions of personal credibility and good will, presidents also negotiate the ethos of their office. A president's credibility on civil rights in some sense has already been rhetorically constituted by previous chief executives' statements.

If speakers are in some sense rhetorical products, so too are audiences. We can discover in a speech an implied audience: an image of what the speaker would have the actual listener become, a model listener who shares the speaker's ideology.[33] Harry S. Truman's 1947 address to the NAACP convention, for example, contains the image of an ideal American citizen committed to the notions of freedom and equality of opportunity. But, while it is possible to locate an audience within the speech text, audiences also exist outside of texts, prior to communicative transactions. A rhetorical approach to public address also examines actual audiences' readiness to be influenced by persuasive messages. Audience members' knowledge, attitudes, perceptions of urgency regarding an issue, and their willingness to participate in communication all influence the outcome of rhetorical transactions. Audiences are not mere passive instruments; a rhetorical perspective emphasizes that audience members are active participants in public discourse. An audience's willingness to be influenced by a rhetor, though, also is a product of contextual influences, previous messages on a subject, and a speaker's prior ethos—a point that underscores the intricacies of rhetoric and the complex network of relationships between texts, contexts, speakers, and audiences. A rhetorical approach to the study of public address emphasizes human communication as a configuration—a process in which the elements are moving relative to the other parts of the process.[34] In sum, rhetorical criticism of public address is concerned with explaining and evaluating the confluence of messages, contexts, speakers, and audiences that lead to or inhibit symbolic inducement.

My specific method of analyzing presidential civil rights rhetoric will be consistent across presidents and speeches. First, I will discuss the president's private and public understanding of civil rights, exploring how personal, philosophical, and political motives likely shaped his behavior and speaking on racial issues. Second, I will analyze the contextual factors that shaped and were, in turn, shaped by the president's speech. For instance, I will explain how crises in race relations influenced presidential discourse and may have been soothed by a presidential address. Third, I will trace the evolution of the speech—its planning, writing, and revision—and analyze closely the language, argument, evidence, and strategies of the speech itself. Finally, I will discuss public and private responses to the president's address by examining reactions broadcast by the media and letters that ordinary citizens and public figures sent to the president. While this description of method may make it seem static, my aim is to use a systematic approach to explain and evaluate presidential civil rights rhetoric while still analyzing the interrelationships between elements of a rhetorical transaction. This systematic method will also help reveal commonalities of presidents' civil rights discourse and allow comparisons of their rhetorical efforts. Finally, although revealing common discursive features is important to this study, its rhetorical perspective will still guide us to consider the integrity of each individual president's rhetorical effort.

Presidential Precedents: FDR and Civil Rights

In order to understand fully the four speeches by Presidents Truman, Eisenhower, Kennedy, and Johnson, it is helpful to consider the racial politics and rhetoric of a man who said very little about civil rights as president— Franklin Delano Roosevelt. While most other chief executives had also said little or nothing about race, FDR's particular way of managing racial issues during his tenure at the White House changed the relationship between the presidency and African Americans. Earlier presidents did nothing that would impinge upon how their successors would manage civil rights, but Roosevelt brought the presidency to the threshold of leadership on racial matters. Roosevelt's occasional public statements, policies, and symbolism on race led many blacks to expect more from the presidency. Roosevelt's words and actions shaped the contexts in which future presidents would be heard.

Franklin Roosevelt left an ambiguous legacy on civil rights. African Americans criticized the nation's thirty-second president as vigorously as they praised him. Some blacks uttered FDR's name in the same phrase as Abraham Lincoln's, while others reminded them that Roosevelt's name belonged in the same phrase as that of John Nance Garner, Roosevelt's first vice president, a Texan viewed suspiciously by most blacks. In 1934, blues singer Joe Pullum praised Roosevelt as the source of his relief from economic troubles in the song "CWA Blues," but in the same year poet Langston Hughes suggested that the president had failed to fulfill his promises to relieve the Depression's stress on African Americans. Hughes's poem "Ballad of Roosevelt" indicted FDR for leaving many blacks homeless, hungry, and jobless while they were "A-waitin' on Roosevelt" for aid. Soon after Roosevelt's death in April, 1945, W. E. B. Du Bois, founding editor of the NAACP's official periodical, the *Crisis,* extended a positive interpretation of the president's efforts regarding race and civil rights, claiming that he "gave the American Negro a kind of recognition in political life which the Negro had never before received." Du Bois's editorial successor at the *Crisis,* Roy Wilkins, however, has expressed a different assessment of Roosevelt:

"I have always felt that F.D.R. was overrated as a champion of the Negro. He was a New York patrician, distant, aloof, with no natural feel for the sensibilities of black people, no compelling inner commitment to their cause."[35]

Roosevelt's record on race and rights was nearly as equivocal as appraisals of his administration. The New Deal's economic programs, for example, were not unequivocally beneficial to African Americans, though they did bring real improvement to the lives of many blacks during the thirties. The Works Progress Administration, begun in May 1935, was the salvation of millions of unemployed Americans, including African Americans. WPA educational and vocational training programs aided many blacks in need, and more than 300,000 blacks learned to read and write in the administration's literacy programs.[36] By 1939, an estimated one million black families depended upon the WPA for their livelihood.[37] Moreover, WPA benefits to blacks exceeded their proportion of the general population, and WPA head Harry Hopkins sought to eradicate discrimination in the administration. Hopkins's deputy, Aubrey Williams, later moved on to craft the relief programs of the National Youth Administration into models of fairness with regard to race. Williams insisted that the NYA include blacks in all its skilled manpower training programs. The administration also had a special Office of Negro Affairs, headed by Mary McLeod Bethune, to eliminate discrimination within its programs. Through the leadership of liberals sympathetic to African Americans' plight, both the WPA and NYA stood as significant departures from previous administrations' policies of excluding blacks from relief rolls during periods of economic strain.

Perhaps even more exemplary was the Public Works Administration, headed by Harold Ickes. The money spent on African Americans under the program tremendously exceeded any previous public or private expenditures for blacks. The PWA built 133 housing projects for blacks only and 40 projects to be inhabited by both blacks and whites. It spent more than $13 million on African American schools and hospitals and granted $3 million to Howard University.[38] The PWA also loaned municipalities and states more than $20 million to construct 225 schools for blacks, improve another 188 schools, and build 64 gymnasiums, auditoriums, and dormitories in African American communities.[39] In addition, Ickes issued an order prohibiting discrimination on PWA projects and ensured that a nondiscrimination clause was included in every PWA contract. Ickes also insisted on equal wage rates for African American workers and developed a racial quota plan for the PWA, where a fixed percentage of its laborers (in proportion to the percentage of black laborers in the local population) had to be black. Overall, the PWA provided tremendous benefits for the African American workforce, which, with an unemployment rate more than double the national average, stood to gain disproportionately from its programs.[40]

In spite of the egalitarian spirit of the WPA, NYA, and PWA, discrimination persisted in distributing jobs and benefits. While the overall numbers of these programs are impressive, aid depended upon geographical location and the local officials chosen to administer the programs: blacks generally fared well in the North and urban South but were regularly discriminated against in the rural South, where local whites attempted to circumvent administration policies in order to maintain white supremacy. And still it took months for these more progressive programs to implement effective policies of nondiscrimination. At the start of the Roosevelt administration, many blacks complained that the New Deal would simply continue discrimination-as-usual. A 1933 editorial in the *Chicago Defender,* for example, claimed: "Without appearing too impatient it might be well to ask the administration just when the 'new deal,' so widely advertised, will begin to include the real 'forgotten men' of America."[41]

Furthermore, several New Deal programs accepted segregation and discrimination as a normal part of administrating aid throughout their tenure. Blacks were especially critical of the National Recovery Act, which often set wages for African Americans below the legal minimum and based wage rates on the previously existing wage differential between black and white workers. *Opportunity* columnist Jesse Thomas claimed that the ability "to prevent the Negro from sharing equally with other wage earners" was the central concern of southern NRA officials. In 1935, John Davis, writing for the *Crisis,* noted that the NRA "tended to continue the inferior status of the Negro." Many blacks had their own ideas of what the acronym "NRA" meant—"Negroes Ruined Again" or "Negro Removal Act"—and came to view the program's symbolic Blue Eagle as a bird of prey. The Tennessee Valley Authority was perhaps even more racially biased in its employment and social planning programs. The TVA practiced thorough discrimination in housing, employment, and job training. Administrators segregated African Americans workers from whites, provided them with inferior accommodations, excluded them from trade schools that would have improved their job prospects, and barred blacks completely from the authority's model village at Norris, Tennessee. In a 1934 essay, *Crisis* authors Charles Houston and John Davis called the TVA a program of "lily-white reconstruction," a label that stuck with many blacks.[42] Although blacks protested vigorously against the NRA and TVA, both programs continued to disregard their official nondiscrimination policies.

Some New Deal programs actually worsened blacks' socioeconomic circumstances. The Agricultural Adjustment Administration went beyond enforcing an existing system of oppression to change economic structures in a way that further oppressed African American farmers. Southern AAA boards ordered the wholesale confiscation of the income of black cotton and tobacco farmers, forcing them into tenancy. AAA benefit payments were to be distributed to black tenants by white landlords, who often withheld those payments. And AAA crop reduction programs often led to the eviction of black farm tenants. The economic plight facing African American farmers became dire. For example, in 1934 author Arthur Raper estimated the average annual salary of black cotton farmers at less than two hundred dollars.[43] In 1935, Will Alexander, Edwin Embree, and Charles Johnson published *The Collapse of Cotton Tenancy,* a year-long study of cotton farming in the South that documented how the AAA had assumed the risks of landowners and placed them on the tenants. Critics of the AAA charged that by pouring money into southern agriculture without addressing the evils of the plantation system, the federal government had shorn up the old system and aggravated the desperate plight of black sharecroppers and tenant farmers.[44] In an essay for the *Journal of Negro Education,* scholar-activist Ralph Bunche argued that the AAA planned to move black farmers into permanent peasantry.[45]

Given its mixture of benefits and discrimination, how should we evaluate, on the balance, the impact of President Roosevelt's New Deal on African Americans? Historians are mixed in their assessments of the New Deal with regard to blacks. Barton Bernstein, for example, argues that New Deal programs were faltering and shallow and that Roosevelt offered blacks little meaningful reform. Harvard Sitkoff, in contrast, claims that the president's reforms were a real boon to African Americans. Given the radical differences in the administration of the numerous New Deal programs, however, Raymond Wolters's interpretation seems more reasonable: "President Roosevelt's program was so diverse and multifaceted that it is difficult to generalize about its impact on Negroes."[46] Besides, it is more important for our purposes to consider how blacks in the thirties and forties responded to Roosevelt: how their interpretations of the New Deal influenced their perceptions of FDR and his administration; how the New Deal helped define their expectations about the relationship between the president, the presidency, and civil rights; how the New Deal shaped the contexts in which future presidential action and discourse on civil rights would be interpreted.

The New Deal, for all its faults, created strong bonds between most African Americans and Roosevelt. Robert Weaver's 1935 essay, "The New Deal and the

Negro," argued that in sum "the New Deal has been more helpful than harmful to Negroes."[47] Blacks' affinity for Roosevelt was strengthened by the fact that prior presidents had done so little to help them. A 1936 editorial in the *Pittsburgh Courier* reflected prevailing black sentiments toward FDR: "Critics will point to discrimination against colored sharecroppers, against Negro skilled and unskilled labor. . . . This is all true. . . . But what administration within the memory of man has done a better job in that direction considering the very imperfect human material with which it had to work? The answer, of course, is none."[48] Similarly, the *Crisis* claimed that "no matter how far behind the ideal he [Roosevelt] may be, he is far ahead of any other Democratic president and of recent Republican ones."[49] Support for the New Deal's departure from previous administrations led many blacks to disavow their allegiance to the party of Lincoln and increased their interest in political participation.[50] This change in politicization led the two major political parties to woo black voters beginning with the 1936 election and led many blacks to demand more from politicians, including public statements on civil rights. While FDR's campaigners targeted written messages at blacks and several members of his administration spoke out on civil rights, the president remained quiet. Many blacks desperately wanted Roosevelt to speak out but were often willing to rest contented with the few actions he had taken to improve their lot—a point that underscores the peculiar relationship between rhetoric and action in demands for presidential attention to civil rights. Overall, memories of the New Deal continued to endear the president to most blacks, in spite of his failure to vigorously champion their cause in one of his eloquent public statements.

Other achievements certainly helped Roosevelt maintain black support. For instance, the administration began the integration of federal rest rooms and cafeterias that President Woodrow Wilson had segregated, and the number of black federal employees tripled during the depression decade. In addition, on February 3, 1939, Attorney General Frank Murphy created a Civil Rights Section in the Justice Department, legitimating for the first time in the twentieth century the notion that the federal government had the right and duty to investigate, mediate, and prosecute civil rights violations.[51] Two years later, in an attempt to halt A. Philip Randolph's plan for a March on Washington, Roosevelt issued Executive Order 8802, creating the Fair Employment Practices Committee (FEPC) and prohibiting discrimination in defense industries. Many African Americans were upset that the president did not take further action to desegregate the armed forces; but still, as civil rights leader Lester Granger noted, to many blacks the president's order "marked the close of an important episode in the drive of Negro citizens toward full respect."[52] FDR's appointment of a liberal Supreme Court was another act that ultimately delighted African Americans. The Court switched from a restrictive interpretation of African Americans' rights to an egalitarian view, which aided the black struggle for equality. In December, 1938, the NAACP won its first major Supreme Court victory when the Court ordered Missouri's all-white law school to admit Lloyd Gaines, a black student. This achievement was a moral victory and strengthened the legal assault on segregation. *Opportunity* called the Court's ruling the "most important legal decision handed down by the Supreme Court in the past quarter of a century, insofar as the civil liberties of Negro citizens are concerned."[53] Possibly more important in sustaining African American support than these achievements, however, were Roosevelt's symbolic deeds.

Roosevelt's most prominent symbolic measures included federal appointments of African Americans, reception of African American entertainers, recruitment of African Americans for the Democratic national conventions, and personal appearances before African American groups. By 1940, more than one hundred blacks had been appointed to posts in the New Deal. The appointment of blacks to federal posts was not new, but some of the appointments seemed unique to many African Americans. Even Ralph Bunche, a frequent critic of the administration, claimed that the "positions held under the New Deal represented a radical break with the past because of their novelty and the entirely different character of the appointee, as well as the method of appointment."[54] For example, Roosevelt appointed William H. Hastie, a brilliant legal analyst and former editor of Harvard University's law review, as the first African American federal judge. The *Crisis* lauded the president for this judicial appointment and all of his federal appointments, claiming that blacks have "penetrated nearer to policy-making desks than ever before."[55] African Americans perceived other federal appointments even more positively. Historian Nancy Weiss claims that the Federal Council on Negro Affairs, or Black Cabinet, was probably the most important racial symbol of the Roosevelt era.[56] The Black Cabinet—a group of African American advisers on the staff of several cabinet departments and New Deal agencies—signified to many blacks that FDR genuinely cared about them.

But even simple acts seemed to signify his concern. When the Tuskegee Choir sang at Sarah Delano Roosevelt's birthday celebration in 1933, the incident received a banner front-page headline in the *Afro-American*.[57] When the Hampton Institute glee club sang at a White House banquet in honor of a French diplomat, the *Crisis* devoted an article to the incident.[58] The *Chicago Defender,*

Crisis, and *New York Age* all gave special attention when the Morehouse College Quartet performed repeatedly for the president.[59] In 1936, the Democratic national convention opened its doors to black reporters and delegates, and an African American minister delivered the invocation at one convention session— acts that might seem like tokenism today. Yet *Opportunity* praised the convention as "an epoch in the political life of the Negro."[60] Indeed, to a race that had been regularly excluded from national politics, the convention was an important symbol. The black press also gave notice when FDR made a rare appearance before an African American audience, even though he usually said little. For example, the *New York Age* gave the president's brief appearance before 200,000 blacks in Atlanta a front-page headline, when Roosevelt merely said, "I'm sorry that I haven't time to speak to you now."[61] Roosevelt's symbolic deeds, however, should not be underrated but rather considered in their historical context. Many blacks found FDR's symbolic deeds impressive because no president in memory had extended even racial gestures. Roosevelt's symbolism deviated from customary political patterns of racial conservatism, if only in a limited way, which was exceptional enough to gain the admiration of many African Americans. Nancy Weiss notes that although perhaps trivial in comparison to action on lynching, disfranchisement, and discrimination, symbolic gestures struck a responsive chord.[62] In the judgment of Rayford Logan, historian and author of the 1944 book *What the Negro Wants,* "Negroes had been so depressed, so frustrated, almost having given up hope, that nearly anything would have created substantial support. . . . The outlook was so bleak . . . that little things counted a great deal."[63] Even then, not all blacks mistook Roosevelt's symbolic gestures for a vigorous civil rights agenda, especially with regard to speaking out on racial issues.

African Americans urged President Roosevelt to speak out on racial problems like lynching, disfranchisement, and discrimination. Occasionally he obliged, but his rhetorical program on race was neither dynamic nor sustained. Many of Roosevelt's public messages to black audiences were insubstantial and avoided issues of great concern to African Americans. For example, in a 1935 statement on a new agricultural building at Tuskegee Institute, Roosevelt praised African American farmers but avoided mention of the problems that they confronted in the South: "The success of Southern agriculture is dependent in great part upon the industry, intelligence and thrift of the Negro farmers."[64] Four years later when FDR visited Tuskegee, he avoided racial issues altogether. Instead, Roosevelt spoke to his black audience about how the visit fulfilled a promise he had made to Booker T. Washington to come to Tuskegee:

"I am fulfilling today a piece of persistency that began nearly thirty years ago when I had my first talk with Booker Washington. He asked me that time to come to Tuskegee and see what he was doing. . . . Well, I am persistent and here I am."[65] In presidential messages that mentioned race, references were often vague and platitudinous. In his address at the dedication of a new chemistry building at Howard University, Roosevelt claimed, "As far as it was humanly possible, the Government has followed the policy that among American citizens there should be no forgotten men and no forgotten races. It is a wise and truly American policy. We shall continue faithfully to observe it."[66] Roosevelt may have failed to address racial problems because he did not fully understand the specifically racial problems confronting African Americans: historian John Kirby notes that many New Dealers believed that there was little difference between conditions facing blacks and whites.[67] Perhaps more important, though, Roosevelt fretted that public statements about race would trigger a backlash from southerners whose support he needed.

This political concern dominated White House discussions about sending messages to the meetings of African American organizations. The administration declined Walter White's invitation to send a message to the 1933 conference of the NAACP, ostensibly because the president was busy "working night and day on vital and pressing legislative concerns and the international situation."[68] In reality, there was chronic worry at the White House about the possible implications of sending messages to black assemblies. For example, White House secretary Stephen Early claimed that before sending a message to the 1935 conference of the NAACP, the administration should consider carefully "the possible political reaction from the standpoint of the South."[69] In preparing a message to the NAACP's 1938 conference, FDR ordered his aides to avoid mention of "lynching and other controversial issues," and directed them to offer "just cordial greetings, etc."[70] White House advisers were anxious about offending the South and believed that any mention of issues like lynching in the message would be "entirely too dangerous."[71] Some scholars charge that southern presidential aides Marvin McIntyre and Stephen Early shielded Roosevelt from requests to speak to black audiences because of their personal racism;[72] but perhaps they also shielded the president because they understood well the racial politics of the South. And many citizens of the South did respond angrily even to perfunctory messages and token appearances before black audiences.[73] African Americans recognized the racial kowtowing to the South by the White House: while many were glad that Roosevelt took the time to send a message to their organization, they still were able to read his strategic silences.

Some of Roosevelt's silences, however, were too much for blacks to concede. African Americans critics began to indict the president for not speaking out against lynching or racial violence in American cities. In 1933, white mobs lynched twenty-eight blacks, three times as many as in 1932.[74] In response, letters flooded the White House urging Roosevelt to take a strong public stand against lynching. For instance, the Writers League Against Lynching—which included W. E. B. Du Bois, Roy Wilkins, and Nella Larsen on its membership rolls—asked that FDR, "as the leader of American public opinion," issue "a statement against the wave of lynchings . . . now sweeping the country."[75] The black press made similar demands of the president: the *Chicago Defender*, for example, asked him to make a speech on racial violence against blacks that would let "the citizens of America understand that whatever others may say, he as chief executive of the nation stands for the full enforcement of the law."[76] Eventually, Roosevelt denounced lynching in a public address to the Federal Council of Churches of Christ in America on December 6, 1933: "This generation . . . is not content with preachings against that vile form of collective murder—lynch law—which has broken out in our midst anew. We know that it is murder, and a deliberate and definite disobedience of the Commandment, 'Thou shall not kill.' We do not excuse those in high places or in low who condone lynch law."[77] But it was not the lynching of southern blacks that had prompted FDR to condemn the lynch law: the president, for example, had remained silent following the notorious lynching of Dan Pippen and A. T. Harden in Tuscaloosa, Alabama, just four months earlier. Rather, Roosevelt's antilynching speech responded angrily to California governor James Rolph, who had congratulated members of a San Jose mob "for making a good job of it" after they had lynched two white men. Despite the troublesome timing of Roosevelt's message and the absence of any significant commitment, African Americans lauded the speech. W. E. B. Du Bois responded for the *Crisis:* "Other presidents have talked about lynching, but they did it as a last resort and under tremendous pressure. It took war, riot and upheaval to make Wilson say one small word. Nothing ever induced Hoover to say anything on the subject worth saying. Even Harding was virtually dumb. Roosevelt, with his great radio audience, has declared frankly that lynching is murder. We all knew it, but it is unusual to have a President of the United States admit it. These things give us hope."[78] The *Chicago Defender* also heralded the speech, claiming that Roosevelt's statement would "do more than any other single factor to bring the nation to a deep and abiding sense of its responsibility to preserve our form of government and perpetuate our ideals of civilization."[79] Once again, Roosevelt's departure from previous presidents gained praise, although he said little substantive and pledged even less. Many African Americans, accustomed to receiving so little from the White House, interpreted the address as a signal to Congress to enact antilynching legislation.[80]

That interpretation was a mistake. Roosevelt had been extremely cautious about even mentioning lynching; certainly he would try to avoid taking a firm public stance for antilynching legislation and risk losing southern congressional support. When NAACP head Walter White—via Roosevelt's black maid, Elizabeth McDuffie—asked FDR to speak out on behalf of antilynching legislation, the president replied that such a speech would turn "too many valuable people" against him.[81] In a personal meeting with White, Roosevelt reinforced his point: "If I come out for the [Costigan-Wagner] anti-lynching bill now, they [southern members of Congress] will block every bill I ask Congress to pass to keep America from collapsing. I just can't take that risk."[82] Roosevelt eventually did speak publicly about the Costigan-Wagner bill. In his May 23, 1934, press conference, FDR claimed that he had problems with this specific bill, but noted "I am absolutely for the objective."[83] Senate Majority Leader Joseph Robinson understood the president's halfhearted support to mean that antilynching legislation could be buried in committee: Congress adjourned its session without considering the measure. When Costigan and Wagner, with help from the NAACP, revived their bill in 1935, Roosevelt avoided comment. When a reporter asked if he would care to comment on the bill during an April press conference, President Roosevelt replied tersely: "No."[84] Without a strong statement of presidential support, the antilynching bill died in the conflict with southern opponents. White's estimate that the Costigan-Wagner bill would "almost surely pass" if the president made clear in an address to Congress that the measure was on his list of "must" legislation was, perhaps, an overstatement.[85] Yet the NAACP leader was right to suggest that without a strong statement from Roosevelt, antilynching legislation would never pass Congress. Attempts to revive antilynching legislation in 1937, 1938, and 1940 failed. By 1940, it became clear to the parties involved that antilynching legislation was effectively dead for the remainder of the Roosevelt administration. In 1940, the *Crisis* evaluated the president's record: while the NAACP periodical rated him a failure on lynching, it gave him high marks for economic and social reform.[86] Most African Americans still supported FDR in spite of perceived failures regarding lynching: a 1940 Gallup poll indicated that 82 percent of blacks approved of the president, and they voted for him overwhelmingly in the 1940 election.[87]

Lynching, however, was not the only issue of great concern to blacks on which Roosevelt remained conspicuously silent. In June, 1943, race riots erupted in Detroit, and many Americans—especially African Americans—began to urge the president to speak to the nation about the situation. The *New Republic* was especially adamant in its demand for a public speech from FDR: "Why, in these months when the peril of open race war hung upon the air, hasn't Mr. Roosevelt come to us with one of his greatest speeches? . . . Why does not the President come to us NOW with such a speech. He must! The race situation is not okay, Mr. Roosevelt, whatever the subtle men whisper." Scores of blacks wrote to the White House urging a presidential message. In a telegram to FDR, Mary McLeod Bethune claimed that "a straight-forward, determined statement . . . is imperative." Walter White urged Roosevelt to deliver a "fireside chat" on racial violence. The Conference of National Organizations—whose membership included the NAACP, the National Negro Congress, the Congress of Industrial Organizations, and the National Lawyers Guild—also recommended that Roosevelt "address the American people over the radio on the subject of the current wave of violence against racial and national minorities." Despite this public pressure, Roosevelt remained silent. Even the claim that racial violence was "rotting our moral position and undermining our purpose" in the war against fascism—a rhetorical *topos* that often induced the president—did not compel him to speak about the Detroit riots.[88]

Roosevelt's advisers had informed him of the demand to speak. Presidential aide Jonathan Daniels even urged Roosevelt to deliver a public speech in a memorandum to the president on June 22, 1943: "The race riots in Detroit must be recognized, it seems to me, as a climax in what almost amounts to an epidemic of racial tensions in the United States—an epidemic still spreading. . . . I can think of nothing which could be more effective in this field than a statement to the people from you. . . . I hope you can find the occasion soon for such a straight talk to American good sense and good will." Daniels's idea of a "straight talk," though, meant emphasizing that racial violence disrupted the war effort—not "a statement of idealism in terms of perfect racial relationships." FDR apparently took Daniels's suggestion seriously, but before he made a decision to speak, he requested Stephen Early's opinion: "Don't you think it is about time for me to issue a statement about racial riots?" Whether or not Roosevelt solicited his opinion is unclear, but on July 15, Attorney General Francis Biddle offered his input on the issue of a possible presidential message on the race riots: "It has been suggested that you should go on the radio to discuss the whole problem. This, I think, would be unwise. However, you might consider discussing it the next time you talk about the overall domestic situation as one of the problems to be considered." Ultimately, Roosevelt heeded Biddle's warning: he did not speak about the Detroit race riots during their immediate wake, nor when Daniels made more detailed, substantive suggestions about what the president should say in a message to the nation about the violence in mid-August.[89]

Some scholars maintain that Roosevelt's decision not to speak out for antilynching legislation or about race riots was not mistaken. Historian William Leuchtenburg, for example, claims that Roosevelt would not have succeeded in pushing the antilynching bill into law and that public statements would only have jeopardized other legislation that benefited blacks.[90] Some of FDR's silences, scholars suggest, were interpreted more negatively by blacks then they should have been. Most often, however, the reverse was true: African Americans regularly interpreted Roosevelt's statements more positively than they probably should have. Many blacks felt hope listening to the president's brief statements and found deep meaning in his messages of little substance. As one African American man put it, "When you're on the outside, just being spoken to is substantive rather than symbolic."[91] Through his departure from his predecessors' rhetorical practices, Roosevelt was able to gain widespread support among blacks and to make many feel that he truly cared about their situation—achievements that required little rhetorical effort. Roosevelt's presidency illustrates a seemingly inadequate mixture of symbolism, infrequent discourse, and ambiguous action on civil rights that still appealed to most blacks during the thirties and forties.

Some historians have seen this mixture as a kind of rhetorical sham, while others claim that African Americans during the FDR years were too astute to be hoodwinked by "mere rhetoric." Barton Bernstein argues that blacks were "seduced by rhetoric, by the style and movement, by the symbolism of effort seldom reaching beyond words." In contrast, Nancy Weiss asserts that blacks were not seduced to the point of being unable to identify the problems of the Roosevelt administration. Besides, she emphasizes, it was the economic relief afforded by the New Deal—not rhetoric or symbolism—that led African Americans to support FDR.[92] Milder versions of both scholars' arguments have merit. That is, the president's rhetoric and symbolism did lead some blacks to develop a blind devotion, yet African American spokesmen regularly criticized Roosevelt's silences and challenged him to do more. And while the importance of New Deal benefits, however limited, should not be underrated, neither should the importance of FDR's rhetoric and symbolism, however limited. In the twentieth century, African Americans have demanded both political action and symbolic action on civil rights. The relationship between civil rights policy and rhetoric was just as important during the Roosevelt administration as it was during subsequent presidencies. FDR shaped that relationship in important ways: his peculiar mixture of racial politics, rhetoric, and symbolism could never be repeated by later chief executives, because even as Roosevelt satisfied most African Americans, he raised their expectations of the presidency. Roosevelt's policies made the presidency seem like an office that could affect blacks in meaningful ways. His public messages to and reception of African Americans hinted at the possibility of an open communicative relationship between the president and blacks. Roosevelt alluded to what was possible for a president—what African Americans might some day hope to receive from the White House—even though he did not fully embody that ideal.

Franklin Roosevelt helped boost blacks' expectations of the president, which, once fulfilled, would lead to even greater expectations. While political action and rhetoric with regard to race had been long overdue, FDR's mixture of symbolism, discourse, and policy made political action and rhetoric on civil rights feel long overdue. Roosevelt also helped accelerate the rhetorical timing of presidential rhetoric on race and civil rights: early in his presidency, Roosevelt's occasional public statements about race or to black audiences seemed ahead of their time, but by the end of his tenure his rhetoric seemed to some blacks to be lagging. Presidential silences on racial problems ultimately became more noticeable during the FDR years although the same troubling circumstances had existed long before. Roosevelt brought civil rights to the threshold of rhetorical leadership: his silences had the quality of becoming ready to speak out about racial problems, though FDR himself was not quite ready to speak. On April 12, 1945, this complex rhetorical situation became the immediate responsibility of Harry Truman—though the effects of Roosevelt's shaping of the relationship between the presidency and civil rights would be confronted by every modern president.

CHAPTER TWO

Harry Truman and the NAACP

When Franklin D. Roosevelt died in the spring of 1945, many African Americans were not sure what to make of the Missourian who suddenly inherited the presidency. But most, in spite of nagging doubts about his border-state background, gave Harry S. Truman their initial backing. In a 1945 song, blues musician "Champion" Jack Dupree urged blacks to support the new president and expressed confidence in Truman's potential as a friend to blacks: "Stand behind our President Truman, each and every one of you, 'Cause you know that's what, FDR would want us to do. It is our duty, put our shoulders to the wheel, Harry Truman would be our friend just as I feel."[1] Even W. E. B. Du Bois, who later became a harsh critic of the Truman administration, gave the new president the slight benefit of the doubt. In an editorial following FDR's death, Du Bois wrote of Truman: "He did not have the opportunity of liberal education and he was born in a former slave state. All this is against him but he deserves charity and sympathy for his tremendous task. He may do far better than his antecedents indicate."[2] The *Chicago Defender* also expressed hope that Truman would rise above the perceived limitations of his background: "Doubtlessly many Negroes will find the man from the Jim Crow state of Missouri suspect. . . . [But] Negro America will remember Truman's pledge to support a permanent Fair Employment Practices Committee. They will recall his promise to assure the Negro a full and equal role in the post-war employment picture. They will keep in mind his renunciation of racial intolerance. . . . They solemnly hope that Truman can prove himself another Justice Hugo Black.[3] If Truman acquired many African Americans' sympathy because of their support for his predecessor, he also seemed to acquire the burden of their expectations. Blacks expected Truman to do something about civil rights as president, whereas they had expected almost nothing from presidents before 1933. Truman, for example, could not return to the racial politics of Calvin Coolidge or Herbert Hoover and still maintain a solid degree of African American support. Upon FDR's death, African Americans waited to see what actions President Truman would take on civil rights and listened closely to hear what he would say about the nation's racial problems.

Students and scholars of American political rhetoric, however, have not listened so closely to Truman's words on civil rights. Communication scholars have attended to the centrality of rhetoric's role in the relationship between the American presidency and civil rights, but the existing scholarship focuses almost exclusively on the 1950s and 1960s. Certainly these two decades were marked by intense civil rights protest and increased demands, and warrant our attention. My purpose is not to question the usefulness or quality of the existing scholarship: studies of Eisenhower's speech following the violence at Little Rock, Kennedy's rhetoric following the desegregation of southern universities, and Johnson's discourse on equal opportunity and urban race riots have made valuable contributions to our understanding of modern presidential rhetoric and public talk about racial issues.[4] Rather, my purpose is to suggest that we broaden the scope of our inquiry into presidential discourse on race and civil rights to include chief executives whose public speaking effected significant changes in the relationship between the presidency and civil rights. In this chapter, I widen our scope to include the Truman presidency. Truman's civil rights discourse has received scant attention from rhetoricians.[5] Yet he was president during a significant civil rights era in which black political activism increased on a national and international level, and he spoke out regularly and forcefully on civil rights issues. I will accompany my broader discussion of Truman, civil rights, and presidential rhetoric with a case study of President Truman's address to the thirty-eighth annual conference of the National Association for the Advancement of Colored People in Washington, D.C., on June 29, 1947.

President Truman's NAACP speech is a significant, clear index of his public stand on racial issues and was the most publicized civil rights address of his career. Truman was the first president to speak before the NAACP. He addressed an immediate audience of more than 10,000, a national radio audience via the four major radio networks and many independent stations, and an international audience that tuned in to the State Department's shortwave broadcast of the speech. In addition, Truman's NAACP speech was rebroadcast in movie theaters nationwide.[6] Truman's address was well received during its own era and has been praised by historians. After the speech, NAACP executive secretary Walter White told Truman that his civil rights message was "the most forthright pronouncement any American president has yet made on this issue." Eleanor Roosevelt praised Truman's address in her "My Day" column, noting that his words were "fearlessly spoken." Historian William Berman lauds Truman for speaking to the nation's racial problems "with frankness and humanity," and biographer David McCullough calls the NAACP speech "the strongest statement on civil rights heard in Washington since the time of Lincoln."[7] By analyzing this lauded address, we can gain insight into Truman's relationship with African Americans, his civil rights policies, the early contributions he made to presidential civil rights rhetoric, and the possibilities of a chief executive's discourse on race.

Truman's speech has many flatterers but few evaluators. Historians have praised the NAACP address but have not explained their admiration or provided evidence for their claims that the speech is laudable. Historical accounts of Truman's address seem to suggest that it is, prima facie, a extraordinary instance of presidential rhetoric on civil rights. Is the speech outstanding, and, if so, why? Whereas historians seem to beg this question, a rhetorical approach to Truman's address can provide an answer. A contextualized close reading of the NAACP speech reveals that it is a meaningful episode of public discourse on racial matters. Truman's speech is a significant departure from his presidential predecessors' approach to civil rights and an important development in his own treatment of the nation's racial problems. Although the speech probably was shaped by political concerns, it still reflects a maturation of Truman's own understanding of civil rights as an important social and political issue. Furthermore, President Truman's address is not merely a symbolic gesture but rather a complex statement of civil rights. He calls for a change in the very concept of rights and is the first president to define civil rights as a crisis. In addition, a close reading of the text shows Truman struggling with the same paradoxes about civil rights that later presidents would encounter: the apparent disparity between historic principles and present deeds, between Cold War ideals and domestic performance. To advance my claims about Truman's speech, the chapter is divided into five sections: (1) a review of the scholarly literature, designed to provide a sense of Truman's personal and political stance on civil rights; (2) an analysis of the historical and political contexts that influenced and were shaped by the president's address; (3) a close reading of the speech itself; (4) a map of the reception of Truman's address; and (5) a discussion of the conclusions and implications of my analysis.

Truman and Civil Rights

Scholars are mixed in their evaluation of Harry Truman's personal stance on civil rights. Most are at least a little puzzled by his ambivalence on racial matters. Truman may have been affiliated with the Ku Klux Klan during the 1920s, or he may have merely flirted with membership, like many politicians seeking support.[8] McCullough suggests that Truman never entirely outgrew his rural Missouri background: "Old biases, old habits of speech continued, surfacing occasionally offstage." For example, William Leuchtenburg notes that even after blacks hailed him as their champion, Truman continued to use the word "nigger" to refer to African Americans.[9] Yet at times he seemed sincerely concerned about civil rights. Although Truman appears not to have had a consuming conviction on racial matters, he did have an attitude of decency and justice and a strong commitment to "fair play."[10] Barton Bernstein has suggested that Truman's convictions matured during his political career, claiming that political necessities seemed genuinely to shape his moral convictions. Alonzo Hamby suggests that Truman was sincere in his stance on racial issues, especially with respect to violence against racial minorities during the war.[11] Most scholars agree that in spite of his lingering racism, President Truman had a strong personal commitment to preventing violence against African Americans.[12] However strong his commitment to certain civil rights issues, Truman drew the line at social equality, still the era's great racial taboo.[13] Robert Donovan claims that Truman's opposition to social equality was personal, not political: his attitude was characteristic of a white Missourian of his time and was shared by most "enlightened" white Americans of that period.[14] Truman could simultaneously support legal rights for blacks and call the waiters at the White House an "army of coons"; his racial attitudes were a peculiar mixture of stereotyping and egalitarianism.[15] Perhaps Donald McCoy and Richard Ruetten best summarize the president's attitude toward civil rights: "Truman was a complex of ideas and impulses, principles and prejudices."[16]

Perhaps because of his border-state background and his southern sympathies, many senators and representatives from Dixie believed Truman would not move forward on civil rights as president. One senator predicted from the funeral train carrying Roosevelt's body, "Everything is going to be all right. The new president knows how to handle the niggers."[17] But Truman's civil rights record as a senator had been good, especially for a border-state legislator.[18] Donovan claims that Truman was astute on the race issue as a senator because Tom Pendergast's Jackson County political machine was politically astute; a significant number of black voters lived in Truman's district, and he learned to court and win their votes.[19] Most scholars agree that his experience with the politics of the African American vote in Missouri shaped Truman's civil rights stance as president, especially during the 1948 election.

Some scholars argue that Truman's civil rights policies were motivated by sheer political expediency during his tenure as president. Berman argues that the president was reluctant to embrace a political cause that might have damaged him, unless the political return promised to be at least as great as the risk: when it was politically expedient he acted; otherwise, he was extremely cautious and prudent about civil rights. Similarly, Bernstein and Chafe claim that Truman acted only when the situation demanded that he act. In *Beyond the New Deal,* Hamby suggests that Truman gave civil rights urgent priority only when it seemed necessary or expedient. Kenneth O'Reilly asserts that President Truman acted purely out of political motives and claims that civil rights always lost out to political concerns when the two were in tension.[20]

The political outcomes of helping racial minorities, though, were unclear. For example, some scholars argue that Truman's creation of the President's Committee on Civil Rights (PCCR) in 1946 was a purely political move calculated to win liberal and African American support and, in O'Reilly's words, to get him off the "hot seat" with minority interest groups. William Juhnke agrees that political concerns motivated Truman's action but suggests that it was not "cynical political maneuver designed primarily to delay or avoid action," as many scholars have suggested. John Egerton, in contrast, claims that the creation of the special committee could have been an instance of "political suicide." Similarly, Ronald Sylvia argues that whereas most scholars treat Truman's desegregation of the military as a move designed to win black votes, the actual gain in electoral support was hardly sufficient for the political risk involved. In *Man of the People,* Hamby criticizes scholars who write Truman off as a "cynical opportunist." McCullough, too, notes that whether support for civil rights was bad or good politics was usually uncertain. To claim that President Truman's motives were purely partisan is to suggest that action on civil rights could be easily identified as helpful or harmful. In fact, the politics of civil rights often involved a precarious balancing act, and the president and his advisers found it difficult to predict the ramifications of particular political actions on racial issues.[21]

Historians provide different interpretations about Harry Truman's personal and political motives on civil rights. Most agree that he did much more than previous administrations and helped put civil rights on the national agenda;

he initiated the momentum on civil rights continued by subsequent administrations.[22] Furthermore, most agree that if Truman's personal commitment was ambivalent and his politics wavered, his public commitment remained strong. Bernstein argues that Truman may have been slow to act, but his rhetoric was ahead of public opinion. Berman notes that the president continued to speak out against racial discrimination in spite of his legislative reluctance. John Hope Franklin claims that Truman's public discourse created a climate in which the status of African Americans could be improved. In short, Truman seemed to have two sets of convictions on civil rights.[23] In an oral history interview recorded in 1976, former Truman aide George Elsey claims:

> He had some public convictions and some private convictions, and I think sometimes there are differences. Publicly, by virtue of his reading, his knowledge of history, and his understanding of the country, he had some very deep feelings about what we needed to do about civil rights, civil liberties. As an individual, given his family background, and the part of the country he grew up in, and simply his generation, it was not as easy for him to deal on a face-to-face and one-to-one basis with members of other races. . . . But this didn't lessen Truman's determination as President to fight hard for civil rights. . . . As President, he saw what he thought was his duty, and he went right ahead with it.[24]

Remarkably, Truman did not let any conflicts between his personal and public convictions on civil rights emerge in his public discourse. Many African Americans took his public statements as indicative of a personal commitment, and a close reading of his civil rights rhetoric does not indicate a disparity in Truman's thinking.

Race and Politics in the 1940s

If Truman was ambivalent in his racial attitudes and expedient in his policies, he certainly was no worse than Franklin Roosevelt. In an oral history interview, Jonathan Daniels, former Roosevelt aide and Truman's press secretary in 1945, claims that Truman was more forthright in regard to civil rights, personally, publicly, and politically.[25] In fact, Truman's civil rights speeches, including the NAACP address, had such impact, in part, because they represented a significant departure from his predecessor's overall silence. By the end of FDR's tenure in the White House, his silence on civil rights became more conspicuous to many blacks. Truman was not so reserved: in his first two years in office, for example, he addressed issues of civil rights in his speech at the closing session of the United Nations Conference on International Organization (UNCIO) on June 26, 1945; in his special messages to Congress on September 6 and November 19, 1945; in a January 3, 1946, radio address on the Reconversion Program; and in his 1946 State of the Union message. President Truman's relative outspokenness was an important contextual factor that influenced how listeners responded to the NAACP speech. But two other contextual factors deserve close attention, as they both influenced and were shaped by Truman's address and also influenced responses to the address. The remainder of this section analyzes those two more immediate contexts: (1) Truman's performance on civil rights issues in 1946 and 1947 and African Americans' evaluation of his performance, and (2) the immediate political climate surrounding the president's speech.

Truman's Performance

Like FDR's, Truman's presidential record on civil rights was mixed. The first civil rights issue to confront the new president was the continued funding of the Fair Employment Practices Committee, which Roosevelt had created as a war measure. As a senator, Truman had supported permanent FEPC legislation, and he continued his support as president, speaking out regularly in favor of the measure in 1945 and 1946. But Truman did not exert pressure on Congress to act on the legislation: only once did he indirectly criticize a Senate filibuster preventing a floor vote on a permanent FEPC bill in 1946; he also failed to rally support for cloture, which would have ended the filibuster and brought the bill to a vote. Several African American newspapers criticized Truman's apparent unwillingness to invest his political capital in the FEPC bill. The *Pittsburgh Courier,* for example, indicted Truman for failing "to use any of his great power to bring pressure on the recalcitrant Southern Senators and Representatives" who opposed FEPC.[26] Similarly, the president voiced his support for an anti-poll tax measure yet stood on the sidelines as the Senate filibustered the bill to defeat in July, 1946. Writing in the *Crisis,* Charles Houston claimed that Truman's vocal support was not enough: "If he cannot produce, well, there is no such thing as gratitude in politics."[27]

Truman gained some African American support by appointing several blacks to government positions in 1946. In August of that year, he garnered some

African American support with a public letter to Charles Bolte, chairman of the American Veterans Committee. Bolte had written to the president in July, urging Truman to give his support and guidance to the development of equal justice and opportunity for all Americans. Truman's response was strong: "Discrimination, like a disease, must be attacked wherever it appears. This applies to the opportunity to vote, to hold and retain a job, and to secure adequate shelter and medical care no less than to gain an education compatible with the needs and ability of the individual."[28] The president's public letter received positive play in African American newspapers: for example, the *Chicago Defender* claimed that Truman "struck at the basic issues affecting the internal peace of the entire nation."[29] During the same month, however, fifteen thousand protesters paraded to the Lincoln Memorial, demanding that the president act against a recent lynching and murder in Monroe, Georgia. The protesters urged Truman to call Congress into a special session to enact antilynching legislation.

Truman's actions in September, 1946, again evoked mixed reactions among blacks. On September 19, the president met with Walter White to discuss the recent wave of racial violence against blacks in the South: at this meeting, the idea of the President's Committee on Civil Rights was proposed. The proposed committee would investigate civil liberties violations and develop programs to alleviate racial tensions; the proposal was lauded by the NAACP, which soon prepared a nomination list of twenty-three people for appointment to the commission. Some black organizations were pleased yet skeptical about Truman's committee proposal: the *Chicago Defender* claimed, "Effectiveness of the agency will be determined of course by the people who compose it."[30] While September's PCCR proposal brought Truman some support, he angered many African Americans on the twenty-third of the month, when he met with a delegation from Paul Robeson's American Crusade to End Lynching. The president and Robeson disagreed sharply and became embittered toward one another: the meeting went poorly, and the black press criticized Truman harshly. The *Amsterdam News* stated that the September 23 meeting was as abominable as President Truman's dismissal of Secretary of Commerce Henry A. Wallace earlier in the year. The newspaper claimed, "We condemn Truman as a fraud."[31]

Early in 1947, Truman pleased many African Americans with his January 6 State of the Union address. In the speech, the president lashed out against the "numerous attacks upon the constitutional rights of individual citizens as a result of racial and religious bigotry" and argued that he "was not convinced that the present legislation reached the limit of federal power to protect the civil rights of its citizens." The *Chicago Defender* editorial labeled the address "a landmark in statesmanship and wisdom," claiming, "Never before in our political annals has a president been so frank, so clear and so uncompromising in championing the civil rights of the oppressed." In contrast, W. E. B. Du Bois worried that Truman would repeat his 1946 performances: "Mr. Truman's message was good; but we know from bitter experience that Mr. Truman does not stand back of his own words and his own convictions." Truman received praise for his January 8 economic message to Congress, which contained a specific proposal calling for the enactment of FEPC legislation; but most blacks realized that Congress would not act.[32]

Truman may have gained some black support with the State of the Union address and economic message, but near the end of the month he again angered many African Americans. On January 23, Truman crossed a Congress of Racial Equality (CORE) picket line that protested Washington's National Theater's refusal to admit blacks to performances. Several black American periodicals, including the *Kansas City Call* and the *Chicago Defender* claimed that the president's action was an insult to all African Americans. With respect to civil rights performance, the months leading up to Truman's address to the NAACP were like most other months: Truman spoke out and took some measures that pleased African Americans. At the same time, however, the president angered many blacks with other actions or inaction.

While some African Americans, such as Du Bois, criticized Truman for not always acting upon his words, the importance of his rhetoric should not be underestimated. Truman's record, like his predecessor's, was mixed, but he spoke out regularly, whereas Roosevelt had remained silent. The *Kansas City Call* praised Truman's outspokenness on civil rights, and PCCR member Channing Tobias claimed that the president's words "have been the chief influence" on a new spirit of optimism among many African Americans.[33] Truman's words gave a yardstick against which actions could be measured, educated the public about racial issues, and encouraged blacks to seek justice. Truman equivocated in his efforts to pass some civil rights measures, but his public discourse on racial matters was unequivocal.

Political Climate

By 1947, Truman already was looking ahead to the presidential election of 1948. Perhaps the greatest threat to Truman's reelection was the possibility that Henry Wallace might make a bid for the presidency. Wallace's criticism of Truman began to fracture the Democratic Party, pulling many liberals into the newly formed Progressive Citizens of America (PCA). The White House realized that if Wallace ran, he would split liberal support, which could likely lead to a victory by Republican Thomas Dewey. Members of the Truman administration began to plan a strategy to retain the support of the members of the Democratic Party. On May 23, 1947, *U.S. News* noted the strategy of Truman's advisers: "In Mr. Truman's daily actions, every step he takes is being studied for political implications in these months during which plans are taking shape for the 1948 presidential campaign."[34]

One action that maintained some liberal support was Truman's veto of the Taft-Hartley bill, a labor bill that shifted the balance of power in labor struggles toward employers. Truman's move also gained him the support of African Americans, many of whom had demanded the veto: an editorial cartoon in the June 14, 1947, issue of the *Chicago Defender,* for example, urged Truman to stand up to the Republican Congress and to veto the legislation. The White House realized that Wallace might carry the African American vote: many blacks saw Wallace as a strong civil rights advocate and had criticized President Truman for forcing Wallace's resignation as secretary of commerce. Wallace also endeared himself with his tour through the South in the spring of 1947 and his insistence upon speaking to nonsegregated audiences. Wallace's candidacy seemed to force Truman to take a stronger stand on civil rights: such a stand might help him cut into the progressive's black—and white liberal—support.[35]

Wallace was not, however, the only challenger who could compete for African American votes; New York governor Dewey was also popular with many blacks. He had appointed a significant number of blacks to important state positions, endorsed state FEPC legislation in 1945, and made public statements in favor of justice for racial minorities.[36] Looking ahead to 1948, the Republican Party also began to court African American voters. In June, House Republicans introduced anti-poll tax legislation, knowing that it would be blocked by a southern filibuster in the Senate. *Newsweek* reported that the legislative move was designed for "reminding Negro voters that the GOP is still the party of Lincoln."[37] Republicans hoped that blacks had supported Franklin Roosevelt the man during the elections of the thirties and forties, not his party, and hoped to bring African Americans back into their party ranks.

African American voters were not to be ignored for the 1948 election. Wartime migration had doubled the number of blacks living in north-central states and increased by half the number in northeastern and western states: every black going North meant another potential voter.[38] In addition, African Americans were becoming increasingly involved in politics. Civic action during the

Roosevelt era and Truman's own rhetoric had encouraged many blacks to participate in politics. Membership in the NAACP had increased sevenfold during World War II, and the organization had stepped up its demands for action by the federal government.[39] By the time special counsel Clark Clifford emphasized for Truman the importance of black voters in his famous November memorandum "The Politics of 1948," strategic actions to gain black support had already begun.[40]

While strong support for civil rights might win Truman African American votes, such a position had the potential to alienate southerners. Early in the administration, southerners seemed willing to excuse Truman's strong stance on civil rights as an obligatory ploy to placate liberals. By 1947, however, many southern Democrats became suspicious. For example, Truman's lashing out against racial discrimination in his 1947 State of the Union address did not disturb the South. When he proposed civil rights legislation in his economic message, however, many southerners were alarmed. The *New York Times* claimed that Truman's recommendation for a permanent FEPC "seemed to dispel the relief among Southern Democrats that was manifest after the State of the Union message."[41] Some white southerners concluded that Truman was no longer acting merely out of expediency but that he had changed.[42] Truman's convictions did mature during his tenure: he developed a stronger commitment to civil rights and was especially moved by violence against African Americans. It would be a mistake to assess Truman's 1947 civil rights program as one marked purely by a desire for votes and political support.

Even a political cynic never could have accused Truman of acting on civil rights solely to secure black and liberal votes: the Cold War loomed over nearly all domestic policies during the late forties, including civil rights. The social and economic status of American blacks had the potential to taint the nation's international image. Since the advent of the Cold War, Soviet propaganda had often scored against the United States for racial discrimination and violence against African Americans.[43] In an April, 1946, memorandum to FEPC chairman Malcolm Ross, Under Secretary of State Dean Acheson claimed, "The existence of discrimination against minority groups in this country has an adverse effect on our relations with other countries. We are reminded over and over by some foreign newspapers and spokesmen, that our treatment of various minorities leaves much to be desired."[44] When Secretary of State James Byrnes pressured the Soviets about their politics in Eastern Europe, they often criticized the violence against African Americans in the South and their exclusion from the voting booths in Byrnes's home state of South Carolina.[45]

The president delivered the Truman Doctrine address only three months before the NAACP speech: strong support for civil rights had the potential to improve Truman's bargaining power in the Cold War and to counteract Soviet propaganda that exposed American white supremacy.

The historical context preceding President Truman's address to the NAACP affected its production and reception. Given the ups and downs in Truman's relationship with civil rights advocates, the speech had the possibility to become a turning point. Considering Roosevelt's reluctance and relative silence, it was a remarkable departure for an American president even to speak before a prominent, national civil rights organization, and the NAACP played up the occasion in advance. A June press release claimed that "100,000 spectators are expected to assemble to hear President Harry S. Truman deliver a major declaration of government policy on racial tensions."[46] Truman did not make a major declaration of policy, but he did use the occasion to attempt to convince African Americans that he supported their cause and deserved their support, in spite of past foibles.

In spite of high expectations among many African Americans, some members of the White House staff were setting their sights low for Truman's speech. Several historians have noted that in a memorandum to sometime speechwriter Matthew Connelly, Truman aide David Niles suggested that "the closing paragraph of the speech, not to exceed one minute, should be devoted to civil rights" and included a suggested speech outline.[47] In fact, this advice and the speech suggestions were first prepared by Philleo Nash, an African American aide working under Niles to whom civil rights issue were often referred. Nash sent a memorandum to Niles on June 2 advising that Truman should avoid focusing on discrimination and civil rights in his upcoming address—a memo that Niles copied verbatim and sent to Connelly under his own name two weeks later.[48] President Truman ultimately rejected Niles's (and Nash's) advice, however, and devoted the entire NAACP speech to civil rights issues.

PCCR member Robert Carr and civil rights adviser Milton Stewart submitted the first draft of the speech. Their draft was a strong statement that emphasized urgency in acting on civil rights problems and the PCCR's role in advising the president.[49] The draft by Carr and Stewart was then revised by George Elsey, then Clark Clifford, and again by David Niles.[50] Elsey and Clifford rewrote several sections of the Carr and Stewart draft and edited it significantly, while Niles made only minor additions to the speech. The White House solicited suggestions from other officials within the executive branch, but few recommendations were incorporated into the final address.[51] The final product is a message that speaks to the history, theory, and practice of civil rights in the United States and the international implications of racial tensions, connecting the Cold War with domestic civil rights. The speech text is a remarkable statement on civil rights that influenced subsequent presidential rhetoric, yet contained possibilities of rhetorical leadership that Truman's successors did not engage. We now turn our attention to the text of President Truman's NAACP speech.

Truman Speaks in Lincoln's Shadow

In an interview with communication scholars Eugene White and Clair Henderlider, Truman said that he preferred to state the essentials of his argument briefly in the introduction so that the audience knew exactly what he was going to do in the remainder of the speech.[52] Truman follows this principle in the NAACP address: the introduction contains the basic themes of the entire speech. He claims: "The occasion of meeting with you here at the Lincoln Memorial affords me the opportunity to congratulate the association upon its effective work for the improvement of our democratic processes. I should like to talk to you briefly about civil rights and human freedom. It is my deep conviction that we have reached a turning point in the long history of our country's efforts to guarantee freedom and equality to all our citizens. Recent events in the United States and abroad have made us realize that it is more important today than ever before to insure that all Americans enjoy these rights."[53] These four sentences outline the speech's principal argument: racial minorities in America should have their civil rights protected because American history, immediate domestic circumstances, and geopolitical circumstances demand it.

These sentences also introduce a sense of immediacy for civil rights, a feeling that pervades the entire address. In the introduction, Truman refers to the present as a "turning point" and notes that "current events" make civil rights issues "more important today than ever before." The whole speech contains ten references to the exigency of the moment. Truman states that America "cannot wait" to remedy racial problems and claims that the nation "can no longer afford the luxury of a leisurely attack" on racial discrimination. He calls progress on civil rights an "immediate task" and argues that the nation "must work as never before" to end racial discrimination. Urgency is the dominant theme of the president's speech. Each of the proofs for his argument is imbued with a sense of temporal imperativeness.

In its marked sense of urgency, the NAACP speech is a departure from Truman's previous civil rights discourse. Neither the 1947 State of the Union nor the economic report—both of which contained strong civil rights statements—underscored the importance of time. In his remarks to the members of the PCCR on January 15, 1947, Truman did note that the nation was "not making progress fast enough" on civil rights, but temporal concerns did not dominate the speech.[54] Whereas Truman directed his appeals in previous civil rights messages almost exclusively toward principle and practicality, in the NAACP address he also directs his appeals toward what Greek rhetoricians called *kairos*, or timeliness. Within the universe of Truman's discourse, action on civil rights is warranted because the times demand it. A significant question to raise at this point is, was there a significant change in historical circumstances between the beginning of the year and June? That is, was there something peculiar about the time external to the speech that demanded immediate action?

The Cold War, which influenced nearly all domestic politics, including civil rights, intensified in the spring of 1947. Truman delivered his plea for aid to Greece and Turkey on March 12, 1947. The particularly brutal lynching of South Carolinian Willie Earle on February 17, 1947, gained national attention and highlighted the terror faced by southern blacks. The upcoming 1948 presidential election also may have affected Truman's NAACP speech. But the urgency of the address is not wholly explainable by external circumstances. The Cold War also had intensified in 1946 with Winston Churchill's "Iron Curtain" address, and already in that same year State Department officials claimed that the Soviets were using racial discrimination in the United States as a political issue to embarrass government officials. The lynching of Willie Earle was brutal, but no more brutal than earlier lynchings in 1945 and 1946, nor more publicized than the terror against the African American community of Columbia, Tennessee, in February of 1946. In fact, as McCoy and Ruetten note, the racial violence of the postwar period had declined by 1947.[55] While the upcoming presidential election probably influenced Truman's discourse, he always could benefit from African American support; his party could have benefited from black support especially in the 1946 congressional elections. Besides, if African Americans perceived that Truman's emphasis on urgency was primarily a product of electoral concerns, he was likely to lose support.

In other words, the temporal moment external to Truman's NAACP speech did not seem to constitute an exigency for civil rights action any more than earlier moments had constituted a crisis. Whereas historians have focused only on the political and historical urgencies that influenced his address, I argue that in the NAACP speech Truman rhetorically constructs an urgency. Truman does not merely respond to events, as many scholars have suggested; instead, his speech becomes part of the events. Truman's speech does not take on its meaning exclusively from historical events; racial discrimination and violence had long been persistent conditions. His speech attempts to give meaning to events by investing them with a sense of urgency. Truman's address is significant because it represents the first instance in the modern presidency when the nation's chief executive defined civil rights as a crisis. That is, Truman attempts to communicate that current developments are critical and that his recommended course of action is necessary to remedy the critical situation.[56]

The rhetorical construction of social problems—that is, moving issues out of the realm of damaging conditions and into the realm of political discussion—always is saturated with ideological concerns.[57] In defining certain circumstances as problems, rhetors give force to their definitions by connecting them with ideologies. In his NAACP speech, Truman defines civil rights as an urgent social crisis and supports his claim by appealing to dimensions of the American ideology. In other words, while Truman does direct his appeals toward the exigence of the moment, he does not argue purely from circumstance. Time is always connected to another issue in the president's address. The three proofs to which Truman connects a sense of urgency have already been mentioned: American history, domestic circumstances (chiefly, racial violence), and international political circumstances. Truman devotes most of his attention to the first and third of these, which are the two most imbued with ideology.

In the first section of the address, Truman argues that immediate action on civil rights is necessary because broader historical concerns warrant it. He begins by referring to the nation's past concern with civil rights: "The civil rights laws written in the early years of our Republic, and the traditions which have been built upon them, are precious to us. Those laws were drawn up with the memory still fresh in men's minds of the tyranny of absentee government. They were written to protect the citizen against any possible tyrannical act by the new government in this country." Here, the president alludes to the Declaration of Independence, the Constitution, and the Bill of Rights and attempts to give those documents a sense of presence in the immediate circumstance. His implied argument is that the nation has been committed to civil rights from its earliest years, a commitment embodied in its founding documents, and must maintain that commitment. Truman's speech reinforces aspects of the American ideology—namely, that Americans understand their nation to be a sacred land for the defense of human freedom. Truman, however, does not allude to the nation's key documents in order to argue from principle. Whereas many later orators who spoke out on civil rights, including Martin Luther King, Jr., used the nation's key documents as a springboard to discuss how the broader principles of liberty and democracy demanded action, Truman seems simply to argue from tradition.

Truman then suggests that the nation cannot rest upon its traditional commitment to civil rights; rather the nation must move ahead: "But we cannot be content with a civil liberties program which emphasizes only the need of protection against the possibility of tyranny by the Government. We cannot stop there. We must keep moving forward with new conceptions of civil rights to safeguard our heritage. The extension of civil rights today means, not protection of the people *against* the Government, but protection of the people *by* the Government." Truman's claim here is significant: rather than merely arguing that the nation needs to live up to ideas conceived in the past, he argues that America must move beyond its historical understanding of civil rights to develop new, enriched understandings. Perhaps the most common theme in the long tradition of American reform rhetoric is that the nation needs to live up to the basic concepts conceived early in its history. Subsequent presidents appealed to this theme of fulfillment in their civil rights discourse. For example, on June 11, 1963, John F. Kennedy claimed, "Now the time has come for this Nation to fulfill its promise." On March 15, 1965, Lyndon B. Johnson argued, "A century has passed . . . since equality was promised. And yet the Negro is not equal. A century has passed since the day of the promise. And the promise is unkept." Activists also appealed to the theme of fulfillment: in his "I Have a Dream" speech, Martin Luther King, Jr., urged the United States to live up to the promises of the Constitution and Declaration of Independence. In his NAACP address Truman, though, seems to be asking for more. Instead of making a case for fulfillment, he argues for growth.

The need for national growth on civil rights is one of the most significant rhetorical possibilities contained in President Truman's speech. Truman seems willing to explore new concepts of civil rights, grounded in cherished traditions, rather than focusing only on the past, which might be limited in its applicability in the present. Although he proposes growth and change, Truman connects his ideas for development with the nation's heritage; his words suggest that change is a logical extension of the nation's history; it will "safeguard our heritage." Truman makes social and political change seem less frightening because, he suggests, it reflects and reinforces the American ideology. The NAACP speech, then, borrows a rhetorical technique from reformist rhetorics of fulfillment even as the address seems to demand more; like those activists who demand that the nation live up to past ideals, Truman makes reform seem safe by defining it in terms of the American way.[58] But, unlike many reformist arguments, Truman suggests that eighteenth-century conceptions of rights are limited in their capacity to help solve civil rights problems more than 150 years later. Without suggesting that the nation's historical understanding of rights is wholly flawed, Truman argues that the nation must develop new concepts to solve the present racial crisis.

While President Truman's argument for national growth is courageous and admirable, it also is peculiar. The overall claim of the first section is that the nation must work immediately to develop new concepts of rights to move beyond its traditions, which include a general commitment to civil rights. Truman does not make clear why the nation's history creates a sense of exigency. If the problem of civil rights has persisted for so long, despite a long-standing national interest in civil rights, why is the present marked by a greater sense of urgency than the past? I will suggest two readings that may help us make sense of the text. First, Truman may have been counting on the power of his words to give America's historical commitment to civil rights a sense of presence for his hearers. In other words, a rejuvenated commitment might create in the audience a strong sense of urgency for immediate action. Second, Truman may have meant to suggest a program of steady, gradual change. To the listener who interprets the president's words in this way, every moment has a sense of urgency: change, however moderate, must continue, or the nation will stagnate.

Truman's historical argument for growth also is peculiar because later in the address he seems to undermine his earlier claims. Near the beginning of the speech he claims that America needs growth, but later he argues that "the desire to keep faith with our Nation's historic principles make the need a pressing one." Near the end of the address, Truman states, "Never before has the need been so urgent for skillful and vigorous action to bring us closer to our ideal." These claims are not necessarily inconsistent with Truman's previous argument for growth; perhaps he means to suggest the fulfillment of fundamental principles of freedom and equality while shaping notions of civil rights to meet the immediate circumstances. But the new concepts of civil rights that Truman suggests are not really new: instead, they are grounded in traditional understandings. About a quarter of the way through the speech, President Truman narrows the discussion of civil rights to equality of opportunity: "As Americans we believe that every man should be free to live his life as he wishes. . . .

If this freedom is to be more than a dream, each man must be guaranteed equality of opportunity." In the remainder of the first section, Truman reinforces the dominant ideological understanding of civil rights. A citizen's achievement, he claims, should be limited only by "his ability, his industry, and his character." Civil rights for Truman include "the right to a decent home, the right to an education, the right to adequate medical care, the right to a worthwhile job." While the beginning of the first section seems to expand the American ideology to include new concepts of civil rights, by the end of the section Truman's vision has contracted. Racial problems are reduced to problems of equal opportunity, and Truman excludes from the political conversation more innovative ideas.

The second section of Truman's address is brief: in it, the president argues that immediate action on civil rights is warranted because of racial violence. He states: "Many of our people still suffer the indignities of insult, the narrowing fear of intimidation, and, I regret to say, the threat of physical injury and mob violence. Prejudice and intolerance in which these evils are rooted still exist. . . . We cannot wait another decade or another generation to remedy these evils." Truman was genuinely affected by hate crimes against minorities, especially against African American veterans, yet his discussion of racial violence is flat, not moving. Truman does not argue for specific proposals, such as antilynching legislation, that would end racial violence. Nor does he describe violence against blacks in such a way to generate pathos in order to goad the nation into supporting action on civil rights. While the immediate audience at the Lincoln Memorial felt the threat of violence, many among his national audience did not. Truman could have acknowledged the fear felt by blacks and encouraged his white listeners to take the perspective of an African American, to imagine the experience of living constantly in the shadow of terror. Giving presence to racial violence has the power to affect public opinion on civil rights; in 1963, for example, images of violence against blacks in Birmingham, Alabama, moved the entire nation. While the social outrage in 1963 was stirred, in part, by the power of the photographic image, that social consciousness was also a product of moving violence out of the realm of the abstract. Encouraging white audience members to imagine themselves as the victims of violence could have had a similar effect.

Instead, Truman underscores the problem of racial violence by connecting it to the nation's history and international politics. At the end of the second section, he claims: "We must work as never before, to cure them [the evils of injury and violence] now. The aftermath of war and the desire to keep faith with our Nation's historic principles make the need a pressing one." These two sentences connect the second section to the first and also mark a transition to third section. President Truman's suggestion that national principles demand an end to violence is inoffensive enough. His claim that the Cold War made the need for progress on civil rights urgent, however, had the potential to offend his African American auditors. Fifteen years later, John F. Kennedy's experiences with civil rights activists would illustrate the negative consequences of dealing with this rhetorical problem ineffectively. During the Kennedy presidency, many black activists criticized the president harshly for the way in which he connected civil rights with international politics in his public statements. Many complained that Kennedy acted or spoke out on civil rights issues only because of the international implications, which tarnished his and the nation's image abroad. Most African Americans did not object to the connection between domestic civil rights and international affairs. In fact, during the Truman administration, several African American organizations petitioned the United Nations to forge a stronger connection between domestic and international civil rights. But they did object when the president subordinated their cause to international affairs and stated the case for civil rights by its negative global implications. It would be an easy mistake for a president, including Truman, to make. International concerns during his presidency most often dominated other political issues, including civil rights.

In the NAACP address, though, Truman seems to avoid the rhetorical problem that would later plague Kennedy. Like Kennedy, Truman understood that racial discrimination damaged the nation's ethos in the struggle against Communism. Yet in subtle but important ways, his discourse does not subordinate civil rights to the Cold War, nor is Truman preoccupied with complaining that civil rights violations are tarnishing America's image abroad. Truman positively states his case for a national-international civil rights connection: "Freedom is not an easy lesson to teach, nor an easy cause to sell, to peoples beset by every kind of privation. They may surrender to the false security offered so temptingly by totalitarian regimes unless we can prove the superiority of democracy. Our case for democracy should be as strong as we can make it. It should rest on practical evidence that we have been able to put our own house in order. For these compelling reasons, we can no longer afford the luxury of a leisurely attack upon prejudice and discrimination." Truman's approach to connecting civil rights at home and around the world fits smoothly into a conversation about civil rights in the African American press in the months preceding the NAACP address. For example, an editorial in the March, 1947, issue of the *Crisis* claimed that in addition to the morality of ensuring all citizens' civil rights at home, such a program also would enhance "our chances of wooing other nations and peoples to our system as against another." A May, 1947, *Crisis* editorial argued that civil rights legislation "will strengthen America's position" in the world.[59] President Truman's linkage also is effective because he depicts the United States as a nation ready to lead a worldwide movement for freedom—including freedom for members of all races at home—rather than as a nation concerned primarily with international politics that considers domestic freedom only when shamed into doing so.

Truman's message appeals to a chauvinistic dimension of the American ideology: he claims that the United States must share its better ways with foreign nations and stand as "a symbol of hope for all men, and a rock of security in a troubled world." One might find this ideological appeal offensive, but it does have rhetorical force with many Americans. While the notion of America-as-chosen-land has been used to justify jingoistic practices like territorial and cultural expansionism, in this speech Truman attempts to put this usually oppressive ideology to use for progressive purposes. The potential danger is that Truman's address becomes a ritual of consensus: his words reinforce the American ideology, restrict the political discussion to dominant myths and values, and exclude alternative understandings.[60] For example, Truman's focus on the United States as the center of civil rights progress seems to exclude the idea that other nations might inform our understandings of civil rights. While Truman does not escape completely this potentially limiting ideological effect, he does suggest that civil rights progress is a cooperative effort. He expresses "confidence in the ability of all men to build free institutions" and notes that the United Nations' proposed International Bill of Human Rights will become "a landmark in man's long search for freedom" that will guide the United States' work toward improving civil rights around the world.

Like subsequent presidents, Truman argues that the geopolitical situation creates an urgent need for action on civil rights, but he does not suggest that the government is merely responding to political pressures. Truman argues that the U.S. government will take an activist role in improving civil rights across the globe. In a peculiar passage in the third section, he also emphasizes that the federal government will take a stronger, proactive approach at home: "But we cannot, any longer, await the growth of a will to action in the slowest State or the most backward community. Our National Government must show the way." While these lines seem slightly out of textual context within the third section of the address, it is one of the most remarkable passages of the entire speech. President Truman suggests that the government must move ahead of public opinion on racial problems to solve the nation's civil rights crisis. Public attitudes, values, beliefs, and habits on racial matters presented a real problem to Truman and subsequent presidents in the modern era. If a president moved too far ahead of public opinion, he risked losing support for civil rights measures and other legislation; if he did not challenge existing attitudes, racial problems might persist indefinitely. When presidents attempted to take federal action on civil rights that moved beyond southern racial attitudes, many southerners complained that the federal government had violated the "States' Rights" clause of the Constitution, and their representatives attempted to block presidents' legislative agendas. When presidents did not act, prejudice, discrimination, and terror continued.

Dwight Eisenhower attempted to cope with the problem of public attitudes through a policy of gradualism and claimed that the government could not "change people's hearts merely by laws." He believed that the federal government's actions should be only slightly ahead of racial attitudes and that presidential persuasion could bring about gradual change.[61] Kennedy's plan for civil rights also was to "keep moving, but move slowly."[62] During the first two years of his administration, Kennedy seemed less willing to take action than had Eisenhower: public attitudes in the South opposed action on civil rights and national opinion did not seem to demand action. Managing public sentiments on racial matters is a difficult endeavor for presidents. Even pushing for moderate change is challenging. How can a president estimate the small amount of pressure to apply that is just slightly ahead of public attitudes? Yet Truman believed that it was the government's responsibility to persuade and to educate the public on civil rights issues. In a meeting with three members of the PCCR, Truman claimed that a program of public persuasion and mass education could help eliminate racial prejudice and, therefore, many civil rights problems.[63] But the president was not willing merely to wait for a program of persuasion and public education to change the American people's minds and hearts. Truman's stance on public opinion in the NAACP address is bold, especially for 1947. He asserts without qualification that the federal government will move ahead instead of waiting "for the growth of a will to action." The president's statement is enhanced by his "Give 'Em Hell Harry" persona: if the nation will not move in the right direction, he suggests, he will make them move.

In his speech before the NAACP, Truman struggled with many of the same rhetorical problems in discussing civil rights that confronted his successors.

The overarching challenge for all presidents is a formidable one—how to speak out on an issue with important moral, political, economic, public, and private dimensions. Truman sought to meet the challenge by defining civil rights in relation to American history, immediate domestic circumstances, and international political circumstances. His speech is a mixture of progressive and conservative appeals, of vision and uninventiveness. Truman's argument for growth in the nation's understanding of civil rights is advanced, yet his reduction of civil rights to equal opportunity is stagnant. Truman was personally moved by racial violence, but his method of claiming that civil rights must be advanced because of violence is flat. He does not make specific proposals for ending violence against African Americans, nor does his rhetoric encourage perspective taking. Truman appeals to a nationalistic aspect of the American ethos but effectively connects civil rights with the Cold War without subordinating domestic racial problems to international political concerns. Truman's speech has limitations but is commendable for attempting to deal thoughtfully with the nation's racial problems after years of neglect and for addressing those problems unequivocally against the advice of the president's advisers. Furthermore, if Truman did not fully develop new concepts of civil rights in his NAACP address, he at least introduced a political ideal to work toward. To condemn Truman for not fulfilling his potential in a single speech would be to efface this early, significant presidential statement on civil rights.

Reception

The contemporary reception of Truman's address is difficult to gauge. Historians McCoy and Ruetten suggest that the speech received positive attention abroad but provide no support for their claim.[64] My findings indicate that many major international newspapers and magazines did not cover Truman's speech. For example, major English-language periodicals like the *Times, New Statesman and Nation, Spectator, Toronto Globe and Mail,* and *Canadian Forum* did not report on the address, nor did *Der Spiegel,* a major German periodical.[65] In the international press, labor strikes in the United States following Congress' overriding of Truman's veto of the Taft-Hartley Act seems to have pushed the NAACP speech off the pages. An international conference on the Marshall Plan held in Paris the day before the president's address to the NAACP also captured the headlines and seems to have taken attention away from the speech. *Hispano-Americano,* a Mexican periodical, however, contained a lengthy article on

Truman's NAACP speech: the article contains extended quotes from the address and emphasizes its international implications.[66] The archives at the Harry S. Truman Library contain another indication of international response—a clipping from the *Daily Service,* the newspaper of the Nigerian Youth Movement, which did not offer editorial comments on the address but did print a transcript of the entire speech.[67] Still, news of the Taft-Hartley Act and Marshall Plan dominated international news coverage of U.S. politics, displacing coverage of the president's civil rights address.

Reaction from whites in the United States also is challenging to assess: major newspapers run by whites, including the *New York Times,* the *Washington Post,* and the *New York Herald Tribune,* printed stories on Truman's speech and reprinted the entire address. Unlike the African American periodicals, though, none of these newspapers contained editorials about Truman's message. The *St. Louis Post-Dispatch* did carry a short editorial on the NAACP speech, claiming, "Seldom is the goal for democracy better put than in these few words by the President."[68] The nation's major news magazines—*Time, Newsweek,* and *U.S. News*—did not report on Truman's speech, either in news stories or opinion essays. Nor was the address covered by the major opinion periodicals of the era, the *Nation, New Republic, Atlantic, Harper's,* and *Collier's.* There was little response to Truman's message in southern white newspapers. The *Arkansas Gazette,* one paper to cover the speech, asked, "Is it in the power of any government to wipe out prejudice? Enforcement of laws against 'discrimination' in fields where the government has not previously entered might only make prejudice more active."[69] As with international periodicals, the editorial pages of most domestic newspapers and magazines were filled with comments on the Marshall Plan, the Paris conference, labor strikes by coal miners and automotive workers, and the politics of the Taft-Hartley Act. Truman's speech to the NAACP speech received basic "who, what, when, where, why, and how" attention from major domestic newspapers but not the in-depth coverage it might have received in different circumstances.

African American response is easier to assess: most blacks applauded President Truman's speech. In a letter to Truman on July 9, NAACP secretary Walter White claimed, "We have been swamped with telegrams, letters, telephone calls, and other expressions of enthusiastic approval of the speech." Nearly all black periodicals praised the president's address. Several, including the *Crisis, New York Age, Norfolk Journal & Guide, Pittsburgh Courier,* reprinted the text of the speech. The *Philadelphia Afro-American* called the message "the strongest address on civil rights ever made by any president." The *Afro-American* especially lauded Truman for his claim that the nation cannot wait for the growth of a will to act: "This probably set back the State's Righters back on their heels. It was something we have been waiting a long time to hear."[70] Rather than just observing that Truman had made a significant statement simply by speaking to the NAACP, African American periodicals examined what Truman actually said (unlike many other news media). Overall, three major themes emerge in the coverage of Truman's speech in the black press: the speech revealed the president's maturation on civil rights; the speech was laudable because it was a "forthright statement" of the nation's racial problems; the speech put domestic civil rights into an international context of human rights.

For example, the *Kansas City Call* suggested that the NAACP speech demonstrated that Truman had outgrown his roots: "Truman so strongly denounced race prejudice and discrimination based upon race, creed, color, and national origin that even his enemies were convinced that the Missourian in the White House had left behind him Missouri's tradition of second-class citizenship for Negroes."[71] The *New York Age* also suggested that the president had matured on civil rights: the speech, one editorial claimed, revealed that "he had re-shaped his thinking."[72] The president's speech, then, convinced some African Americans that Truman's prior ambivalence on civil rights was an attitude of the past and that he had developed a new vigorous, personal commitment to the nation's racial problems.

Several African American periodicals also commended Truman for his forthrightness. The *Crisis* called the president's speech "the most comprehensive and forthright statement on the rights of minorities in a democracy, and on the duty of the government to secure and safeguard them that has ever been made by a President of the United States." The *Chicago Defender* applauded Truman's "historic speech" for its "bold, unequivocal language." The *Norfolk Journal & Guide* also praised the message as a "forthright speech" that was a climax to "a great occasion." The *Pittsburgh Courier* lauded the president for his "sincerity and forthrightness," which one editor claimed was a notable turn away from his record of "double-talk and political expediency." An editorial in the *Chicago Defender* praised Truman's straightforwardness but emphasized that blacks must hold the president accountable to his new vigorous commitment: the author claimed that Truman must act to give meaning to his statement; "Otherwise it would be one more puff in the wind." The *Defender* may have been guarded in its praise, but blacks overwhelmingly praised the speech as forthright, most likely because of Truman's departure from the timid, shallow nature of earlier presidents' discourse on civil rights.[73]

Many African American newspapers also emphasized the international aspects of Truman's speech. An editorial in the *Philadelphia Afro-American* lauded Truman for acknowledging that "America's claim to world leadership is at stake each time a right is abridged or a privilege denied" at home. The author claimed, "We were glad to hear him admit it officially." The *New York Age* led its story on the address with the global implications of the president's message, emphasizing that Truman spoke to an international community about human rights, not just a domestic audience. The *Norfolk Journal & Guide's* coverage of the speech also led with the president's discussion of the international context for civil rights. The *Chicago Defender,* too, underscored Truman's treatment of freedom as a global issue.[74] Truman's arguments about the global importance of domestic civil rights spoke not only to his international audience, but also to many among his African American audience. As historian Brenda Gayle Plummer shows in her book *Rising Wind,* many blacks were actively interested in international affairs during the 1940s and had long related the domestic race problem with global concerns.[75] African Americans also identified with the struggles of African colonial nations and the plight of people of African descent throughout the world, as demonstrated by the convening of a Pan-African Congress in 1945. Unlike most white Americans, who usually viewed civil rights as a domestic problem, black Americans saw civil rights in an international context—as did the White House. President Truman, unlike some of his successors, was able to address this international context of civil rights in a way that appealed to many African Americans.

Conclusion

Harry Truman's address to the NAACP is a remarkable instance of presidential rhetoric on civil rights. The speech is more eloquent than most of Truman's rhetoric: like Lyndon Johnson—another president not known for his eloquence—Truman seemed to rise to the rhetorical occasion for important civil rights addresses. While the address did not remove all doubts about the president's willingness to put the full weight of his office behind civil rights legislation, it was a turning point in his relationship with African Americans. The speech convinced most blacks that his commitment to civil rights was personal, sincere, and vigorous. Channing Tobias told Truman that the speech "made known to the country where you stand personally on the ideals that you would have the country at-large embrace"; Raymond Alexander, whose wife was a member of the PCCR, told the president that the speech "left no doubt as to . . . where you stand on the basic, fundamental, civil, and political rights of your fellow Americans."[76] Truman's words injected a sense of excitement into the drive for civil rights: the black press was abuzz with discussion of the NAACP message and the president's strong assurance that the United States would solve the problems of prejudice and discrimination. The June 29, 1947, address also provided an impetus to action for civil rights activists; many began to petition more adamantly for redress of their grievances. In addition, Truman's NAACP speech, like many of his civil rights addresses, provided activists with a means to prod him into action: they could use the president's words as a benchmark against which they could measure his deeds. Truman did make small policy contributions to advance the cause of civil rights during his tenure, but more important was his public discourse.

Truman helped bring civil rights to the public sphere as a major topic of discussion after years of neglect, and his outspokenness helped sustain the discussion. He committed not only himself to civil rights rhetorically, but also the office of the American presidency. Subsequent presidents would find it difficult to remain silent on racial matters, in part, because Truman's frequent public address placed the presidency at the center of public discussion about civil rights: this is a major, often overlooked accomplishment of his administration. Before Truman, presidents needed not make strong public statements on civil rights: blacks had been inspired by the few general comments about social relief in Franklin Roosevelt's rhetoric, in spite of his silence on civil rights in particular. After Truman, however, African Americans criticized presidents severely for remaining silent or making small gestures toward civil rights in their public discourse. Executive action and legislative initiatives also were important, but a public commitment to civil rights became an important demand upon the president during the fifties and sixties.

Presidential addresses on civil rights can educate the citizenry, goad the legislature toward action, and sustain this important social issue as a topic of discussion in the public sphere. Rhetorical studies can inform the historical understanding of presidents' civil rights legacies and illuminate current rhetorical practices on racial matters. The existing scholarship has made significant contributions by examining the political rhetoric during the Eisenhower, Kennedy, and Johnson years, but we should broaden our scope to include the civil rights rhetoric of Harry S. Truman. Truman's address to the NAACP reflected a maturation in his own thinking on civil rights, stood as a turning point in his relationship with many African Americans, and influenced how future presidents would speak about race and rights.

Truman's speech also exhibited several key rhetorical struggles that would become a regular feature of the discourse of his successors. Should the president move ahead of public opinion, attempting to educate the people, or wait for public attitudes to change? In either case, once a decision is made, the particulars are difficult to manage. Should the president emphasize moral growth on civil rights or focus on fulfillment? The rhetoric of fulfillment is a familiar aspect of American public discourse and makes social change seem less frightening by fitting it into the American ideology; yet such an approach can lead to a stagnant understanding of important social issues, including civil rights. Advocating a change in the nation's understanding of civil rights can seem radical or too farsighted: why should the president advocate advanced concepts of civil rights when the nation cannot even live up to past ideals? Finally, most presidents have discussed the concept of equality in a confounded way. While "freedom" and "equality" are treated as universal ideals in presidential discourse on civil rights, often the term "equality" is used to mean equality of opportunity. The inconsistent use of the term "equality" in presidential rhetoric is harmful for public discourse: such discourse holds out the possibility of equality of condition even as it limits the political discussion to equality of opportunity.

And addressing these issues would become in some senses more complicated for Truman's successors. Civil rights activists stepped up their demands, changed their tactics and strategies of protest, and received more media attention in the subsequent decades. Moments of dramatic crisis and violent clashes between protesters and local citizens and officials arrested the public's attention. Legislative action moved beyond the stage of establishing committees and passing civil rights laws confined to federal and government-sponsored activities. Yet subsequent presidents would still struggle with many of the same issues that confronted Truman in the NAACP speech. Truman's immediate successor, Dwight D. Eisenhower, would struggle with the role of presidential rhetoric in managing public opinion on racial attitudes and with the tensions between his personal sentiments on civil rights and his sense of public duty as president. The desegregation crisis of Central High School in Little Rock, Arkansas, would bring this rhetorical struggle to its boiling point in the fall of 1957.

CHAPTER THREE

Dwight Eisenhower against the Extremists

President Truman still resided at the White House when the Supreme Court began hearing oral arguments in the five school segregation cases known collectively as *Brown v. Board of Education*. Unexpectedly, in its last days, the Truman administration aided the plaintiffs by filing an amicus curiae, or friend of the court, brief arguing against the constitutionality of school segregation. But the actions of Truman's successor, not the man from Missouri, shaped the Court in such a way that it declared the policy of "separate but equal" unconstitutional—a declaration that ultimately led Dwight D. Eisenhower to send U.S. Army troops to Little Rock, Arkansas, to protect the entry of nine African American children into Central High School. During the *Brown* case, Chief Justice Fred Vinson died, and Eisenhower appointed California governor Earl Warren to fill the post. Ike is rumored to have later called the appointment "the biggest damfool mistake I ever made."[1] Eisenhower's Justice Department also filed an amicus curiae brief with the Warren Court, concluding that segregation in public schools was unconstitutional. After reargument of the *Brown* case in December of 1953, Chief Justice Warren battled and bargained for nearly five months behind closed doors to gain a unanimous decision in favor of school desegregation.

That the *Brown* decision, issued on May 17, 1954, was one of the first and perhaps most significant civil rights events of the Eisenhower years seems fitting, given the president's stand on racial issues. The Warren Court's decision revealed the character and weaknesses of Eisenhower's approach to civil rights. Ike expressed hope that the United States would one day guarantee true equality of opportunity to all its citizens but warned that the president could do little to ensure such a society. Unlike Truman, who declared in his NAACP address that the federal government—including the chief executive—had a duty to advance civil rights, Eisenhower located the responsibility for advancement elsewhere. In the *Brown* decision, the Supreme Court took responsibility for guaranteeing equality of opportunity in education, leaving the president to deal with the consequences. Eisenhower refused to comment publicly on the decision or on the morality of school desegregation, suggesting to some a tension between the president's public and private sentiments. The president focused on the legal aspects of desegregation following the Court's decision, but some Americans wanted to hear about the morality of ensuring civil rights. Ike wanted civil rights to remain largely a local issue, but local officials acted in radically different ways in response to *Brown*. The Court's decision forced Eisenhower to take decisive action at Little Rock, the second great civil rights event in his administration, one perhaps equal in significance to *Brown* and one that he perceived as the most troublesome of his presidency.

Blatant defiance of the court-ordered desegregation of Central High School by Arkansas governor Orval Faubus and local citizens led Eisenhower to send federal troops into Little Rock, "a constitutional duty which was the most repugnant to him of all his acts in his eight years at the White House," and to deliver a radio and television address to the nation about school desegregation.[2] The president would have preferred to remain silent on this civil rights issue: he found much political speaking to be a waste of time and was not interested in using his office as a "bully pulpit" to lead the nation with regard to civil rights.[3] But the Little Rock crisis forced Ike's hand, although he avoided commenting on the morality of desegregation or the broader civil rights issues raised by the segregationists' stand, focusing instead on the legal issues and framing the events at Central High as an isolated problem. Eisenhower's speech of September 24, 1957, provides scholars of the presidency and civil rights with the president's interpretation of the events at Little Rock and stands as his most sustained discourse on civil rights. His speech reveals the problems presidents face in addressing moments of domestic crisis, difficult moments that his successors came to share. Furthermore, since Eisenhower was involved directly in the preparation of the address and the drafts of the speech are extant, we can read the address as disclosing elements of Ike's personal and political understanding of civil rights and as expressive of his political philosophy. The White House's position on desegregation and racial discrimination was one of the most significant factors in setting the pace of the struggle for civil rights, and as a significant statement of a president's position on the issues, Eisenhower's address of September 24 deserves close attention.

Eisenhower's speech is revealing because of the subjects it addresses and those on which it remains silent, and also because the address illustrates the difficulties of his political and rhetorical approach to civil rights more clearly than any episode during his tenure. The unfolding of events at Little Rock represented a significant challenge to Eisenhower's rhetoric: just two months earlier he had claimed, "I can't imagine any set of circumstances that would ever induce me to send Federal troops . . . into any area to enforce the orders of a Federal Court."[4] My inquiry into Eisenhower's address is motivated by questions about his justification for federal intervention—how the president attempted to make a compelling argument for federal involvement given his prior rhetoric and his nonintervention in previous desegregation cases, especially the defiance of court-ordered desegregation in Mansfield, Texas, in the fall of 1956. I will also discuss the consequences of his rhetorical justification, especially its focus on the law; the relation between personal sentiments and public responsibilities expressed in the speech; Eisenhower's argument regarding the international implications of the Little Rock incident; and contemporary responses to the message. I also aim to explore whether Eisenhower's political and rhetorical stand on civil rights and desegregation was competent on its own terms. Or, if not, could it have been made to be feasible? Most scholars either have criticized Eisenhower for not having a principled understanding of civil rights or have attempted to get him off the hook merely by claiming that Ike did have an understanding of civil rights, just not one acceptable to many of his critics. Few, however, have indicated what, specifically, the president might have done and said within his own understanding of civil rights while indicating the limitations of the president's understanding. During the Little Rock incident, Eisenhower became the victim of his own politics and rhetoric. His September 24 speech shows he still did not fully understand the limitations of his approach and beliefs in regard to civil rights.

To guide this inquiry and to aid in the development of my claims, the chapter is divided into the following sections: (1) a discussion of President Eisenhower's personal and political understanding of civil rights, aiming to indicate the possibilities and possible limits of his approach to the nation's racial problems; (2) a chronicle of the context in which Eisenhower's speech was located—the historical, political, and rhetorical circumstances that shaped the address and had the potential to be shaped by it; (3) an analysis of the Little Rock speech itself, focusing closely on the development of the address and its rhetoric; and (4) an account and interpretation of the responses to Eisenhower's speech—internationally, nationally, regionally, and racially.

Eisenhower and Civil Rights

Born in Texas and raised in Kansas, Dwight Eisenhower had little contact with African Americans as a boy or young man. Few blacks lived in his hometown of Abilene, a midwestern city infused with the bigotry common to most of the nation but still a long way from Dixie. No blacks attended West Point during Ike's education there, and he had few interracial contacts in the Army that might have broadened his racial understanding. If anything, his post assignments in the American South and overseas only contributed to stereotypes of servility and inferiority. For instance, in 1943, writing from North Africa, Eisenhower told his son that he was living in a comfortable house staffed by "a group of darkies that take gorgeous care of me."[5] And while serving as supreme commander of Allied forces, Ike reportedly chuckled over a propaganda film that showed black troops carrying rifles in battle, something he said that he had never seen in real life.[6] Eisenhower did desegregate Red Cross and USO clubs and integrate some military units during World War II, but these actions were the product of practicality and necessity, not a desire to advance black civil rights or desegregation in the military. During his testimony before the Senate Armed Services Committee in 1948, Ike argued that because African Americans were less educated, they would not rise through the ranks of a fully integrated military. He also expressed a sentiment that later became a mainstay of his discourse on civil rights, that change in racial attitudes and conduct would come through education, not through laws: "I do believe that if we attempt merely by passing a lot of laws to force someone to like someone else, we are just going to get into trouble."[7]

Yet for his apparent paternalism, Eisenhower often took forthright action when he witnessed racial bigotry throughout his life. For example, he resigned from a high school sports team because the coach had harassed a black teammate, and later in life he refused to register for lodgings on the Florida coast, where he and Mamie were vacationing with Lucius Clay, because a resort announced, "Negroes and Jews not welcome."[8] In his memoirs, Eisenhower also claims to have always had a strong personal belief in equal opportunity: "Since my boyhood I had accepted without qualification the right to equality before the law of all citizens of this country, whatever their race or color or creed." But, like Truman and many of his presidential predecessors, Ike was not an advocate of social equality. He once told White House speechwriter Arthur Larson that political and economic opportunity did not mean that everyone has to mingle socially or that a "Negro should court my daughter." Some have taken Eisenhower's views against social equality to mean that the president was a segregationist at heart. Journalist Roy Reed even goes so far to claim that "Eisenhower almost certainly was more of a segregationist than [Orval] Faubus was." Eisenhower's former press secretary, James Hagerty, in contrast, claims that the president "didn't have a segregationist mind or a segregationist bone in his body."[9]

Ike may not have been a staunch segregationist, but he did not hesitate to separate himself from African Americans socially or to have a good laugh at their expense. Kenneth O'Reilly notes that Eisenhower was "habitually uncomfortable in black company" and that he told "nigger jokes" to the men around him on the campaign trail.[10] Once in the White House, Eisenhower repeated to his family and friends racial jokes and stories he had heard about "darkies" that he had picked up from his southern golfing friends in Augusta, Georgia.[11] Eisenhower may have once turned away from a place of public accommodation that denied access to blacks, but he played golf regularly with bigoted friends like Cliff Roberts on courses that did not allow African Americans on their grounds, except as servants.

These friendships influenced deeply his racial understanding and actions. Ike had a fondness for the South and its people; he also developed sympathy for their racial customs, culture, and fears. For example, in his memoirs, former chief justice Warren claims that at a White House dinner, Eisenhower expressed sympathy with southern fears of miscegenation and myths regarding the sexual aggressiveness of black males: the president told Warren that he could understand why southerners would want to see that "their sweet little white girls are not required to sit in school alongside some big black buck." Historian Robyn Ladino notes that close friendships with southern leaders also contributed to Eisenhower's gradual, moderate approach to civil rights. Ike gave the racial opinions of his friends in Dixie substantial consideration with regard to civil rights policy and became upset when their racial convictions were not accommodated. In a talk with speechwriter Emmet John Hughes, Eisenhower complained about the *Brown* decision and the school desegregation troubles facing the nation, noting that southerners' deep feelings on the issue had not been considered adequately. He claimed, "You take the attitude of a fellow like Jimmy Byrnes [then governor of South Carolina]. We used to be pretty good friends, and now I've not heard from him even once in the last eighteen months—all because of bitterness on this thing." Above all, the president's personal ties to the South led him to believe strongly in the good will of southerners eventually to solve the racial problems within their borders.[12]

Larson contends that Eisenhower's understanding of civil rights was more than "a little Southern." In his evaluation of the Eisenhower presidency, Larson claims, "I realized that this man, whose views on so many other subjects were easy for me to identify myself with, had views on race relations that to me were distinctly old fashioned or of another generation." O'Reilly argues that Ike had a nineteenth-century understanding of racial issues. Many of Eisenhower's notions of race and rights did hark back to an earlier era. He quoted Booker T. Washington in an address to the National Newspaper Association, an African American organization. He continually addressed blacks as "you people" in his public statements. He agreed with the "separate but equal" reasoning of the 1896 Supreme Court ruling in *Plessy v. Ferguson*. Eisenhower's inaction on many civil rights issues was not necessarily a product of indifference, then, but of a set of beliefs that seemed outdated to his critics.[13]

In addition to the influence of southern sympathies and antiquated understandings, Eisenhower's political philosophy determined his actions on civil rights. Ike favored what some scholars call a "weak presidency," an institution that would have few dealings with the other branches of government and would not try to force its will on Congress.[14] Eisenhower believed that presidential influence should be confined to the sphere of clear constitutional authority and that Franklin D. Roosevelt had pushed the boundaries of executive power. With regard to civil rights, this political philosophy meant that Ike took action to desegregate public schools in the District of Columbia and on U.S. military bases—areas of undisputed executive jurisdiction—but was reluctant to let Attorney General Herbert Brownell file an amicus curiae brief on the 1954 *Brown* case, which the president believed might infringe upon the duties of the Supreme Court. Communication scholar Martin Medhurst expresses sympathy with Eisenhower's limited conception of power, claiming: "Eisenhower knew what the constitutional limits of executive authority were and he consciously tried to stay within those parameters. . . . Eisenhower respected the functions of the three branches and insisted that each do its own job, as envisioned by the Founders."[15] Ladino, however, argues that what Medhurst identifies as Ike's understanding of and respect for the separation of powers was not a product of knowledge or respect at all; rather, his view was the result of a lack of legal understanding and political inexperience with complex domestic issues.[16] And other historians see what Medhurst calls knowledge and respect as excessive timidity or a lack of initiative to take decisive action on racial problems requiring executive intervention.[17] James Duram claims that Eisenhower's perspective on federal power was more than just cautious: he had a more limited conception of the scope of executive power than most presidents before and after him.[18] Holding steadfast to a minority opinion, however, does not make Eisenhower necessarily wrong.

But specific civil rights cases during Ike's tenure clearly illustrate his trepidation to act. The 1956 Eighth U.S. Circuit Court of Appeals ruling in *Brewer v. Hoxie* gave the executive branch the authority to intervene in desegregation cases when private individuals conspired to prevent compliance with the *Brown* decision. Although the limits of that authority were unclear,[19] the Eisenhower administration was unwilling to locate the exact boundary through a test case, and the White House refused to act even in cases where citizens clearly were conspiring to obstruct desegregation. In addition, Autherine Lucy's efforts to attend the University of Alabama demonstrate Ike's unwillingness to exert any executive power. When university officials expelled Lucy soon after her enrollment and a federal district court judge upheld the expulsion, Eisenhower refused to intervene or even to direct the Justice Department to research the case.[20] President Eisenhower's political philosophy emphasized separation of powers but failed to take account of the unwillingness of federal district courts in the South to execute their duties faithfully. Perhaps equally important, then, in determining the president's limited exercise of executive power in these and other instances was his belief in voluntary cooperation, that states, private groups, and local citizens should be encouraged to do the right thing by themselves.[21] Eisenhower believed in restraint by the federal government in general—not just in the exercise of executive authority at the expense of the other branches—and was sympathetic to the states' rights doctrine. As such, he was willing to wait for the South to act on its own racial troubles, as long as gradual progress was being made. Historians Chester Pach and Elmo Richardson claim that civil rights "revealed more dramatically than any other issue the shortcomings of Eisenhower's philosophy of government restraint."[22]

Given the limitations and shortcomings pointed to by many scholars, one might be inclined to think that Eisenhower had no accomplishments on civil rights, which is untrue. The Civil Rights Acts of 1957 and 1960 became law during his administration. While the drive for the 1957 civil rights bill revealed Ike's unwillingness to invest political capital in part 3 of the bill—which would have expanded federal authority in cases of the obstruction of court-ordered desegregation—the Act still was the first piece of comprehensive civil rights legislation since Reconstruction. And although the administration could have pushed harder to prevent the dilution of the 1960 Act, Eisenhower's initiative indicated a genuine concern regarding voting rights, about which Brownell claims the president "had a very deep emotional feeling."[23] The Civil Rights Act of 1960 also contained provisions to prosecute perpetrators of racial violence, an apparent White House concern,[24] but Eisenhower neither said nor did anything in response to instances of terror against blacks—such as the notorious 1955 murder of fourteen-year-old Emmet Till in Money, Mississippi. Apart from legislative action, the Eisenhower administration also made federal appointments that had the potential to advance blacks' interests. For instance, E. Frederic Morrow became the first black presidential aide in 1955, and other African Americans were appointed to posts in the Departments of Labor and Health, Education, and Welfare. O'Reilly claims that these appointments were merely an attempt to entice some African Americans to vote Republican, but Morrow believed that he was not merely a black "window-dressing" for the White House.[25] Finally, some scholars count Eisenhower's establishment of the President's Committee on Government Contracts (PCGC) as an accomplishment, while others indict it as an ineffective alternative to a reestablished Fair Employment Practices Committee.[26] True to Ike's political philosophy, the PCGC encouraged private firms accused of employment discrimination to work out the problem themselves.

Historian Michael Mayer claims that Eisenhower's "personal attitudes on race combined elements of sympathy, understanding, and empathy with paternalism and some racist notions." Eisenhower's public attitudes on civil rights were marked by these same characteristics and by his political beliefs in restricted executive action and voluntary cooperation. Perhaps the aspect of Eisenhower's sentiments on race most baffling to many of his critics, both liberal and conservative, was the relationship between his public and private attitudes. For example, Eisenhower may have been distressed personally by acts of racial violence, but publicly he seemed unmoved. Individual acts of bigotry may have invoked his horror, but as Mayer notes, Ike could not translate his reaction to specific cases into outrage at the larger issues of racial injustice in American society.[27] That is, Eisenhower seemed unable or unwilling to translate private concerns into public ones. As a consequence, many Americans during the Eisenhower years (as well as in recent times) did not believe that Ike was genuinely interested in civil rights. In a 1957 memorandum to Sherman Adams, assistant to the president, Morrow wrote, "In all my trips and speeches about the country, my greatest difficulty is convincing people during the question and answer period that the Administration is sincere in its attitudes on civil rights."[28] By his own account, Eisenhower indicated that his private opinions on civil rights did not matter, that the law was supreme. He also disliked the idea that a president should use the office as a "bully pulpit," which he believed would require one to "preach and yell" at the American people.[29] But his un-willingness to exercise personal, moral leadership led to interpretations of Eisenhower's motives at odds with both his public and private beliefs—inter-pretations that forced him to become involved in situations he wanted desper-ately to avoid, situations like the crisis at Little Rock.

Legal, Historical, and Rhetorical Dilemmas
The Schools, the Courts, and the President

Probably the most significant contextual factors shaping the Little Rock crisis were the Warren Court's rulings on school desegregation and President Eisen-hower's responses to those decisions. The *Brown* ruling mandated the deseg-regation of public schools, but in the ruling referred to as *Brown II,* the Court deferred enforcement, requiring only that desegregation efforts proceed "with all deliberate speed." As former attorney general Brownell notes, many southerners interpreted this phrase to mean "at some indefinite date in the future."[30] Many southern political leaders opposed to school desegregation formulated plans to undermine the philosophy underlying the Supreme Court decision, espousing a philosophy of interposition and nullification. In March of 1956, 101 senators and congressmen issued a Southern Manifesto urging states to refuse to obey the Court's desegregation order, which they called "contrary to the Constitution" and "unwarranted." The southern legislators claimed that the Court did not have the power to demand an end to segregation and that only a state can decide upon the racial makeup of public schools. The mani-festo also acted as a catalyst for the proliferation of chapters of the White Citi-zens' Council—an organization formed in 1954 to fight desegregation—across the South.[31] In a press conference, Eisenhower tried to put the best face on the manifesto, noting that its signers did not advocate violent resistance or state nullification of federal law.[32] Some southerners took Ike's statement as a tacit endorsement of their cause, and most interpreted it to mean that he would not interfere with their efforts to resist the *Brown* decision. Any hopes for inte-gration at "deliberate speed" were dashed as many southern communities stalled until faced with a federal court injunction, forcing African American parents and civil rights attorneys to file individual desegregation legal suits across the South.

While Eisenhower had not wanted the Supreme Court to mandate the immediate desegregation of public schools, his Justice Department had recommended that the Court require local school boards to submit desegregation plans within ninety days of the *Brown II* ruling. Brownell claims that the Court's decision regarding enforcement "created major administrative problems for the President."[33] The Court's decision in *Brown II* did create serious enforcement problems and contributed to massive resistance in places like Clinton, Tennessee, and Little Rock, Arkansas, but the president made his own significant contribution to these problems. Eisenhower's rhetoric on civil rights, school desegregation, and the Court decisions also encouraged delay and resistance, which helped create the "major administrative problems" the attorney general disliked. In addition, one must not automatically equate Justice Department recommendations with Eisenhower's personal or political attitudes. For example, in 1953, some southerners became concerned that Eisenhower personally supported the Court-ordered desegregation of public schools when, during a November 18 press conference, the president indicated that he was involved personally in shaping the Justice Department's amicus curiae brief. In a personal letter to the president, James Byrnes expressed surprise and dismay at the press conference comment: Byrnes wrote that the dominant southern perspective that the Court's interference was unwarranted was "in accord with the position you have consistently taken, that the states should have the right to control matters that are purely local." Eisenhower's personal reply to Byrnes on December 1, 1953, must have reassured the South Carolina governor, as the president's letter seemed to indicate a difference of opinion between his personal views and the recommendations made in the Justice Department's brief.[34]

After the *Brown* decision, perhaps in response to the interpretations of his press conference remark, Eisenhower became more guarded in regard to his personal opinion on school desegregation. As Eisenhower notes in his memoirs, he was unwilling to express his personal opinion on the *Brown* decision: "After the Supreme Court's 1954 ruling, I refused to say whether I either approved or disapproved of it. . . . This determination was one of principle. I believed that if I should express, publicly, either approval or disapproval of the Supreme Court decision in one case, I would be obliged to do so in many, if not all cases. Inevitably I would eventually be drawn into a public statement of disagreement with some decision, creating a suspicion that my vigor of enforcement would, in such cases, be in doubt."[35] When a reporter at his May 19, 1954, press conference asked if the president had any advice about how the South should respond to the Supreme Court's decision, Ike claimed, "Not in the slightest. . . . The Supreme Court has spoken, and I am sworn to uphold the Constitutional process in this country." Eisenhower did indicate distance, though, between the Court and his administration when asked if the decision would alienate his political supporters in southern states: "The Supreme Court, as I understand it, is not under any administration."[36] While many Americans looked to the president for moral leadership, Ike repeatedly claimed that his own opinion on *Brown* was irrelevant and refused to say whether or not the Court decision was right, just, or fair. Eisenhower had indicated early in his administration that rhetorical leadership was necessary to solve civil rights problems: in the 1953 State of the Union address, he claimed that the answer to discrimination problems lay "in the power of fact, fully publicized; of persuasion, honestly applied; and of conscience, justly aroused."[37] Personally, however, Ike was unwilling to provide the moral leadership he identified as crucial, believing that the president should not "be leading crusades of a moral, humanitarian, or civil rights nature."[38] Because of his reluctance to take sides in partisan conflicts, Pach and Richardson assert, Eisenhower did not know how to provide the effective moral leadership that would hasten popular acceptance of school desegregation.[39]

Ike did take some initiative, however, although it did not rely on the moral authority of the presidency. Eisenhower called on ministers, especially the Reverend Billy Graham, to use their moral influence to enlighten and persuade citizens to accept moderate progress on desegregation. In a meeting at the White House on March 20, 1956, Graham promised the president that he would advise moderation and try to get southern ministers to advocate that position with their congregations.[40] Soon, however, Eisenhower lost interest in the "Graham operation" and continued to hope that southerners would somehow sort out this problem in time.[41] The president continued to decry the "extremists on both sides," and he avoided moral leadership on his own, remaining convinced that a strong personal stance would inflame an extremely emotional situation. Ike distrusted popular passions and worried that a comment either way about his personal attitudes toward the morality of the *Brown* decision would destabilize an already volatile situation.[42]

Despite his carefully calculated plan of refusing personal comment, Eisenhower's silence actually helped destabilize the emotional situation regarding desegregation. Ike's "vigor of enforcement" was cast in doubt by his refusal to express approval or disapproval of the *Brown* case. By his own silence, Eisenhower gave organized southern resistance to school desegregation room to grow, as some opponents of desegregation took his refusal to comment as license to resist. Writing in 1959, William Peters claimed that Ike's failure to support the Court's decision had "obviously strengthened the hand of die-hard segregationists." Former Justice Warren argues that southern resistance "was aggravated by the fact that no word of support for the decision emanated from the White House." And Richard Kluger claims that Eisenhower's attempt to "stand above the battle" was tantamount to siding "with the legions of resistance." These perceptions apparently were shared by the public: a 1955 Gallup Poll reported that the fourth most frequent criticism of Eisenhower was that he "encourages segregation." Even if Ike did not encourage segregation by word or intent, he said little that assisted the moderate and undecided citizens who looked for White House guidance. Some critics argued that Eisenhower's silence aided in the polarization of public opinion. For example, *Arkansas Gazette* editor Harry Ashmore asserted: "There is no evidence that the Eisenhower administration is genuinely concerned with the lot of the Negro— none, certainly, in the record of the President's flaccid inaction in the quiet time after the Supreme Court decision when the moral weight of his office might well have headed off the polarization of public opinion." In short, the volatile popular passions that Eisenhower worried he would upset with public rhetoric were just as provoked by his attempts at neutrality.[43]

The president's statement that his personal opinion on the *Brown* decision had no bearing on the public issue still was, after all, a rhetorical utterance. In a sense, Ike was not wholly silent on his personal opinion, because he could never avoid answering the public question about his private sentiments. Citizens interpreted Eisenhower's answer to reveal some opinion—and in most cases it was not read to mean neutrality. Could Ike not see that articulating his philosophy of moral leadership as an answer would not release him from the tensions he wanted to avoid? He had, in other instances, avoided reporters' questions skillfully: could he not do so in this case? Admittedly, such tactics would have been difficult to execute. But Eisenhower certainly did not need to state his principle that his personal opinion did not matter. To supporters of integration and undecided citizens, his response must have had the same feeling of cold indifference ascribed to Stephen A. Douglas's "don't care" argument regarding the expansion of slavery. To these listeners, Eisenhower seemed preoccupied with legal and constitutional issues but uninterested in moral ones, and, like Douglas, Ike's apparent indifference was taken to mean a positive defense of racist practices. To opponents of desegregation familiar with Eisenhower's fondness for the South and states' rights, his apparent indifference implied sympathy with their cause. Complicating matters further, however, his response had the feel of pleading the Fifth Amendment in a court-room drama: why would the president not offer his personal testimony unless it would incriminate him? As such, his refusal to testify could incriminate him before both opponents and advocates of desegregation. Perhaps Ike could have articulated a stance of principled neutrality at another time or on another public issue; but—like the circumstances facing the nation during the Lincoln-Douglas debates—the gravity of the racial problems facing the nation in the 1950s made Eisenhower's rhetoric of neutrality on the moral issue untenable. Hardly anyone interpreted the president's statement as a purely neutral stand, and the passions he wished to soothe became more excited. On its own terms, Ike's discourse failed.

Revisionist historians and former members of the Eisenhower administration claim that the president's stance against taking a public, moral stand was principled: it was not the product of a lack of initiative, weakness, or indifference, as critics often have charged. But might Eisenhower's stance also have been the product of his confusion and lack of political and rhetorical understanding demanded by civil rights issues? For instance, it remains unclear whether Ike personally supported or disagreed with the *Brown* decision. In his memoirs, Eisenhower claims that he had "definitely agreed with the unanimous decision." In the wake of the Court's ruling, however, he apparently expressed dissatisfaction with the decision. Hughes recalls the president claiming, "I am convinced that the Supreme Court decision *set back* progress in the South *at least fifteen years*," and remarks on Ike's "abiding dissent from the Supreme Court action." Larson claims that during one private meeting with the president, Eisenhower expressed his personal opinion clearly: "As a matter of fact, I personally think the decision was wrong."[44] Perhaps Eisenhower's claim about the Court decision in his memoirs is a patent falsehood aimed at influencing the public memory of him and his administration. Perhaps, however, Eisenhower was simply ambivalent about *Brown* during his tenure as president. Were his personal convictions about the decision so decisive as Hughes and Larson make them seem? Ike was unsure about what the Court decision would bring: possibly he feared southerners might close public schools rather than desegregate. Yet he believed in equal opportunity regardless of race. But he also worried that Court-ordered desegregation was unnecessary. Eisenhower believed that African Americans could advance themselves through education. Still, he was sympathetic with southern fears regarding integration. The school desegregation issue was exceedingly complicated, and Ike had little legal or political expertise that prepared him to sort out the complexities. The president could not express his confusion and uncertainty to the nation. Maybe for this reason Eisenhower refused to express his personal opinion on the *Brown* decision.

Regardless of the impetus behind Eisenhower's statement that his personal opinion was irrelevant, Ike became committed firmly to that statement. If the president worried abundantly about the potential effects of articulating a personal stand, he did not worry enough about the consequences of not articulating a personal stand. Eisenhower failed to understand that southern resistance would not yield to mild exhortation or gradual persuasion from ministers or other local moderates. If Eisenhower's political faith rested in the gradual power of persuasion, as Hughes claims, then he failed on his own principles.[45] His stand against using the persuasive power of the presidency was impractical, and Ike did not adjust his beliefs about the "bully pulpit" for the limitations imposed by unique, acute circumstances. Eisenhower's principles, sympathies, and confusion regarding school desegregation combined to create a race situation that caused serious problems for his presidency and for many Americans.

Given President Eisenhower's public stance—constrained by political philosophy, sympathy, and inexperience—could he have said something following the *Brown* decision to prevent some of the desegregation problems that troubled the nation? I believe so. First, Eisenhower could have encouraged southern compliance with the Court's ruling more vigorously. He did indicate that he would uphold the Court's orders, but his rhetoric was not threatening—nor did it need to be. Instead, Ike needed to make a compelling, thorough public statement encouraging compliance. Second, Eisenhower could have encouraged public school districts to submit their plans for desegregation quickly after the *Brown II* ruling. The White House supported gradual desegregation, but the administration also wanted school districts to submit plans soon—within ninety days. If Ike believed that the Court's "all deliberate speed" mandate was too vague a timetable, he should have made public statements supporting timely submission of desegregation plans, which would not have been a violation of the separation of powers or required commentary on the morality of the decision. Third, Eisenhower could have used the law, as declared by the Supreme Court, to criticize the resistance of southerners opposed to school desegregation. Again, Ike indicated that he would—as was his constitutional duty—uphold the *Brown* decision, but never did he condemn vigorously southern efforts to circumvent or obstruct the Supreme Court ruling. Instead, Eisenhower merely decried "extremists" on both sides of the desegregation issue, though he never stated explicitly who these "extremists" were. Moreover, he continually expressed hope that the South would solve the problem. If Ike's hope was raised by the fact that some public schools had integrated without major incident, then he should have highlighted specific cases in his public speech and made a compelling argument that they set an example for other southern school districts to follow. Finally, President Eisenhower's public statements advocated gradual desegregation, but many school district plans that were submitted presented extremely slow schedules for full integration. Ike could have stated more clearly what he meant by gradualism. Most Americans also favored gradual desegregation, but the term "gradual" was interpreted to mean very different things.[46] Eisenhower could have shaped the public discussion of school desegregation in a meaningful way by defining this important term more clearly.

Historical and Rhetorical Precedents

Eisenhower's inadequate response to the *Brown* and *Brown II* decisions abetted public confusion and polarized public opinion, and also invited southern resistance to the desegregation of public schools, including the defiance at Central High School. But before Little Rock, resistance broke out in Texas and Tennessee in the fall of 1956: both of these circumstances helped shaped the Arkansas crisis and constrained Eisenhower's Little Rock speech. In August, twelve African Americans entered the public high school in Clinton, Tennessee, but were met by mob resistance led by John Kaspar. Local segregationists forced the removal of the black students, which led Governor Frank Clement to send in the Tennessee National Guard to maintain order and to attempt to uphold the Court-ordered desegregation plan. Resistance to the desegregation of Clinton's high school continued throughout the fall, and the federal government did not intervene. That same fall, Texas governor Allan Shivers sent Texas Rangers to Mansfield High School in the name of preserving public order—which meant barring African American boys and girls from attending the all-white high school. Shivers, a Democrat who had supported the president in the 1952 election, boasted publicly about defying federal authority in his state's school desegregation attempts.

When asked about the Clinton and Mansfield cases in press conferences, Ike did not criticize local citizens or officials specifically. Rather, the president decried "extremists on both sides" and replied that he could intervene only when a state could not maintain public order: "Well, in each case I think the local governments have moved promptly to stop the violence. . . . The Texas authorities had moved in and restored order, so the question [of federal intervention] became unimportant." Ike demonstrated in his public statements a strong concern with ending mob violence but little concern about ensuring the enrollment of black students in the face of mob violence. He also emphasized local law enforcement in desegregation efforts and indicated that federal intervention was extremely unlikely. In his September 5, 1956, press conference, Eisenhower stated that he would not intervene until "the State is not able to handle the matter," and in a press conference six days later, he claimed that the federal government would not intervene in state desegregation cases "unless called upon by the governor."[47] Southern segregationists took this rhetoric to mean that Eisenhower would never interfere in their affairs. After all, the resistance in Texas had been effective, sponsored by the governor, and violent—yet still reasonably acceptable to the president. NAACP attorney Thurgood Marshall vigorously criticized Eisenhower's responses to the obstruction of school desegregation in the fall of 1956, noting that citizens "continue to look to our president for forthright leadership in enforcement of the Constitution and laws of the United States Supreme Court." Marshall criticized the president's remarks following the Clinton and Mansfield incidents, charging that they had given "support to many in this country who have sought to confuse the issue by trying to divide responsibility for such situations between lawless mobs and other Americans who seek only their lawful rights."[48] Marshall resented an apparent implication of Ike's public statements—that the racist mobs and the African American children were both "extremists." Rather than making a clearer public statement, specifically condemning the confluence of forces that obstructed desegregation, or advocating a stronger role for the federal government, Eisenhower responded to his critics by ordering Attorney General Brownell to have the Tennessee and Texas desegregation case records sent to the Justice Department for study.[49]

While Eisenhower may have refused to take a stronger public stand because of his principles and beliefs about how to manage this domestic crisis, some scholars have offered different interpretations of the president's reasons. Historian Robert Burk, for example, suggests that Ike's motives for not responding more vigorously in the Mansfield case were largely political—noting that 1956 was a presidential election year, that Texas was a key campaign target for Ike's reelection bid, and that Governor Shivers was a personal friend and political ally of Eisenhower.[50] Regardless of any possible political motives, many citizens viewed the president's statements and nonintervention regarding the 1956 desegregation cases as a true expression of his personal and political faith. Ike's discourse and actions also might have led some southern resistors to interpret his previous statements about the *Brown* decision as a veil for his personal objection to the Court's verdict. The president's rhetorical responses to the 1956 desegregation cases shaped the confrontation at Little Rock—the expectations that Americans had about Ike and civil rights, the actions taken by the participants, the discourse preceding the confrontation, the need for a major speech to explain federal intervention, and the arguments the president used to explain his decision to intervene.

Confrontation at Little Rock

The confrontation at Little Rock was an extremely complicated incident: any attempt to analyze fully the confluence of forces that shaped it would be necessarily imperfect. The genesis of Little Rock school superintendent Virgil Blossom's desegregation plan in 1954, the revision of the Blossom plan by the school district in the summer of 1955, the local NAACP's legal challenge to the revised desegregation plan, the efforts to obstruct school desegregation through enacting a doctrine of interposition, the gubernatorial politics of Arkansas, and the passage of the Civil Rights Act of 1957 all shaped the confrontation in significant ways. But for the purpose of explaining Eisenhower's rhetorical response to the events at Little Rock, the quickening of the crisis during the late summer of 1957 is most telling. The court-approved plan for the desegregation of Central High School was scheduled to begin in September, 1957. By the end of July, 1957, it seemed possible that the plan might be implemented without incident. Little Rock school officials, after all, had developed a school desegregation plan voluntarily soon after the *Brown* decision; that plan had been tempered by the school board; the plan had withstood a challenge from the NAACP in *Aaron v. Cooper;* and many white leaders in Little Rock supported the desegregation plan; indeed, many offered to help prepare the way and to aid in its peaceful implementation.[51]

But in August, local segregationists who had not been consulted during the plan's development—led by the Mothers' League of Little Rock—took strong measures to attempt to block the attendance of African American students. On August 27, the League filed suit in the Pulaski County chancery court, as arranged by Governor Orval Faubus. The next day, Justice Department official Arthur Caldwell met with Faubus to discuss the enrollment of the black students. Caldwell communicated a lack of enthusiasm about federal intervention in Little Rock, which encouraged Faubus and other local citizens to pursue a plan of calculated obstruction that they believed Eisenhower would not oppose.[52] On August 29, the chancery court issued a temporary injunction against the desegregation of the local high school. School officials, who were ready for the desegregation to begin, filed in federal district court for an injunction against the citizens seeking to interfere with the school board's plan. Judge Ronald N. Davies reversed the chancery court's decision and ordered that desegregation to proceed. Following the precedent set by Texas governor Shivers, Faubus then asked Arkansas attorney general William J. Smith to draw up a proclamation to mobilize the state's National Guard for the purpose of blocking the black students' entry into the public high school. On September 2, Faubus appeared on television to announce that units of the Arkansas National Guard were stationed at Central High School to preserve "peace and good order," not to enforce either segregation or integration. Although Faubus claimed in his meeting with Caldwell that he could not produce credible evidence of impending violence, he insisted in his televised speech that violence would occur if the scheduled school desegregation were to take place. Contradicting his claim about the purpose of the National Guard's presence, Faubus also noted that preventing the enrollment of black students would stop the forced integration of Little Rock's schools.

Judge Davies continued to call for the unobstructed desegregation of Central High over the next few days, and the president became increasingly involved in the Little Rock situation. Davies repeated his order on September 3, without effect. In a press conference that afternoon, Eisenhower noted that the Justice Department was trying "to find out exactly what [had] happened" at Little Rock and planned to "discuss this with the Federal Judge." Ike also expressed his political philosophy regarding civil rights laws: "You cannot change people's hearts merely by laws. Laws presumably express the conscience of a nation and its determination or will to do something. But the laws here are to be executed gradually."[53] The president was calm, did not criticize Faubus, and indicated that the trouble in Arkansas would likely be handled without federal intervention: "Now there seems to have been a road block thrown in the way of [the school board's] plan, and the next decision will have to be by the lawyers and jurists."[54] But the next decision was made by Governor Faubus, who on September 4 ordered the Arkansas National Guard to block the entry of the nine African American students. Photographs of Little Rock segregationists harassing Elizabeth Eckford—a black student who, through miscommunication, attempted to enter the school alone—were circulated worldwide. The dramatic moment had captured national and international attention. On September 5, Judge Davies asked the Justice Department to investigate the causes of the disruption at Central High, which the department already had begun in secret. The local school board had asked Davies to call in U.S. marshals to carry out the desegregation order, but Davies apparently wanted to avoid conflict between federal and local agents. So, instead, he took the cautious approach of asking for a federal investigation and for the Justice Department to consider possible legal action against Faubus.

After Davies's rulings, Faubus began to initiate contact with the president, and the White House commenced meetings to discuss the Little Rock situation. In a September 7 meeting with the president, Attorney General Brownell informed Eisenhower that the Justice Department's report to the district court would probably lead Davies to ask the federal government to file an injunction petition against Faubus and the Arkansas National Guard. Still, Ike expressed a desire to give the governor every possible chance to take an "orderly retreat." Faubus notified the White House, through Arkansas representative Brooks Hays, that he wanted to confer about the situation in Little Rock and desired to find a way out of the predicament.[55] In the meantime, as expected, Judge Davies ordered the Justice Department to file a petition for an injunction against Faubus on September 9, ordering the governor to comply with the desegregation plan immediately. Davies gave Faubus ten days, however, to prepare for a hearing if he refused to comply. After careful negotiations about the rhetoric of their meeting (the governor was to send a public request for a visit indicating his desire to comply with the court order), Faubus traveled to the vacation White House in Newport, Rhode Island, on September 14 to confer with the president and his staff.[56] Eisenhower believed he had obtained agreement from Faubus not to obstruct the court order: a diary entry about the Newport meeting reads, "I got definitively the understanding that he was going back to Arkansas to act within a matter of hours to revoke his orders to the Guard to prevent re-entry of the Negro children into the school."[57] The president's secretary, however, recorded a different impression of the meeting's outcome in her diary: "I got the impression that the meeting had not gone as well as had been hoped, that the Federal Government would have to be as tough as possible in the situation."[58] Faubus's public statement following the meeting was vague: he did not express clearly whether or not he would obey the district court order. Despite Ike's perception, the administration's strategy meetings and its conference with Faubus had not produced the desired outcome—a clear indication from the governor that desegregation plans would not be obstructed.

The period between the Newport meeting with Governor Faubus and September 20 was an unsettling time for the president. With Faubus refusing to act and African American leaders demanding a meeting with the president, Ike found himself in a situation that might not be resolvable through persuasion.[59] Still, Eisenhower seemed hopeful that the situation could be resolved without federal intervention. On September 18, the Justice Department acknowledged that it would not seek an injunction against the governor if he would remove the National Guard troops: the White House wanted to give Faubus every chance to retreat without making it seem that he had backed down. Congressman Hays suggested that the president federalize the National Guard, thus displacing Faubus's authority. The White House opposed this idea, however, and negotiations between the governor and the administration terminated. On September 19, Faubus's attorneys filed an affidavit contesting the jurisdiction of Judge Davies, which indicated more clearly that the governor's noncooperation would require presidential involvement. Following the actions of the governor's legal team, White House staff secretary Andrew Goodpaster informed press secretary James Hagerty that "Governor Faubus is not going to carry out the order of the Court, but is going to engage in some legal manoevering [sic] to try to block and frustrate the order of that Court." Special assistant Sherman Adams and the attorney general advised that Eisenhower should not make a public statement—as the president wanted—but instead should wait to address the country after "the Court issues a directive to admit the children forthwith, and Governor Faubus refuses to comply."[60] On September 20, Judge Davies issued an injunction against Faubus, whose attorneys promptly marched out of the courtroom. Faubus did comply with the court order within two hours by removing National Guard troops and leaving Little Rock for a conference in Georgia. His compliance prevented a showdown between himself and Eisenhower, but it still required an important decision from the president.

The White House realized that the withdrawal of the Guard could create a serious law enforcement problem in Little Rock that would prevent the entry of the nine African American students but remained unconvinced that federal law enforcement was necessary. The Justice Department refused even to authorize the use of federal marshals, counting instead on Arkansas state troopers to ensure the enrollment and protection of the black students. Even Texas governor Shivers, who met with Ike at Newport during the crisis, suggested that the president might want to send U.S. marshals to Little Rock to prevent uncontrollable violence.[61] Archival documentation of White House conversations about Little Rock indicate little concern with protecting the nine children and overwhelming concern with preserving states' rights.

Scholars have thoroughly interrogated Ike's conservative interpretation of federal authority, but we should also interrogate his rhetorical stance at this moment in the Little Rock crisis.[62] If Eisenhower was unwilling to test the limits of federal intervention, he at least could have used the persuasive powers of his office, as demanded by some civil rights advocates. A speech to the nation after Davies's September 20 ruling urging calm, restraint, and nonviolent compliance with the court order might have soothed the situation. The American Friends Service Committee, in fact, made this recommendation on September 20, urging Eisenhower to warn "of the danger in the growing resort to violence as a way of solving problems."[63] A forceful address could have made it clear that the president would not stand for a series of unlawful episodes of resistance to desegregation. An editorial in the September 21 issue of the *New York Age* did urge the president to speak out about the "violation of the law," but still he remained silent.[64] Eisenhower also could have indicated at what point federal intervention would come if obstruction of the federal court order took place and articulated a forceful rationale for that intervention. A strong proactive stance in a national address could have corrected the perceptions of segregationists who had interpreted Ike's earlier discourse to mean that the president would never intervene. Given his apparent unwillingness to intervene until severe, unmanageable violence had erupted, President Eisenhower should have used his persuasive powers in a national, televised speech to attempt to prevent the violence and law enforcement problems that seemed possible, even likely, at Little Rock.

Instead, Eisenhower issued a written statement from Newport on September 21 that reviewed Faubus's actions, the school board's intention to desegregate Central High, and the preparedness of local law enforcement. Ike also expressed optimism that the citizens of Little Rock would "vigorously oppose any violence by extremists" and "welcome the opportunity to demonstrate that in their city and in their state proper orders of a United States Court will be executed promptly and without disorder."[65] Not only did the president's written statement lack the force of a televised address, but it also placed unwarranted faith in the local citizenry to solve the problem itself. Although some citizens in Little Rock did not oppose desegregation, they were not the citizens Eisenhower needed to address. Moreover, how were the "persons of good will" of whom Ike wrote to oppose violence by "extremists" in a meaningful, effective way? A carefully crafted message to the nation might have prevented the situation the president wanted to avoid—without lambasting local individuals or groups and without constraining the administration's options. Or, at least, a public speech could have demonstrated to some of Eisenhower's critics that he was willing to exercise rhetorical leadership. Even some liberal critics simply wanted the president to "appeal to the South's essential patriotism and respect for law and order" and to put the "authority and prestige of his office and person behind the lawful orders of the court."[66]

The tensions that smoldered in Little Rock over the weekend of September 21 and 22 erupted on Monday, September 23. A crowd of segregationists had gathered at Central High early Monday morning. Angry whites from the pack attacked four African American newspaper reporters mistakenly believed to be acting as decoys to permit the entry of the black students. Instead of arresting the offending whites, city and state law officials attempted to reason with the growing crowd, estimated at between five hundred and several thousand. Eight of the nine African American students entered Central High through a side door while the mob was distracted at the school's front entrance. One woman in the crowd exclaimed, "Oh, my God . . . the niggers are in." A man shouted in response, "Come on, let's go in the school and drag them out." The mob surged against the line of police officers. At 11:30 A.M., assistant police chief Gene Smith decided that the students had to be removed quickly, as law enforcement officials could no longer hold back the angry whites.[67] Police officers took the students through the basement to two cars ready to drive them home: the children sat with their heads down as the drivers sped through the sea of people trying to stop them. The children had attended Central High for just over three hours. Although Faubus was absent from Little Rock during the mob action, Mayor Woodrow Wilson Mann and others believed that the governor was aware of what was going to take place, given the presence of his friend and former henchman, James Karam.

At the White House, scores of messages poured in about the trouble in Little Rock. Arkansas congressman Hays was unable to reach anyone in the administration by telephone until late afternoon. Mayor Mann sent a telegram to the White House describing the situation and the inability of police forces to ensure the black students' safety. Soon after receiving Mann's telegram, Eisenhower issued a statement decrying "violations of law and order by extremists" and issued a proclamation of obstruction of justice—a cease and desist order that also justified the use of federal troops to end unlawful resistance to the court-ordered desegregation. White House officials realized that if violence continued on Tuesday, the president would need to deploy federal troops to Little Rock. Minorities adviser Maxwell Rabb worked out plans for the use of troops with Mann and approved the wording of the mayor's request for federal assistance.[68]

On September 24, a militant mob substantially larger than the previous day's contentious crowd assembled outside Central High—in spite of the fact that the African American students had decided not to return to school until President Eisenhower guaranteed their safety. The president remained in Newport, believing that it would look better if he appeared to go about his normal routine.[69] Yet things were not normal, as the administration discussed how to use federal authority to quell violent obstruction in one of the united states. That morning, White House aide Maxwell Rabb received a telephone call from a distressed Mayor Mann requesting federal intervention in the crisis. The president waited. Brownell informed Eisenhower that General Maxwell Taylor preferred to use National Guard rather than regular army troops. The president agreed.[70] Back in Little Rock, police were powerless to restrain the pugnacious pack. Just after nine o'clock, Mann sent a telegram to Eisenhower requesting immediate law enforcement support from federal troops:

> The immediate need for federal troops is urgent. The mob is much larger in numbers at 8 a.m. than at any time yesterday. People are converging on the scene from all directions. Mob is armed and engaging in fisticuffs and other acts of violence. Situation is out of control and police cannot disperse the mob. I am pleading to you as President of the United States in the interest of humanity, law, and order, and because of democracy worldwide to provide the necessary federal troops within several hours. Action by you will restore peace and order and compliance with your proclamation.[71]

Following Mann's telegram, Ike seemed to change his mind about what kind of force to use. He not only federalized the Arkansas National Guard but also ordered the secretary of defense to use any means necessary to overcome the resistance, including the deployment of U.S. Army forces. The president's command was carried out through Executive Order 10730. Ten thousand members of the Arkansas National Guard and one thousand Army troops were mobilized to Little Rock to put down the resistance. The 101st Airborne Division paratroopers were in place at Central High by Tuesday evening, and the remainder of the federal troops would be ready by early morning. With federal forces deployed to protect them, the Little Rock Nine prepared to attend Central High School on Wednesday, September 25.

Eisenhower Addresses the Nation

As federal troops mobilized and the black students readied themselves to enter school, Eisenhower turned to the task of explaining his involvement in the Little Rock confrontation to the American people. The rhetorical challenge facing Ike was formidable. The appearance of Army soldiers at Central High stunned many members of the local community and citizens across the nation. Given the president's earlier statement that "the Federal Government is not allowed to go into any State unless called upon by the governor," how would he now explain his use of federal force over Governor Faubus's resistance? Given the president's earlier insistence that sending Army troops into the South to enforce federal court orders never "would be a wise thing to do in this country," what would he say now?[72] Given the photographic juxtaposition in many newspapers of the president playing golf at Newport while angry crowds raged in Little Rock, how would the president demonstrate that he was in command of the situation? To many Americans it had seemed that the school desegregation at Little Rock might ultimately proceed without incident. Eisenhower had placed his faith in the local citizenry in his public statements, and many newspaper accounts—although concerned about "rumors of impending violence"—made it seem like the African American students might enter Central High without disorder or massive resistance.[73] Feeling confused about the apparent incongruity between the president's earlier rhetoric, media accounts of the confrontation, and the actuality of violence and federal intervention, many Americans wondered what exactly had happened at Little Rock and what it meant. For answers to these questions, they waited to hear from the nation's interpreter-in-chief.

Attorney General Brownell had completed a draft message on September 23 and sent it to Press Secretary Hagerty at Newport, offering the text as "a possible television speech or statement to be made by the president if and when he issues the executive order" on the twenty-fourth.[74] Most of Brownell's proposals appear in the final speech text, although his words were edited significantly in places. The attorney general's draft outlined the Supreme Court decisions preceding the disturbance at Little Rock, detailed the history of its implementation in the South, justified the president's intervention, indicated the limits of federal power, and called upon southerners of good will to preserve law and order. At 8:35 A.M. on September 24, Eisenhower telephoned Brownell, informing the attorney general that he was working on the proposed public statement, which would not be issued "unless or until something happened in Little Rock this morning." Ike also noted that he had softened Brownell's language about the law being defied, substituting phrases about his sympathy with the people of Little Rock.[75] The president's message went through at least seven drafts before the speech was completed: Brownell, Hagerty, Adams, Secretary of Defense John Foster Dulles, and others aided the president in completing the address.[76] Dulles, for example, suggested that President Eisenhower would be "in a stronger position if he talked more broadly than he apparently has done in recent days."[77] With a revised text in hand, Ike traveled from Newport to Washington, D.C.; he delivered his radio and television address to the nation at 9 P.M. from the Oval Office. The final speech does not address civil rights issues more broadly, as Dulles proposed, nor does it speak to the moral issues involved as some civil rights advocates hoped. The speech is, however, a clear explanation of the president's rationale for using troops, a detailed interpretation (from the White House's perspective) of what happened at Central High, and a direct call for an end to the obstruction of federal court orders in Little Rock.

Eisenhower's speech unfolds in six parts: an account of his decision to speak from the White House, a description of the scene at Little Rock as extreme, a rationale for his intervention based on legal decisions, a chronicle of the events leading up to the crisis, a rationale for intervention based on executive power, and an appeal to the South and world opinion. The central arguments that emerge during the address include Eisenhower's assertion that he has been involved with the crisis despite his absence from Washington, D.C., and that his decision to intervene in Little Rock was inevitable given the extreme situation there. He also contends that a moderate approach to civil rights (which represents the good will of most southerners, despite its frustration at Little Rock) still should be pursued. Eisenhower suggests that the law is the singular justification for school desegregation and its violation is the central problem of the crisis at Central High School. In addition, the president argues that the problems in Little Rock must be remedied in order to repair the damage done to the reputation of the United States on the international stage.

Eisenhower begins the speech by noting that he has come to the White House from Rhode Island to deliver his talk. The apparent strategy of the first paragraph of the address is to demonstrate that Eisenhower is not too busy vacationing to deal with the grave situation in Little Rock. The president attempts to establish his ethos, damaged by unflattering media accounts, by connecting his personal credibility with the ethos of the presidency—which apparently is located in a specific place, the White House. Ike seems to acknowledge a kind of scenic effect—what critic Kenneth Burke would call a scene-agent ratio—whereby the place itself reveals elements of the character of the person located in it.[78] Drawing upon the ethos of his office could facilitate Eisenhower's arguments about his intervention in Little Rock, but Ike states what is patent to his audience and communicates defensiveness by calling attention to his decision to address the nation from Washington: "To make this talk I have come to the President's office in the White House. I could have spoken from Rhode Island where I have been staying recently."[79] The conditional verb construction "could have spoken" in the second of these sentences implies a mood. The speaker's attitude toward his subject is one of legitimacy: for Ike to have spoken from Newport would not have constituted shirking his presidential duties. But it is an unnecessary mood to express. To an audience member aware of the accusations that Eisenhower was out of touch with the desegregation crisis in Little Rock, the tone of this overly conspicuous, justificatory passage might seem petty, which would detract from the very credibility the president attempts to bolster.

Eisenhower completes his conditional sentence by providing reasons for his choice to speak to the nation from the White House: "but I felt that, in speaking from the house of Lincoln, of Jackson and of Wilson, my words would better convey both the sadness I feel in the action I was compelled today to take and the firmness with which I intend to pursue this course until the orders of the Federal Court at Little Rock can be executed without unlawful interference." Eisenhower's words, however, do not make explicit why the White House—literally or synecdochically—conveys the sentiments he describes. The building that occupies 1600 Pennsylvania Avenue is not a site strongly identified with the civil rights movement or court desegregation orders. And the relation between the three men whom Ike mentions as former White House residents is ambiguous. Only one of these former chief executives has a clear relationship to the circumstance Eisenhower describes—Andrew Jackson, who objected to the rights of individual states to nullify federal law. The reference to Abraham Lincoln may refer to his conciliatory tone toward the South during Reconstruction or his emancipation of the slaves. The meaning of the reference to Woodrow Wilson is unclear. Wilson was an advocate of states' rights, perhaps even more so than Ike on issues of race, but he also instituted segregationist policies in the federal government during his administration. None of these former presidents had a particularly positive reputation with southern segregationists, and only one—Lincoln—was a positive symbol to African Americans. Moreover, nearly any audience member would have a difficult time understanding how these presidential references clearly convey Ike's sadness and firmness. Effective allusions must be appropriate to the rhetor's point and within the audience's experience: the president's historical allusions are strained on both counts. As such, they do not help bolster Ike's ethos, because the allusions do not connect his personal credibility with the character of the office of the presidency in a meaningful way.

Eisenhower's efforts to enhance his ethos were part of a challenging rhetorical situation. The press had created obstacles to his credibility, and his prior refusals to endorse school desegregation personally only contributed to ethos-based problems. The office of the presidency, while respected by many Americans, did not lend specific credibility to a president involved in a school desegregation crisis. The history of presidential action on civil rights did not constitute a compelling rationale for federal intervention. Eisenhower usually staked his credibility on the ethos of his office—his constitutional role and commitment—when speaking about civil rights: the first paragraph of his Little Rock address illustrates the limitations of his rhetorical strategy. Some Americans had questioned Ike's personal commitment to and involvement in the situation. Although he attempts to illustrate his personal interest and involvement by mentioning his return to Washington, D.C., Eisenhower does not issue a strong personal statement, which he was in a position to make. President Eisenhower could have said with reasonable cause, for example, "I am speaking tonight from the nation's capital, an area in which school desegregation has been implemented peacefully at my urging."[80] Such a statement, however, might have suggested personal support for school desegregation, since the District of Columbia school board had looked to the White House for guidance in its desegregation plans. Instead, Eisenhower appeals to a place and an office that communicates virtually nothing about his personal feelings of sadness or his firmness regarding the situation in Little Rock. Ike often claimed that his personal sentiments had no significant relationship to the issue of school desegregation, but as framed in the opening paragraph of his address to the nation, neither did the sentiments of the American presidency.

After focusing on the White House, the president shifts attention to the capital of Arkansas. The second section of Eisenhower's address is aimed at depicting the situation in Little Rock as extreme. The people who obstructed the court orders were organized into "disorderly mobs" and were led by "demagogic extremists." The mobs could not be controlled by "normal agencies." As depicted in Ike's speech, the whites organized in front of Central High are both radical and severe: the words "mob" and "extremists" separate them from the rest of the people of Little Rock. The president's rhetorical depiction in this section of the address is central to the speech's argument as a whole and its capacity for success. Eisenhower's depiction deploys what Kenneth Burke would call a scene-act ratio that ultimately functions to explain his intervention: as part of the scene in Little Rock, the extreme and deviant crowd depicted by the president required him to take a radical and severe action.[81] Ike argues implicitly that forceful action, which was a departure from the executive's normal behavior, was demanded by the scene, which was a departure from the local citizenry's normal behavior. Only by accepting his rhetorical depiction of the scene and its agents does an audience member come to understand Eisenhower's conclusion that his "responsibility [to act forcefully] is inescapable." The president does not refer to Sections 332, 333, and 334 of Chapter 15, Title 10 of the United States Code, as he did in his proclamation of September 23. In the absence of a strong legal justification in this section of the speech, only the president's depiction of the radical, extreme scene stands as a compelling explanation of his inescapable response.

The depiction in this section contextualizes the remainder of the address: Ike is not trying to justify regular or casual federal intervention in states' affairs, as many southerners worried—especially in their objections to Title III of the Civil Rights Bill of 1957.[82] Close attention to the president's words indicates that federal intervention will come exclusively in response to an extreme situation. Eisenhower justifies only this kind of federal response in the rest of his speech. Ike's depiction reflects his commitment to states' rights, but unfortunately it does not discourage other acts of resistance aimed at obstructing court-ordered desegregation. The president does not criticize the racist motives behind the obstruction at Little Rock, only the fanatical and disorderly behavior of those involved. In contrast, depicting the scene as one in which rabid segregationists attempted—but inevitably failed because of federal intervention—to enact their beliefs in the constitutionality of separate schools would imply a different rationale for Ike's actions. Such a depiction would indicate that the racial beliefs of mob members also were central to their defeat by the president and imply that any effort to subvert desegregation would be unsuccessful. A chief problem throughout Eisenhower's address is his failure to criticize the racist nature of the obstruction at Little Rock: he focuses instead on the extreme disorder. This rhetorical approach was ill-suited to head off the succession of southern resistance to come. In this early section of the address, before his detailed justification, Ike needed to make clear that his actions came in response to the conduct of racially motivated, constitutionally mistaken seg-regationists who were also "disorderly " and "demagogic."

Eisenhower also could have improved this section of the address by refer-ring to his own previous discourse on school desegregation, to make his words and deeds seem consistent. The president needed to depict the scene in a way that addressed a question on many Americans citizens' minds: Why did Eisenhower intervene in Little Rock when he had claimed earlier that he could not imagine such a scene? To speak to this question, Ike could have included a passage similar to the following: "Only two months ago I claimed that I could not 'image any set of circumstances that would ever induce me to send Federal troops . . . into any area to enforce the orders of a Federal court, because I believe that the common sense of America will never require it.' Unfortunately, the circumstances in Little Rock have exceeded the level of impediment and senselessness I imagined possible. Therefore, I have been required to take ac-tion I imagined impossible and unnecessary just over sixty days ago." Such a statement would have clarified the president's overall rhetorical stand on school desegregation and federal intervention and indicated that this scene was more extreme than other cases of obstruction in which he did not authorize federal intervention.

In the third section of the address, Eisenhower begins a detailed argument for his decision to authorize federal intervention: "It is important that the rea-sons for my action be understood by all our citizens." Ike begins his rationale by appealing to the Supreme Court's decisions in *Brown* and *Brown II.* He re-minds the audience that segregated school laws are unconstitutional and that federal courts have been charged with the authority to issue orders necessary to ensure the admission of all students, regardless of race, to public schools "with all deliberate speed." He then notes that some southern public schools already have instituted plans of "gradual progress" to comply with the law. These schools, Ike argues, "have demonstrated to the world that we are a nation in which laws, not men, are supreme." However, Eisenhower remarks, this fun-damental principle was not observed in Little Rock. The president then indi-cates that the violation of this basic principle also upset normal federal-state relations: a "localized situation" had to be controlled by federal powers; the "traditional method of leaving the problems" of a state in that state's hands could not be followed. Ike portrays himself as a forbearing man who hoped that the situation would be brought under control. But ultimately, he claims, "the law and national interest demanded that the President take action." Eisenhower's use of the passive voice in this final sentence and the reference to himself using the title of his office convey a feeling of objectivity, inevitability, and depersonalization. His language implies that he did not authorize the intervention but rather that the American presidency—its hand forced by the violation of core democratic principles in Little Rock—authorized the use of federal troops.

Overall, this section of the speech is convincing. Eisenhower argues from law and principle, confirms the authority of the federal district court's ruling in Arkansas, and demonstrates that lawful enactment of the high court's ruling is possible in the South. He avoids character attacks against Governor Faubus, whom he does not mention by name here or elsewhere in the speech. He depicts himself as having waited patiently for the citizens of Little Rock to comply with the court orders. The president's words are faithful to his commitment to gradual progress and states' rights.

However, one sentence in which Ike utters a common refrain of his civil rights rhetoric is troublesome: "Our personal opinions about the decision have no bearing on enforcement; the responsibility and authority of the Supreme Court to interpret the Constitution are very clear." The second clause of this sentence does not support the first completely: Eisenhower presumes that the audience understands that the president's responsibility to uphold the Court's interpretation of the Constitution also is very clear. That this sentence is unnecessary or misconstrued, however, is most troublesome. The adjective "our" indicates that Eisenhower is referring to his own opinion and the opinions of the American people. This sentence, like his earlier claims about the *Brown* decision, suggests to some that the president does not agree with the high court's ruling. When Ike replied during press conferences that his personal opinion was unimportant, his claim was, in one regard, less problematic than in this address. In his answers to reporters, he presumably aimed to direct attention toward his strong commitment to enforcement, which, to a man with an overwhelming sense of constitutional duty, was not wholly dependent upon his personal opinion. In this message to the nation, however, Eisenhower is not responding to reporters' questions about his personal sentiments. There is no need to direct attention away from his opinion to the issue of enforcement, since the entire speech act is about an enforcement decision already enacted. The president's claim that "our opinions have no bearing" adds nothing positive to the speech. If Ike meant to suggest that the opinions of the American people about the *Brown* decision have no bearing on his duty to enforce the ruling, then he should have spoken only that restricted claim.

By saying the word "our," the president casts a shadow of a doubt on his personal commitment. Eisenhower's claim about his personal opinion in this speech could not be interpreted to mean that he would not enforce the Court's ruling, as it was during his press conferences. But each intimation by Eisenhower, intentional or unintentional, that he did not personally support the decision wholeheartedly undermined the moral legitimacy of the *Brown* decision. Eisenhower demonstrated clearly at Little Rock that he would enforce the court decisions in a particular kind of circumstance. His claim that "our" personal opinion has no bearing, however, is not true. The president's opinion matters not only because it necessarily determines his willingness to enforce court decisions but also because the American people look to him for moral leadership. The opinions of the public matter because they can lead citizens to obstruct efforts to enforce court orders. Eisenhower undermines the moral legitimacy of desegregation when he should be engaging in a rhetorical effort to head off continued southern resistance to public school desegregation. Several scholars claim that it was Eisenhower's intimation that he did not support the *Brown* ruling and his refusal to provide moral leadership that led to his involvement in Little Rock, a situation that he desperately wanted to avoid.[83] His speech of September 24 indicates that the president still did not understand fully his failures nor how to use public rhetoric to prevent further obstruction of school desegregation.

After offering an initial rationale for his intervention, Eisenhower presents a chronicle of the unfolding situation in Little Rock: "Here is the sequence of events in the development of the Little Rock school case." The president begins his account by noting that the local school board approved the current desegregation plan in May, 1955, which required that "a start toward integration would be made at the present term in the high school, and that the plan would be in full operation by 1963." Ike then interjects that public school integration already has begun in other communities in Arkansas without violence, implying that desegregation can be fitted to local folkways. As Eisenhower continues his chronicle, this section of the speech evolves into more than a retelling of events; it becomes an implicit argument for moderation in school desegregation. He observes that the Little Rock plan was challenged by some who believed it was too slow and that this challenge was dismissed by the federal court. Ike claims that this dismissal confirms the rightness of a "gradual rather than an abrupt change from the existing system" and that "the school board had acted in good faith in planning for a public school system free from racial discrimination." He calls the Little Rock school board's schedule a "moderate plan" for "gradual desegregation."

Eisenhower's tacit endorsement of the so-called moderate, gradual approach in Little Rock deserves close scrutiny. The Phase Plan for desegregation was designed to proceed in stages, beginning desegregation in the high schools in 1957, continuing at the junior high level in 1960, and finishing in the elementary schools. Contrary to the president's claim, however, no specific date for completing the plan was set, although 1963 was considered a strong possibility. But this moderate plan provided for limited integration of only one local high school, Central High, while ensuring that Horace Mann High School would remain all black and that Hall High School would remain all white. Moreover, only a token number of African Americans students were to be enrolled at each stage. Significant integration was to be put off for years, perhaps generations. One school board member claimed, "The plan was developed to provide as little integration as possible for as long as delay was possible."[84] Some local citizens called it a plan of continued segregation, not integration. This approach was seen as the middle way by many citizens of Little Rock and apparently by President Eisenhower, too. The plan was not ardently segregationist; it was not racially progressive. Ike's chronicle of events indicates for perhaps the first time in public what he meant by a gradual approach to public school desegregation.

Eisenhower's words in this section of his speech indicate that the Little Rock plan is not too slow, given the district court's ruling, and that the plan is not too fast, since other schools in Arkansas have begun desegregation. Eisenhower also suggests that the local NAACP's legal challenge to the Little Rock plan was an extremist move tempered by the gradual, moderate Phase Plan, which subsequently was upheld by the district court. However, the actual reason the local NAACP filed suit in the 1956 case *Aaron v. Cooper* was to ensure the integration of Central High School and eventually of all other public high schools in Little Rock. Local African Americans protested when Horace Mann High opened as a segregated school and objected that only a handful of children would be integrated into all schools. Local NAACP leaders also believed that Little Rock school board officials would not move forward unless directed by court orders. Moreover, the NAACP lost in federal court primarily because prosecuting attorney U. Simpson Tate's arguments focused on constitutional issues—contrary to the local NAACP's strategy—instead of on the vague, limited nature of the Phase Plan or the hardships it created for black children.[85] Judge John Miller ruled that the Phase Plan was "a prompt and reasonable start," but the federal court did not rule on the basis of the local NAACP's actual complaints in the case. Ike may have believed the Little Rock plan to be moderate and gradual, but his implied rationale that the school board's plan was moderate and gradual because it was upheld against the legal challenge in *Aaron v. Cooper* is misleading.

Eisenhower's chronicle continues by describing the frustration of the court-ordered desegregation at Little Rock. He claims that some people at Central High School had interfered with the school board's efforts to "comply with the law" and subsequently failed to demonstrate "proper and sensible observance of the law" expected of all citizens. The president asserts that these "misguided persons" persisted in defying and sought to discredit the law. Eisenhower shows restraint here by not mentioning Faubus, despite his personal indignation toward the governor. This passage offers support for Ike's continued belief in a moderate, gradual approach to desegregation: it was only the "misguided persons" who frustrated that approach. And—in an interesting reversal of a *topos* later used by the opponents of civil rights directives—he claims that many of the troublemakers were "imported into Little Rock by agitators." Eisenhower suggests that the wise, unrebellious population of Little Rock was prepared to follow the moderate, gradual, court-sanctioned plan but were disrupted by deviants. As we will see later, he also suggests that the moderate southerners of good will ultimately will prevail in the desegregation issue. We will also see that his focus on the law here and throughout the speech ultimately frustrates his effort to advance an argument for moderation and gradualism in school desegregation.

After narrating the events leading up to Little Rock and the unfolding drama there, Eisenhower resumes his rationale for federal intervention. He explains that Americans' individual rights and freedom rest upon the certainty that the president "will support and ensure the carrying out of the decisions of Federal Courts," using all the means under his power. Ike focuses on executive force (or the threat of force) rather than voluntary cooperation as the ultimate safeguard of civil liberties. Without force, he claims, there would be anarchy and a lack of security. This line of argument is consistent with the president's earlier claims that civil rights issues are in part a matter of the heart—and that the law will not change people's hearts. One might also read Ike's principled statement about the relation between force and liberty to mean that the federal troops do not represent an intrusion upon states' rights or local freedom from federal intervention but rather stand boldly as a symbol of rights and freedom. Eisenhower encourages this interpretation by then claiming that "Federal troops are not being used to relieve local and state authorities. . . . Nor are the troops there for the purpose of taking over the responsibility of the School Board." Using language similar to that of Governor Faubus's television address,

Ike claims that the maintenance of "peace and order" lies with local officials. The Little Rock incident, however, is a "special case" in which federal help was requested by the state. The president asserts that federal action is taken only in "extraordinary and compelling circumstances," such as the "extreme situation" that was created in Little Rock. Still, Eisenhower does not explain why this situation was more extreme than in others in which he did not intervene. Nor does he explain why he responded to the mayor's call for federal assistance when earlier he had claimed that the president could intervene only upon a governor's request. The president does explain, however, that federal troops are in Little Rock "solely for the purpose of preventing interference with the orders of the Court," suggesting that they are not there to enforce desegregation or oppose segregation per se.

Eisenhower completes his rationale with a single, crucial sentence: "This challenge [in Little Rock] must be met and with such measures as will preserve to the people as a whole their lawfully-protected rights in a climate permitting their free and fair exercise." The word "climate" here merits close attention. The president seems to suggest that the force of the federal government will preserve civil rights and create a climate suitable for their exercise. While the first of these claims might be true in many circumstances, the second is uncertain. Would force create a climate suitable for African American children to enjoy their right to attend public schools? Force may be a necessary step to secure that right, but ultimately an appropriate climate would come when whites accepted the principle of integrated education, not just the enforcement of the law. By focusing on the law and the federal government's duty of enforcement, President Eisenhower neglects the importance of educating the citizenry to accept the principle behind the law. Furthermore, since the president had declared previously that laws will not change people's hearts, his speech holds out no hope that the law itself might create habits of heart that ultimately could contribute to the climate necessary for the "free and fair exercise" of all Americans' right to a public education.

Having completed the second part of his rationale for sending federal troops to Arkansas, Eisenhower then lauds the people of the South. He begins generally, claiming that the "overwhelming majority of our people in every section of the country are united in their respect for the observance of the law—even in those cases where they may disagree with that law." Ike then observes that the Supreme Court's rulings on school desegregation affect the South more seriously than other parts of the nation. He speaks of his fondness for the South and of his friendships with many of its citizens. The president asserts that his "intimate personal knowledge" has convinced him that the majority of southerners, including most Arkansans and citizens of Little Rock, are "of good will and united in their efforts to preserve and respect the law even when they disagree with it." Not only does the president try to create identification between himself and the South, he also tries to create identification between the South and the rest of the nation. He argues that the majority of southern citizens have the same respect for the law, the same good will, the same occasional disagreements with the law as citizens across the nation.

The form of address in this section of the speech is peculiar. Eisenhower seems to address the nation as a whole, drawing on his personal experience to inform the American citizenry about the southern ethos and belief system. Eisenhower also seems to address the southerners of "good will," calling on the prudent citizens of Arkansas "to assist in bringing to an immediate end all interference with the law and its processes." And Eisenhower seems to address his audience as though the very act of saying that southerners are of good will and respectful of the law might make them so. Each of these three forms of address is problematic. First, Ike privileges his personal experience as a way of knowing (his "intimate personal knowledge") over other ways of knowing about southerners' character, attitudes, and beliefs. As a result, he underestimates and miscommunicates the level of resistance to school desegregation in the South. Second, Ike expresses an unwarranted faith in the ability of the Arkansans of "good will" to stop the obstruction in Little Rock. How could they bring an immediate end to the resistance? The inability of these prudent southerners to carry through their plans to comply with the law illustrates that the level of resistance to school desegregation was more severe than Eisenhower understood. Finally, Ike avoids speaking directly to the people who created the crisis, including Orval Faubus, an official elected to represent the people of Arkansas. Instead of addressing the legal and moral dimensions of school desegregation, the president seems to attempt to make all southerners become sober and legally responsible by verbal fiat.

In a final point of identification with the South, President Eisenhower claims that southerners, like all Americans, understand that the situation at Little Rock has disgraced Arkansas in the eyes of the nation and our nation in the eyes of the world. That Eisenhower closes his speech with remarks about the international implications of the situation in Little Rock is significant. Medhurst argues that "Eisenhower was not particularly concerned with segregation or integration per se, except as they became issues in the battle for hearts and minds around the world."[86] In his September 24 address, Ike emphasizes "the harm that is being done to the prestige and influence, and indeed to the safety, of our nation and the world" as a result of the crisis in Little Rock. He states that the United States' Communist enemies "are gloating over this incident and using it everywhere to misrepresent our nation." That Communists would use this incident to harm the United States is ironic, the president suggests, since Communism bears hatred "toward a system of government based on human rights," such as American democracy.[87] Still, Eisenhower claims: "We are portrayed as a violator of those standards of conduct which the peoples of the world united to proclaim in the Charter of the United Nations. There they affirmed 'faith in fundamental human rights' and 'in the dignity and worth of the human person' and they did so 'without distinction as to race, sex, language, or religion.'" The president ends his address by asserting that if the resistance in Little Rock ceases, the "blot upon the fair name and high honor of our nation in the world will be removed" and "the image of America and of all its parts as one nation, indivisible, with liberty and justice for all" will be restored.

Eisenhower is correct to say that the situation harmed the nation's image abroad. U.S. Information Service had warned White House officials that news photographs of the mob assembled at Central High School "were particularly damaging to U.S. prestige."[88] Privately, Dulles bemoaned that "this situation was ruining our foreign policy."[89] *Pravda* used the incident to mock Dulles's public claims that U.S. foreign policy was based on moral principles: "The reports and pictures from Little Rock show that Dulles's precious morals are in fact bespattered with innocent blood." In France, several men scrawled "Vive Faubus" on the walls of the U.S. embassy, and the Italian periodical *Il Paese* printed a political cartoon depicting the Statue of Liberty dressed in a Ku Klux Klan robe, holding a burning African American child in place of its torch.[90] The Little Rock crisis also damaged America's image in Asia and in Africa, where colonial nations—some of which had come to identify with black Americans through organizations like the Council on African Affairs—saw racism against African Americans as indicative of American attitudes toward black people in general. One Ethiopian official, for example, claimed that the events had made the United States "an object of scorn and disgust."[91] The administration monitored international responses to the situation in Arkansas closely: the Foreign Broadcast Information Service submitted a report on world media reactions to the events in Little Rock to the White House on September 27. It is clearly a Cold War document, reporting on the reactions of Communist nations and the implications for the conduct of foreign relations.[92]

The persuasive effect of President Eisenhower's appeal to internationalism is more difficult to assess. Medhurst suggests a disparity existed between the opinions of the citizenry and the president regarding race relations: "To most Americans, civil rights was a purely internal domestic problem. To Eisenhower it was a serious issue in the ongoing Cold War."[93] In one sense, Medhurst is correct. The president's speech had the capacity to influence American public opinion about the international implications of the Little Rock crisis, as many Americans, unlike Ike, did not perceive that racial problems at home affected world opinion. Yet it is unclear to what extent most citizens could be persuaded to see the Cold War implications of racial tensions. Exposure to Eisenhower's speech could move racial moderates and those on the margin to change their attitudes and beliefs toward desegregation, which could promote African Americans' integration into dominant culture. Such a change, however, would be superficial and ephemeral since it would be grounded in a situation subject to change and not inherent to the issue of race relations. And the racial conservatives whose cooperation was necessary to avoid future situations like Little Rock were unlikely to be persuaded at all by Ike's appeals to the Cold War. Moreover, Medhurst's claim that civil rights was a purely internal issue to most Americans neglects the fact that many African Americans saw domestic civil rights issues in an international context. For example, in a letter dated September 13, Jackie Robinson urged Ike to deliver a speech on the Little Rock situation, noting "As it is now, you see what the Communist nations are doing with the material we have given them." Nearly a week before Eisenhower's speech, NAACP executive Roy Wilkins wrote to the president, claiming that the "events of past three weeks . . . have humiliated the United States before the family of nations." On September 21, the *Norfolk Journal & Guide* reported on international reactions to the situation in Little Rock, noting that "American integration problems in the South have furnished the Communists with new ammunition to smear the United States."[94]

Although Eisenhower claims in his address that civil rights is an important issue in the Cold War, in another sense, few officials in the State Department or White House saw civil rights as anything other than a purely internal matter. That is, the administration had made the states' rights approach to domestic civil rights its international orientation. It refused to allow international concepts of human rights or international organizations committed to civil rights to determine federal thinking or policy. Brenda Gayle Plummer notes that the State Department saw internationalism in civil rights as a threat rather than a challenge.[95] Eisenhower's speech illustrates the administration's orientation. For example, Ike quotes from the U.N. charter but does not argue that it is a standard the nation should live up to; instead he claims that America has been "portrayed" as violating the principles of the charter. The president is preoccupied with "the image of America" across the globe, not with striving to meet or spread international concepts of civil rights. Unlike Harry Truman's speech to the NAACP, Eisenhower's address does not suggest that the United States has the potential to advance civil rights abroad by putting its own house in order and exhibiting the virtues of democracy. Rather than showing concern with leading a worldwide movement for freedom and human rights against totalitarian and Communist regimes, the president focuses solely on removing the stain on America's "fair name and high honor."

As an alternate rhetorical strategy, Ike could have mentioned that Communism's promise of equality might lure away third-world nations unless America demonstrates its commitment to civil liberties at home and cooperates with other nations to promote it abroad. Then, Ike could have articulated the philosophy that makes desegregation an important national and international goal. Such a rhetorical approach would have been consistent with Cold War goals and might have defused criticism that the administration's "New Look" Cold War strategy was ineffective at portraying the United States as a vanguard force for a better way of life in the global arena.[96] Eisenhower also might have referenced the findings of the United Nations Sub-Commission on the Prevention of Discrimination of Minorities, which had undertaken a study of discrimination in education months before the *Brown* ruling, to make an argument about the legitimacy and desirability of school desegregation. Such a rhetorical approach still would not have persuaded the intransigents at home to support desegregation but might have appealed to moderate and undecided citizens. It also would have promoted a principle of human rights and global freedom rather than a political concern with national image. In short, Eisenhower should have made his appeal to foreign concerns a truly international argument about civil rights. A truly international rhetorical orientation would have avoided subordinating domestic civil rights to Cold War concerns about national image, would have urged the nation to put its own house in order so that it might promote democracy abroad, and would have used international principles and declarations, such as the United Nations Universal Declaration of Human Rights, to advocate the advancement of human rights everywhere.

Response and Reaction

A Gallup poll indicated that most Americans nationwide (64 percent of those polled) supported Ike's decision to send troops to Arkansas, while a clear minority of citizens in the South (36 percent of those polled) endorsed the president's judgment.[97] Responses to Eisenhower's justification for federal intervention also fell along regional lines. Following the influx of letters and telegrams responding to Ike's address, White House secretary Ann Whitman noted that response to the speech "was about even, with a sharp delineation as to geographical location of the sender of the messages."[98] Most Southerners did not demonstrate their "good will" or preference for moderation in their responses to Ike's speech. No polling or survey data is available to indicate the level—or causes—of overall public support or distaste for Eisenhower's televised address. However, by examining personal letters and telegrams to the president, media coverage, public speeches, and international responses, we can ascertain some of the strengths, weaknesses, meanings, and consequences of Eisenhower's September 24 speech. Such documents also can help us understand how Ike's message shaped the rhetorical situation in which his speech participated.

In Congress, southern legislators indicated that they did not find Eisenhower's interpretation or justification compelling. Senator James Eastland of Mississippi argued that federal intervention was aimed "to destroy the social order of the South," and Georgia senator Richard Russell claimed that the president did not have any right to "take over the functions of any state."[99] Russell sent a telegram to Ike on September 26, comparing the troops in Little Rock to "the officers of Hitler's storm troopers." More significantly, Russell accused the president of putting the Little Rock schools "under military control" and claimed that "the laws of this country give ample authority to United States marshals to deputize a posse of sufficient strength to maintain order and carry out any decision of the courts."[100] Alabama congressman Armisted Selden, Jr., also sent a telegram to the president urging him "to permit the states to solve their own problems in an orderly manner."[101] These legislators' claims indicate that several of the president's rhetorical strategies may have failed. Ike's argument that the federal government was not trying to destroy southern society but rather adapting the court ruling to local folkways in a moderate fashion did not succeed. His distinction between federal intervention in this extreme case and a total disruption of normal state-federal relations was unpersuasive to at least three prominent southerners. The president's contention that the maintenance of public safety and the management of public schools remain "strictly local affairs" also fell flat. Russell's telegram also suggests that perhaps Eisenhower should have justified his decision to use federal troops rather than U.S. marshals, which some southerners and a few administration officials had supported.

Other key rhetorical strategies in Eisenhower's speech also seemed to fail to persuade his southern listeners. Stephen Ambrose claims that the South did not see Ike's distinction between using troops to uphold the law and enforcing integration.[102] Responses from a few prominent southerners support Ambrose's claim. For example, Texas governor Price Daniel expressed his shock that Eisenhower had ordered troops into Little Rock given his "previous statements against the use of force," and asked whether the president would "occupy every non-integrated school in the South." The governor did not respond to Ike's depiction of Little Rock as an extreme case, nor did he perceive the president's claim that force would be used only to support court-ordered desegregation—not to enforce integration in every southern school. Ike underscored this point in his reply to Governor Daniel: "I am sorry to see that your . . . telegram wholly misses the point in respect to the mission of the federal soldiers in Little Rock. They are not there to enforce desegregation; they are there to support our Federal Court system, to uphold the law." Mississippi senator John Stennis also apparently did not accept Eisenhower's distinction. In a letter of reply to Senator Stennis on October 7, the president wrote, "As to the mission of Federal soldiers in Little Rock, I emphasize that they are there not to enforce or to advance any governmental policy respective to integration, desegregation or segregation. They are there, simply, because the normal processes of law have been frustrated."[103] Again, these responses suggest that Eisenhower was not wholly successful in articulating the crucial distinctions upon which his rationale hinged. Eisenhower's distinction between using troops to enforce court orders and to enforce desegregation may have failed, in part, because it was similar to the language Faubus used when he dispatched the National Guard to Central High: the governor had claimed that he was not enforcing segregation but rather maintaining public order. To be sure, many southerners also were unwilling to be persuaded to see recent events as Eisenhower understood them. The rhetorical obstacles Ike faced were numerous and substantial, and he seemed unable to overcome them completely.[104]

Responses from sympathetic southerners and white citizens outside the South reveal less about the impact of the president's rhetoric. *Arkansas Gazette* editor Harry Ashmore, for example, sent a simple, brief compliment to Eisenhower: "Thank you sir for your masterful statement on television last night. . . . You have made it possible for us to restore calm and good feeling to this community." Ashmore's letter does suggest that the liberal and moderate supporters of desegregation in Little Rock (of which the editor was one) may have found pleasing the president's rhetorical efforts to separate them from the "demagogic extremists" outside Central High. Harry Bullis, chairman of General Mills corporation, revealed even less in his telegram to Ike: "Hearty congratulations for your excellent television address Tuesday evening . . . This is the sentiment I am finding among business executives in New York and Washington." Nelson Rockefeller also sent his brief congratulations, "What you said last night and the way you said it makes us all proud to be Americans."[105] Unfortunately, these responses and other letters contained in the Eisenhower Library's archives tell us little about the reasons that the president's message was satisfactory to supporters of the speech.

Mainstream newspaper and magazine accounts also reveal little about Eisenhower's rhetorical act. The *New York Times* reprinted the speech text but merely commented that it "was a firm address, with some language unusually strong for President Eisenhower." The *Washington Post* stated simply, "Mr. Eisenhower was never more effective than in his description last night of his combination of sadness and firmness of purpose." The *Post* also argued that the blame for the confrontation at Central High should not be placed upon the citizens of Little Rock—perhaps indicating that Ike's claim that the crisis was precipitated by "demagogic extremists" was compelling to some listeners. In fact, the *Post* editorial lays blame at the feet of "supposedly responsible leaders . . . who have preached massive resistance, interposition, and other counsels of defiance." Other media accounts suggest that the president's rhetoric was less convincing to some audience members. For example, the *New Republic* seemingly did not accept Eisenhower's insistence that the people of Arkansas were not to be blamed for the crisis: writer Ronnie Dugger claimed, "Orval Faubus is not the cause of Little Rock. He *does* represent his people: they are the cause." Some of the writers and readers of the *New Republic* also were unlikely to find Ike's speech forceful overall, since he did not address the morality of school desegregation. In the issue prior to the deployment of federal troops to Little Rock, the magazine prodded the president to speak about "the moral inevitability of integration—not just the desirability of abiding by the decrees of the Court, but the essential rightness of those decrees." The writer also claimed that President Eisenhower should make "an effort to highlight the moral consequences of continued opposition."[106] Coverage of Eisenhower's address by many prominent periodicals was neither specific nor sustained:

insights gleaned from these media accounts about the rhetorical action of Ike's message within its rhetorical configuration are speculative.

Most African American newspapers claimed that Eisenhower's speech and his decision to intervene came late, but many still applauded his actions and words—although with some reserve. Many blacks had longed for the president to speak: the *New York Age,* for example, had claimed just three days before Ike's address that every black American was wondering why he had not "made some sort of speech to the entire nation." Following the speech, the *Pittsburgh Courier* declared that the president had acted "forthrightly if reluctantly" and that although Ike had temporized and acted hesitantly, he still deserved credit for his "forthright stand." The newspaper did scold Eisenhower mildly, however, for allowing Faubus "to slide gracefully out of a bad situation." The *Courier* also featured the response of Channing Tobias, chairman of the NAACP board of directors, who claimed that "law abiding citizens of every race and creed in the South, as well as in the North, will applaud [Eisenhower's] heroic utterance." Tobias did not indicate, however, why citizens should applaud the president's address. The *Norfolk Journal & Guide* reported that Ike deserved "the highest praise" for his "long-delayed but firm and forthright stand."[107]

Two prominent African American newspapers were less supportive of Eisenhower's message. The *Chicago Defender* reported on the events in Little Rock but said nothing about the president's address. The *Philadelphia Afro-American* continued to criticize Ike after his military and rhetorical intervention. The newspaper decried him for failing "to give the Supreme Court decision on school integration his personal approval and enthusiastic backing." The *Afro-American* also reported that Eisenhower did not understand the willingness of Governor Faubus and other southern leaders to obstruct desegregation and that he "underestimated the lengths to which Southern states are willing to go to defy the Supreme Court and the law of the land." And the newspaper persisted in its critique of the president's prior rhetoric: "The President failed to realize the encouragement he gave 'mobs and demagogic and misguided extremists' when he counseled patience, moderation and education after *Brown.*" In the eyes of one prominent black media outlet, Eisenhower's September 24 speech did not correct the basic flaws in his civil rights rhetoric, nor did it demonstrate an astute understanding of the school desegregation problem facing the nation.[108]

Like the American press, international news media focused more on the events in Little Rock and the troop deployment than on the president's words.

Scant international media coverage was not a result of a lack of effort by the administration, which took steps to promote Eisenhower's address. The speech was translated into forty-three languages, and copies were dispatched to seventy United States Information Service posts around the world for distribution.[109] And according to administration reports, the speech did receive some attention. Radio Warsaw and Radio Moscow reported factually on the president's address. The Ankara (Turkey) Home Service noted that Ike's speech had appealed to the citizens of Little Rock to respect the law of the land.[110] One of the few international media outlets to give the speech sustained attention was the *Manchester Guardian,* which printed Alistair Cooke's two-column commentary. Just days before the deployment of troops, Cooke claimed during a BBC Home Service radio program that the situation at Little Rock "should not be prejudiced by a resounding radio or television talk from the President," given the delicate constitutional (state-federal relationship) questions involved.[111] Perhaps not surprisingly, then, Cooke's report for the *Guardian* applauded Eisenhower's address. Overall, however, most international reports emphasized that the president had spoken and acted too late: for example, the *Rhein-Neckar-Zeitung* (Heidelberg) claimed Ike should have adopted a firmer stand at the beginning of the integration conflict to prevent the Little Rock crisis. The singular element of Eisenhower's speech that may have influenced international opinion was his distinction between the extremists assembled outside Central High School and the remainder of the American citizenry. Hilversum Radio (the Netherlands) decried the agitation by the "extremists," who had damaged the United States' prestige, and the French periodical *L'Aurore* reported that "a fraction of the American people are guilty of excesses." Even Soviet official Nikolai Andreyev distinguished between "ordinary Americans" and "racists" like Governor Faubus.[112]

Interestingly, while President Eisenhower's radio and television address did not receive abundant international commentary, it did seem to move the mainstream press at home to focus on the Cold War implications of civil rights. Unlike the African American press, most mainstream American periodicals did not report on how foreign nations—especially Communist-bloc countries—used civil rights obstructions to denounce the United States. However, after the president's address, which closed with a commentary on the nation's tarnished image in the world's eyes, many newspapers and magazines gave sustained attention to this effect of civil rights resistance. *Newsweek,* for example, devoted three columns to global reactions to the "serious internal difficulty" in Little Rock; the article included quotes from foreign newspapers condemning the United States.[113] The *Newsweek* writer, like the president, defined civil rights as a wholly domestic issue that created a "propaganda windfall." The *New York Times* also reported on the international aftermath of the Little Rock situation. The *Times* reported that Eisenhower's claim that the desegregation crisis "would play into the hands of the Communists" had been confirmed by reactions in the international press.[114] For the many Americans (or at least the mainstream media) who had been inattentive to the international effects of domestic civil rights issues, the president's speech seemed to heighten their awareness of a global context, though that global context was image-centered.

Conclusion

The trouble at Little Rock did not end following federal intervention and the president's speech. Eisenhower attempted, but failed, to goad Faubus to declare that he would assume responsibility for maintaining law and order and enforcing the court order. Federalized National Guard troops eventually displaced regular Army troops at Central High, but a reduced federal force remained there until the end of the school year. Ike continued to argue—usually without success in the South—that although the problem in Little Rock "grew out of the segregation problem . . . the troops [were] not there as part of the segregation problem." He emphasized that troops were present only "to uphold the courts of the land."[115] The Mothers' League challenged the Phase Plan and Eisenhower's use of troops in federal court, and Faubus appealed Judge Davies's ruling against him. In the absence of strong leadership from Eisenhower, the moderate local school board requested postponement of the Phase Plan on the grounds that questions remained about the legal and constitutional issues involved in the desegregation of Little Rock's schools.[116] Desegregation of Central High was postponed following a district court ruling, which was subsequently overruled. Arkansas also established private school corporations to ensure segregation; when the private corporations went bankrupt, the state enacted pupil placement laws to limit severely the extent of integration. Throughout these events Ike continued to articulate his belief in gradualism and moderation and refused to address the moral issues involved or to urge the South to hasten its acceptance of public school integration.

Yet Little Rock represented the frustration of Eisenhower's moderate approach to civil rights and school desegregation. The obstruction at Central High demonstrated that a gradual, moderate approach was not necessarily a feasible approach. The president's claim that the resistance in Little Rock was led by extremists implied that gradualism still might succeed. Without a proactive stance from the federal government, segregationists—even if unrepresentative of the southern people as a whole—could continually obstruct and frustrate court orders. A moderate approach also placed an often unbearably heavy burden on the African American students and their families to fight for their entry into public schools. Moreover, Eisenhower overestimated the good will of some southerners and underestimated their commitment to resistance. Ike's address of September 24 illustrates that he still did not understand the troubles that a moderate approach to desegregation would encounter, even after its frustration. Eisenhower's speech also focused on immediate restoration of law and order rather than the prevention of similar circumstances in the future.

Given Eisenhower's claim that some of the "misguided persons" in the mob at Central High were "imported into Little Rock by agitators," he should have recognized the potential for massive resistance to desegregation outside of Arkansas. Ike's depiction of Little Rock as localized, isolated, and aberrant allowed him rhetorically to separate segregationists from the nation's citizenry, which some international responses indicate was a successful strategy. This depiction, however, prevented him from addressing—and perhaps from understanding—the breadth of defiance. Eisenhower could have criticized other segregationist leaders, such as John Kaspar, who was being tried for his role in the obstruction in Clinton, Tennessee, in 1956. By mentioning other segregationists, Ike might have avoided making the obstructionists at Little Rock feel isolated (which seemed to increase their intransigence) and would have indicated that segregationist resistance would be defeated wherever it occurred. Ike also could have urged all school districts to follow the example set by other communities rather than justifying the single situation in Little Rock and urging order only there. Both of these hypothetical strategies would have urged broader compliance with desegregation orders without appealing to moral principle, which Ike wanted to avoid.

Any avoidance of moral rhetoric, however, ultimately would have been limited in its effectiveness. Eisenhower's civil rights rhetoric consistently focused on the law and court rulings when speaking about school desegregation, as did many southern moderates. Little Rock school superintendent Virgil Blossom also had stressed a legal justification for desegregation and focused on compulsion, not consent. Historian Tony Freyer notes that Blossom and other Arkansas moderates appealed to the rule of law, a value they hoped would transcend disagreement. What Blossom and other Little Rock leaders failed to understand, Freyer argues, is that what constituted the law would itself become an issue of controversy. For example, the doctrine of interposition deflected attention away from questions of moral principle and equal justice, emphasizing a legal abstraction in it opposition to desegregation. In Little Rock and throughout the South, obedience to the law itself, not the substantive value of equal educational opportunity, became the basis of both compliance and massive resistance. Freyer also claims that the use of force to guarantee desegregation obscured the moral issues involved in access to public education regardless of race.[117] Eisenhower's address on September 24, then, perpetuated the problems of focusing on the rule of law by southern moderates: it deferred a discussion of the rightness or desirability of integrated public education. If the law had been a solid rationale for desegregation, perhaps this deferment would have succeeded—although it still would have been an uneasy agreement and placed undue burden on African Americans. Since the law and its interpretation became issues of contention, however, Ike's rhetoric appealed to a principle that did not transcend the conflict of opinions and interests. Close attention to the rationale used by Little Rock's moderate leaders would have informed the White House that a rhetoric of legality and constitutionality was unlikely to deter resistance, since such a rhetoric had not actuated unobstructed desegregation of Central High.

Appealing to higher principle other than the law or Constitution was against Eisenhower's rhetorical instincts, given his aversion to the "bully pulpit." But the president did not need to be bombastic or didactic to speak about higher principles. Ike might have appealed to international principles of human rights developed by the United Nations. This orientation would have put civil rights in a global context and might have avoided a polarizing effect whereby the South felt the North was imposing its integrationist will on them—though southerners probably would have challenged international authority as they had challenged federal authority. Eisenhower could have argued that civil rights and equality are important national principles rather than focusing on force as the guarantor of civil rights. Yet these concepts would be interpreted as consistent with segregationist principles by some southerners: these concepts would not transcend the conflicts of opinion. In fact, the notion that Eisenhower could have achieved rhetorical transcendence might be simplistic. Some scholars imply that if the president had simply appealed to morality, he would have transcended the conflict—that the higher ethical principles would have persuaded citizens to hasten integration. Ike might have been able to appeal to morality in a careful way that would have persuaded some listeners and shamed them into compliance. And by participating in a larger presidential discourse on civil rights, any individual president's rhetoric would make an important contribution to the moral acceptance of civil rights. In the short term, however, the real force of moral rhetoric would be to provide the struggle for civil rights (approved by the Court) with greater moral legitimacy. By moralizing civil rights, Eisenhower could have helped demoralize the forces of segregation. Such a moral orientation to civil rights discourse ultimately would have persuaded blacks to persist and persuaded white obstructionists to desist. A principled argument would have made clear that morality is against the segregationist side, and demonstrated that the United States is a nation of laws *and* of morals, not of men. A moral approach to civil rights would have been politically risky and rhetorically difficult. Public moral arguments are challenging to articulate effectively on any issue. We should not fault Eisenhower for encountering rhetorical difficulties in general in 1957. We can and should analyze and scrutinize his civil rights discourse, but we also should be sympathetic to the formidable challenges he faced.

Depicting Ike as a rhetorical bumbler is too easy an explanation of his discourse on racial problems. Although he could have spoken more forcefully and effectively about civil rights, we should remember that the rhetorical situation confronting the president was extremely complex and challenging. Moral rhetoric was not only against his impulses as a speaker but also a highly complicated enterprise. The political and ethical complexities of racial issues thwarted presidents considered to be more rhetorically skilled than Eisenhower, such as Franklin D. Roosevelt and John F. Kennedy. In fact, the rhetorical career of Ike's successor on public school and university desegregation issues reveals that Dwight Eisenhower was not alone in his problems in speaking about civil rights. In fact, Eisenhower's Little Rock address bears a close resemblance to President Kennedy's 1962 address following the confrontation and federal intervention at the University of Mississippi. JFK's speech also focuses on law and order, and although considered an instance of crisis rhetoric, it does not depict the situation in Oxford, Mississippi, as a crisis in order to talk about the larger problem of civil rights confronting the nation. Kennedy's civil rights rhetoric is instructive. He also resisted moral rhetoric during his tenure, but ultimately he spoke with moral authority and thereby demonstrated that the forces of segregation would be defeated. His speech following the desegregation at the University of Alabama at Tuscaloosa was a turning point in presidential discourse about civil rights and race.

CHAPTER FOUR

John F. Kennedy and the Moral Crisis of 1963

During the same period that many southerners began to turn on Dwight Eisenhower for his stance at Little Rock, Ike's presidential successor transformed himself from a symbol of southern opposition into an adopted southerner. In 1957, John F. Kennedy spoke throughout the South as part of his campaign to win the 1960 Democratic Party presidential nomination. Kennedy intended to ensure that the party did not split along regional lines and aimed to secure southern support. The senator's efforts were largely successful: Victor Lasky notes that by the summer of 1957, the South had accepted JFK as one of their own and came to know him as "Dixie's favorite Yankee."[1] The *Christian Science Monitor* claimed that Kennedy handled civil rights issues adeptly in the South by "combining traditional southern suspicion of Republicanism with the reaction against the administration for using federal troops in Little Rock."[2] Only when pressed did Kennedy indicate his support for the *Brown* ruling, and oftentimes his rhetoric sounded similar to Eisenhower's: "Whether we favor the decision or oppose it, it is going to be carried out. It is the law of the land."[3] Still, JFK frequently criticized Ike's handling of the Little Rock situation, claiming that the president should not have let events reach a crisis stage that required intervention by federal troops. Kennedy repeated his critique of Eisenhower's handling of Little Rock throughout the 1960 campaign. During one speech he claimed, "There is more power in the presidency than to let things drift and then suddenly call out the troops."[4]

Kennedy's public criticism of Eisenhower came to haunt him as president, when in September, 1962, he was forced to call out federal military forces to control violence during the desegregation of the University of Mississippi.

Critics accused JFK of letting things drift too far, then calling out the troops: the president's actions, some noted, contradicted his words during the campaign. President Kennedy's address to the nation on September 30, 1962, paralleled Eisenhower's rhetoric following intervention at Little Rock: it focused on law, order, and constitutional duty. Kennedy claimed that "the observance of the law is the eternal safeguard of liberty" and noted that the law should be "uniformly respected and not resisted" whether or not people agree with it. He argued that his "obligation under the Constitution" to enforce the federal court orders was "inescapable."[5] JFK had considered Little Rock "to be a great failure in the Eisenhower administration," yet he made a similar mistake and echoed Ike's public discourse.[6]

Despite his political mistakes and rhetorical similarities to Eisenhower during the first two years of his administration, President Kennedy ultimately became known as a champion of civil rights, the leader of a "Second Reconstruction." Manning Marable notes that "millions of poor and working class black families framed photos of the late president . . . and displayed them proudly in their homes."[7] This conversion in Kennedy's image was largely the product of a single rhetorical event. The most significant episode marking JFK's transformation in many Americans' eyes from a dispassionate, pragmatic politician on civil rights to a powerful friend of civil rights is his address to the nation in the summer of 1963, following the successful desegregation of the University of Alabama at Tuscaloosa.

On June 11, Kennedy spoke to the moral dimensions of civil rights for all Americans and urged the end of racial discrimination in public education, in places of public accommodation, in economic life, and at the ballot box. He also urged Congress to enact civil rights legislation, which he soon would propose. In the most important civil rights address of his administration, JFK put the full weight of his office behind civil rights by declaring, "We are confronted primarily with a moral issue." In this speech, he subordinated the legal arguments that had characterized his earlier discourse on civil rights, emphasizing instead the moral imperative. Kennedy claimed: "This is not even a legal or legislative issue alone. It is better to settle these matters in the courts than on the streets, and new laws are needed at every level, but law alone can not make men see right." The ethical component of Kennedy's televised speech addressed the concerns of civil rights leaders who had criticized the president for failing to address the moral imperative of racial integration. JFK's address made an important contribution to its own historical moment and to the tradition of presidential civil rights rhetoric by speaking in ethical terms and confirming the justness of civil rights activism.

The stakes involved in Kennedy's "moral issue" speech were high. Many African Americans felt a heightened discontent with the nation's racist beliefs and practices; southern white resistance to integration had swelled at Birmingham, Alabama; and the consciences of many American citizens had been raised to the existence of a serious race problem. But President Kennedy had done little to alleviate the tensions involved in any of these situations. Kennedy needed to find discourse that provided a satisfactory interpretation of the circumstances facing the nation in 1963, including the immediate situation at the University of Alabama. He needed to explain the events at Tuscaloosa and to show that the desegregation of the university was not just another event in an endless series of local battles against the racial integration of public education. Kennedy was under pressure to justify his actions as commander in chief and to speak about civil rights more broadly.

Scholars have written extensively about the evolution of JFK's leadership on civil rights: many identify the June 11 speech as a turning point in the Kennedy presidency.[8] Several rhetorical critics have written about the development of JFK's address, its general claims, and its relation to his civil rights discourse in general. Theodore Windt identifies the speech as the moment when President Kennedy finally used crisis rhetoric to speak to civil rights issues. Steven Goldzwig and George Dionisopoulos examine the June 11 address as part of their discussion of Kennedy's evolution from "principled bystander" to "public advocate." Craig Smith and Kathy Smith discuss briefly JFK's speech as a policy address in the tradition of "the American Jeremiad."[9] Yet the character of Kennedy's value appeals to the American public and his attempt to define the state of American race relations as a moral crisis demand a closer, sustained textual reading. Important questions about the president's speech remain unanswered: How did he define civil rights as a moral issue? According to the president, what moral code was being defied, and who was defying it? How, according to President Kennedy, could the American public redeem itself? What are the consequences of defining civil rights as a moral issue?

This chapter analyzes the contextual influences leading up to Kennedy's address, the speech text itself, and the influence of the president's words on the configuration of public discourse on race in 1963. I will demonstrate how JFK's speech used immediate circumstances to interpret the nation's broader racial problems in light of national ideals, to supply the citizenry with a sense of power to surmount its problems, and to present a vocabulary for moral action. Kennedy's speech is remarkable and stands as the first sustained moral argument by an American president on civil rights. He attempted to goad the citizenry toward civic virtue as he affirmed the civil rights movement. He appealed to Christian ethics and traditional American values as the grounds for ethical behavior with regard to race. The president's rhetoric was consistent with the discourse of many civil rights activists but seemed unlikely to change the deeply entrenched racial beliefs of many southerners. Yet his national address made clear that the moral strength of the office of the presidency was on the side of civil rights, and Kennedy established that the forces of segregation would now be compelled to fight an ethical battle in which the president declared them to be on the losing side. In one sense, Kennedy's speech seemed to be a timely response to a critical moment in American race relations, yet we also can understand it to be overdue and too late. In order to illuminate the context of President Kennedy's speech and evaluate its moral argument, the chapter will: (1) examine JFK's attitudes and approach toward civil rights; (2) interpret the historical circumstances that preceded the address and that shaped its production and rhetorical strategies; (3) analyze the speech text closely, especially its moral argument; and (4) discuss the responses to Kennedy's address and its impact on the configuration of events that made his speech possible and on the nature of presidential discourse about race.

JFK, Race, and the Politics of Civil Rights

The manner of John Kennedy's convictions angered many liberal Democrats, as he was devoted to rationalism instead of instinctive belief. Kennedy was "always a bit detached and emotionally uncommitted" to issues about which others felt deeply—including civil rights.[10] The most common words that friends, former colleagues, and scholars have used to describe the Kennedy persuasion are cool, skeptical, and pragmatic. Biographer Richard Reeves argues that a philosophy characterized by cool objectivity, dispassionate analysis, and decision making unswayed by sentiment or subjective and moral argument was a point of pride to Kennedy. Historian Stephen Oates asserts that JFK had "detached, dispassionate views toward social problems." Kennedy's friend and attorney Clark Clifford claims that the president had a pragmatic cynicism toward events and people, and former special assistant on civil rights Harris Wofford states that Kennedy "was the candidate of reason in politics, not passion in politics." If Kennedy's initial proclivity was to be cool in all things, this was especially true of civil rights.[11]

Assessing JFK's attitude toward civil rights, Wofford claims: "He considered it irrational. He was not knowledgeable about it. It was alien to most of his experience." Kennedy's privileged lifestyle did not provide him with a deep knowledge or feelings about the racial prejudices that his fellow citizens possessed or confronted. He had little interaction with blacks in Boston or Hyannisport, except as servants. Perhaps his only sustained association with an African American as a young man was with his valet, George Thomas, whose services had been given to the junior congressman as a gift from family friend and *New York Times* columnist Arthur Krock. Still, Kennedy was not a bigot: he opposed discrimination intellectually, "but there was little in his experience to create a passion about the subject."[12] He did not know any blacks well enough to understand more fully the awful effects of prejudice, though it is not certain that personal interaction would have ignited a burning sentiment on civil rights. Each meeting with African American leaders, however, seemed to advance Kennedy a little in his own commitment to civil rights.[13] But until 1963 (and a few argue even then), JFK's opposition to racial discrimination was more abstract than felt; he thought prejudice was a waste of emotion and time. White House speechwriter Theodore Sorensen claims that Kennedy was against discrimination before assuming the presidency but notes that "it was an academic judgment rather than a deep-rooted personal compulsion."[14]

Civil rights leaders perceived Kennedy's detachment on issues of race during his senate years and during the first two years of his presidency. Although former special assistant to the president Arthur Schlesinger, Jr., claims that Kennedy's openness, interest, and sympathy impressed activists in spite of his hesitance to act, most leaders still worried that he lacked the moral commitment necessary to effect significant social change.[15] For example, Martin Luther King, Jr., told Wofford: "I'm afraid the fact is he's got the understanding and he's got the political skill . . . but the moral passion is missing." King believed that the president did not have "a depthed understanding" of civil rights problems.[16] Members of the Student Nonviolent Coordinating Committee (SNCC) also grumbled that Kennedy "lacked any deep moral commitment to the cause of civil rights."[17] JFK may not have understood the kind of commitment civil rights leaders wanted from him: David Halberstam notes that Kennedy "felt that if he wasn't an active racist himself, then he was on the right side of the issue, and that black people would understand the essential goodness of his heart."[18] Many leaders worried, however, that because racial issues did not touch the president deeply, he would not understand the full nature of their problems or the stirrings of social change.

These worries were well founded. Kennedy did not comprehend the significance of race as the dominant factor in African Americans' troubled lives. In a peculiar sense, JFK had an egalitarian attitude toward blacks: they were no different to him than any other group of people, nor were their problems special or unique. Sorensen notes, for example, that, as a senator, Kennedy was more likely to talk about the general problems of education, unemployment, and slum housing than to focus directly on the race issue."[19] Kennedy was often sympathetic to the problems confronting many blacks, but he was not sensitive to the racial element of those problems. As president, he often wondered why African American leaders criticized his record on "civil rights," when he was working to ensure passage of employment, housing, education, and tax measures that would help improve circumstances for blacks. Only through increased exposure to African Americans' problems and through the influence of others did Kennedy eventually begin to understand the centrality of race.

Compounding many civil rights leaders' apprehension about JFK was that he seemed to treat their cause as just another political issue to be managed. Harvard Sitkoff claims that civil rights leaders viewed the president as "a temporizer and a manipulator, devoid of any true sense of moral urgency concerning the race issue" and as someone who "saw the struggle against racism as a conundrum to be managed, not a cause to be championed."[20] Halberstam asserts that Kennedy viewed civil rights activists as "something to be handled, lest they get in his way and cause unwanted problems," and Reeves argues that to JFK "civil rights, Negro demands, were just politics, a volatile issue to be defused."[21] Kennedy's actions during his congressional and early presidential years seem to prove the charges that he treated civil rights as a strictly political issue. During the legislative process to pass the Civil Rights Act of 1957, Senator Kennedy voted with the South to send the bill to the Senate Judiciary Committee, headed by racist James O. Eastland (D-Mississippi), and sided with the South on the bill's jury trial amendment—which would provide for local, all-white juries to decide cases of voting rights infractions in Dixieland.[22] Both votes angered advocates of civil rights, who charged that JFK was "playing politics" in order to maintain southern support for his bid for the presidency. As president, Kennedy's actions during the 1961 Freedom Rides and the Albany protests also seemed politically motivated: he appeared to possess a strong interest in the maintenance of civil order and southern political support but little interest in the advancement of civil rights.[23] Still, Kennedy attempted to play civil rights both ways as a political issue. He was interested in gaining black votes as a candidate and, therefore, often made platitudinous statements and symbolic gestures on race aimed at securing African American support. The influence and impact of JFK's call to Coretta Scott King during the 1960 campaign and his inaugural address, however, demonstrate that blacks sometimes took Kennedy's words and deeds to be genuine, not perfunctory and crudely political.

Overall, race was often just another political issue to Kennedy: in fact, he usually saw civil rights as a peripheral issue and wanted to keep it that way. The international implications of civil rights, however, prevented the president from pushing civil rights to the periphery. Critics charge that Kennedy was most concerned about domestic racial difficulties as a foreign policy problem: "he didn't want to see the problems give the country a bad name abroad."[24] Kennedy worried that the Freedom Rides, for instance, would damage America's international image and obstruct his ability to negotiate international agreements. Perhaps JFK's central aim with regard to civil rights was to prevent international publicity about domestic racism, which would help the Communists exploit America's racial problems for their benefit. Historian Carl Brauer suggests that Kennedy's international outlook on civil rights was not wholly bad, that he understood integration to be profoundly important in a global context.[25] However, for the president the key element in the global context was the United States' image, not an international perspective on human rights. Especially during the first two years of his presidency, Kennedy was concerned primarily with the international political effects of domestic civil rights abuses, not with the political possibilities of locating civil rights in an international context.

Kennedy's political approach to civil rights reflected his worldview. Political scientist Bruce Miroff claims that above all, JFK was a political pragmatist—an orientation that led him to focus on behind-the-scenes negotiation, tangible outcomes, political contexts, and executive leadership. Kennedy's political pragmatism assumed a bounded political context in which elites competed, bargained, and compromised; the primary skill for a political leader, then, was the ability to maneuver among and manipulate those elites.[26] JFK seemed unequipped to deal with the civil rights movement's program of mass politics and direct action, which was unpredictable and created political volatility. Moreover, he was skeptical of the movement's moralistic tone, which was an anathema from Kennedy's perspective, and its distrust of elite politics, which was fundamental to Kennedy's perspective. That President Kennedy treated civil rights as a political issue should not be surprising or necessarily damning. Civil rights is a political issue involving the distribution of power, and the presidency is a political office whose occupants "play politics" with every issue. Any criticism of Kennedy's political approach to civil rights should not be leveraged against his penchant for playing politics. Rather, it should charge that JFK's style of politics was uncomfortable with blacks' intrusion on the political scene and that he failed to give civil rights—and domestic issues in general—high rank on his political agenda until the year of his death.

When in 1963 Kennedy ultimately took strong action on civil rights and spoke about the moral imperative of racial equality, he still was motivated in part by political concerns. He needed to satisfy the scores of Americans who protested against prolonged federal inaction, reduce the potential for racial violence, and attempt to maintain the shred of confidence African Americans still had in the federal government. Additionally, JFK believed it necessary to aid moderate civil rights leaders like Roy Wilkins, James Farmer, and Martin Luther King, Jr., in securing their objectives lest the movement be taken over by radicals. Schlesinger claims that the president saw no alternative but to lead the fight for civil rights in order to prevent the final isolation of the black leadership and the embitterment of the African American people. Yet Kennedy's decision to speak and act was not "based on a cold political calculation," as Kenneth O'Reilly asserts.[27] Rather JFK's sense of morality on civil rights developed while in office, and perhaps politics and his understanding of the presidency intensified his concern about racial discrimination. Kennedy became very sensitive to criticism of his moral leadership, and when forced to meet with civil rights leaders and to negotiate racial disturbances, he came to understand the profundity of racism. Historians and political scientists have found Harry Truman's maturation on civil rights while in the White House honorable, but some scholars seem unwilling to grant the same possibility to JFK, who apparently was supposed to know better all along. Some civil rights leaders, however, came to regard the president as a friend, "a man who had grown in office and who had sincerely grappled with the complexities of America's racial dilemma," despite the limitations of his leadership.[28] Kennedy's strong leadership in 1963 was a product of a political concern and a matured personal understanding: both convinced him that civil rights was an issue of "such national gravity that it must transcend normal political considerations."[29] As such, President Kennedy declared on the evening of June 11 that civil rights was a "moral crisis."

In short, JFK, like most modern American presidents, seems enigmatic on civil rights. As a senator, he voted to weaken civil rights legislation in 1957 but proposed his own antibombing bill a year later. As a presidential candidate, Kennedy chose as a running mate Lyndon Johnson, the senator who had gutted the Civil Rights Act of 1957 but supported the strong civil rights plank in his party's platform.[30] As president, he worried about the damaging effects of discrimination on the economy, on health, and on education but took little initiative to overcome the racial aspects of the economic, medical, and educational problems facing the country. Kennedy shared modern liberals' faith that the federal government, led by a dynamic chief executive, could solve acute social problems, but he did not provide vigorous, active leadership on civil rights during the first two years of his administration. Former White House officials claim that JFK's convictions "were reached gradually, logically, and coolly," yet with regard to civil rights, the president seemed to lose his coolness. And although "the best spirit of Kennedy was largely absent from the racial deliberations of his presidency" in 1962 and 1963, contemporary writers still praise his speech of June 11, 1963, as a model of rhetorical leadership during a time of trial.[31]

Moral, Global, and Domestic Crises

In order to illuminate how Kennedy's speech of June 11 was a product of and a response to a particular set of circumstances, I will advance three central claims about the historical and rhetorical contexts that shaped the address. First, the moral tone of JFK's campaign rhetoric created an appetite that his early presidential discourse did not satiate. Activists later turned Kennedy's own words against him in order to pressure him into a moral stance on civil rights. Second, the Cold War shaped Kennedy's early presidential rhetoric on racial issues. This rhetoric, which reflected his preoccupation with international affairs, alienated civil rights leaders further and intensified their criticism of the president's failure to speak out about the moral dimensions of civil rights. Third, the crisis in Birmingham and George Wallace's interference at the University of Alabama raised the national conscience and the conscience of the White House. The confluence of these contextual factors eventually made the costs of not speaking out about the moral aspects of racial equality too high. As a consequence, President Kennedy delivered his June 11 radio and television address—a speech that also expressed his own developing sense of moral urgency about civil rights.

Throughout the 1960 presidential campaign, Kennedy's civil rights rhetoric was moral in tone—at least in many of his speeches outside the South. He claimed that racial discrimination was wrong and argued that the nation's next president must act as a moral leader on civil rights issues. Kennedy's promise of moral leadership was more important to many civil rights activists than his promises of decisive executive action, such as ending housing discrimination with "the stroke of a pen," and his promises of legislative leadership. President Eisenhower was disliked by many civil rights leaders, in spite of his executive action and the passage of two civil rights bills during his administration. Ike attempted to use moderate legislative action to improve the nation's racial problems but did not deliver the strong moral rhetoric that many African Americans longed to hear from a chief executive. Executive action and legislation were important steps in blacks' journey toward freedom equality, but they also wanted to know that the president was on their side during that journey.

Kennedy's demand for strong moral leadership was a common theme in his public speeches throughout the presidential campaign. In an address to the National Press Club on January 14, he claimed, "The White House is not only the center of political leadership. It must be the center of moral leadership—a 'bully pulpit,' as Theodore Roosevelt described it."[32] Later in the speech, he invoked the spirit of other moral leaders: "[Franklin] Roosevelt fulfilled the role of moral leadership. So did Wilson and Lincoln, Truman and Jackson and Teddy Roosevelt—they fought for the great ideals as well as the bills. And the time has come to demand that kind of leadership again." Candidate Kennedy used similar appeals during a campaign speech in Springfield, Ohio, on October 17: "The next president himself must set the moral tone, and I refer not only to his language, but to his actions in office. For the Presidency, as Franklin Roosevelt himself has said, is preeminently a place of moral leadership. And I intend, if successful, to try to restore that leadership and atmosphere beginning in 1961."[33] And in a response to questions by the Associated Press, JFK claimed, "The President must be a moral leader—using the educational and inspirational powers of his office to achieve the goals of harmony and justice our national responsibilities require."[34] In these three speeches, Kennedy's promise of moral suasion was not confined to civil rights. Rather, he indicated that his very conception of the presidency was grounded on the principle of moral leadership.

In other campaign addresses, Kennedy made explicit the connection between moral leadership by the president and the nation's civil rights crisis. Addressing a crowd in New York City on June 23, he claimed, "Moral persuasion by the president can be more effective than force in ending discrimination against Negroes." And in a campaign speech in Los Angeles on September 9, Kennedy claimed: "When our next President takes office in January, he must be prepared to move forward in the field of human rights in three general areas: as a legislative leader, as Chief Executive, and as the center of the moral power in the United States. . . . He must exert the great moral and educational force of his office to help bring equal access to public facilities from churches to lunch counters, and to support the right of every American to stand up for his rights." Kennedy claimed that he would establish a "New Frontier" for the nation's young people by using "the full moral and political power of the presidency to obtain for all young Americans, and others similarly affected, equal access to the voting booth, the schoolroom, to jobs, to housing, and to public facilities, including lunch counters."[35]

Senator Kennedy repeated his argument for moral leadership on civil rights during the presidential debates with his Republican challenger, Richard M. Nixon. In the second televised debate with Vice President Nixon, Kennedy claimed, "What will be done to provide equality of education in all sections of the United States? Those are the questions to which the President must establish a moral tone and leadership. And I can assure you that if I am elected president we will do so." JFK's claim was an implicit indictment of the Eisenhower-Nixon administration's failure to put the moral power of the White House behind civil rights. Throughout the campaign, Kennedy had criticized Eisenhower for his failure to morally sanction the *Brown* decision. In a question-and-answer session following campaign remarks in Minneapolis on October 1, Kennedy claimed, "I think that the failure of the President to indicate his endorsement of the Supreme Court decision has cost us heavily. I hope the next President of the United States states that he stands for equal rights."[36] In a speech in New York on October 3, Kennedy claimed, "The world must know that America's Chief Executive . . . [will] fully support and endorse the Supreme Court's decisions to translate civil rights from a slogan into a reality that can be enjoyed by all."[37]

In addition to crafting speeches indicating support for civil rights, Kennedy's campaign staff searched for other, less public ways to communicate to the black community that their candidate had a moral interest in civil rights. In October, 1960, the Kennedy machine found success when JFK made a symbolic gesture that was interpreted by many African Americans as indicative of his moral commitment. Martin Luther King, Jr., had been jailed in Atlanta, Georgia, on October 19 for protesting against racial discrimination by local merchants. Coretta Scott King—worried that her husband would be killed while in jail—contacted Kennedy aide Harris Wofford. Wofford comforted Mrs. King and later telephoned the candidate to ask him to call her. On the evening of October 26, Senator Kennedy called Mrs. King to express concern over her husband's arrest and incarceration, and he asked her to let him know if there was anything he could do to ease her burden. Mrs. King later described the phone call as "unexpected but very uplifting" and called it a turning point in Kennedy's relationship with many members of the African American community.[38]

Kennedy's symbolic act was praised by many African Americans, and convinced them that as president he would provide moral leadership on civil rights issues.[39] Martin Luther King, Sr., praised JFK before the Ebenezer Baptist Church congregation: "It took courage to call my daughter-in-law at a time like this. He had the moral courage to stand up for what he knows is right." Martin Luther King, Jr., claimed, "Senator Kennedy exhibited moral courage of a high order"—a claim amplified by Baptist minister Garner Taylor, who stated, "This is the kind of moral leadership and direct personal concern which this problem has lacked in these last critical years."[40]

In addition to campaign messages and symbolic gestures that suggested he would provide moral leadership, Kennedy's Pulitzer Prize-winning book *Profiles in Courage* emphasized moral leadership by politicians. The book is a study of eight U.S. Senators who exhibited political courage, which JFK defined as risking one's career to uphold principle, to act on one's conscience regardless of the political consequences. Kennedy wrote, "A man does what he must—in spite of personal consequences, in spite of obstacles and dangers and pressures—and that is the basis of all human morality."[41] Although the book was published in 1956, it received considerable attention during the 1960 campaign. During the race for the presidency, the Kennedy campaign staff sent autographed copies of the book to key contacts and grassroots supporters, party leaders, labor leaders, and fund-raisers; Kennedy himself also referred to the book in many of his campaign addresses.

Liberals initially criticized Kennedy for lacking the political courage that his book described. For example, after the 1956 vote to censure Joseph McCarthy (from which Kennedy abstained), Eleanor Roosevelt described JFK as "someone who understands what courage is and admires it, but has not quite the independence to have it." By the 1960 election, however, Roosevelt changed her assessment of his political courage. In radio and television advertisements for the Kennedy campaign, she stated, "I urge you to vote for John F. Kennedy for I have come to believe that as a president he will have the strength and moral courage to provide the leadership for human rights we need in this time of crisis."[42]

Kennedy's promises of moral leadership, however, eventually would be turned against him: his campaign rhetoric activated a desire for moral rhetoric that his presidential discourse did not satisfy. James Farmer, chairman of the Congress of Racial Equality (CORE), claimed, "The beautiful rhetoric of his campaign . . . inspired people and served as a catalyst for much of the action. Blacks all over the country, especially young blacks, said, 'I want to get the country moving too.'"[43] Kennedy's rhetorical and political action during his presidency, however, disappointed many civil rights supporters. SNCC activist Robert Moses claimed, "I don't think Kennedy anticipated that his words would touch people who were looking for new expectations from this country."[44] But JFK's words about civil rights did touch many African Americans. *Ebony* magazine, for example, noted that many African Americans looked to the Kennedy era "to become the most hopeful, the most encouraging period for racial progress in U.S. history" in large part because of Jack Kennedy's campaign promises to exercise moral leadership as president.[45]

By 1963, though, activists' expectations had seriously eroded. Journalist Victor Navasky claims that "the civil rights program of the new Administration was more limited than John Kennedy's campaign rhetoric would have suggested or than civil rights activists hoped."[46] During the Freedom Rides, Dr. King noted that President Kennedy had "failed to come through with certain promises he made prior to his election."[47] In 1962, Roy Wilkins also used the president's pledge against him: "We've come to collect what you promised us in 1960."[48] On March 30, 1963, King criticized the White House for its failure to back civil rights: "The demand for progress was somehow drained of its moral imperative." Later that spring, King suggested that if the president did not speak to the country about the moral imperatives of integration, civil rights leaders would sponsor a March on Washington. On June 10, 1963, King once more charged JFK with not having lived up to his campaign promises. He argued that above all, the president must talk in moral terms, "which we seldom if ever hear the President of the United States speaking." King also said that Kennedy must demonstrate his "personal and moral" commitment to civil rights.[49]

Other civil rights activists also criticized the president's civil rights stand with his own rhetoric. Author and activist James Baldwin charged the administration with "spinelessness" and demanded that the president "take a moral position and stop playing politics."[50] Whitney Young, Jr., executive director of the National Urban League, claimed that Kennedy should "place human rights above regional politics" and "exhibit the kind of guts that he himself described in his book *Profiles in Courage*."[51] In another address, Young—again alluding to Kennedy's book—claimed that the president should defend civil rights "on moral as well as legal grounds." He argued that JFK should issue a statement claiming, "If this be political suicide, so be it, for I must live with myself."[52] The rhetorical situation immediately preceding Kennedy's televised address was serious, and the demands for moral leadership had increased. The June 10 issue of *Newsweek* proclaimed that the president was "under heavy pressure" to demonstrate his commitment to civil rights.[53]

Cold War Worries

The moral rhetoric of the 1960 campaign had swelled expectations for change, but once elected, Kennedy found it increasingly difficult to fulfill his promises. Events in the Cold War quickly grabbed the president's attention, and the civil rights issue usually was pushed aside. As JFK turned his attention to international exigencies like the Bay of Pigs, Laos, Berlin, and nuclear test resumption, he left most civil rights matters to his brother, Attorney General Robert Kennedy.[54] Civil rights was only a small part of the president's larger agenda, which was primarily concerned with international relations.

Kennedy turned away from moral rhetoric on civil rights issues in his first speech as president. His inaugural address contained no pleas or promises for freedom and equality for African Americans. The president spoke about freedom, but his focus was on international events. When he proclaimed, "The rights of man come not from the generosity of the state but from the hand of God," President Kennedy was speaking to the problem of oppression "around the globe," not about discrimination at home. When JFK claimed, "Let both sides unite to heed in all corners of the earth the command of Isaiah—to 'undo the heavy burdens . . . (and) let the oppressed go free,'" his plea was for improved East-West relations, not improved white-black relations. Kennedy asked Americans to join in the fight against the common enemies of man, which included "tyranny, poverty, disease and war itself," but not against racial discrimination and segregation.[55] Yet the idealism of the speech, coming on the heels of the moral rhetoric of the campaign, moved some blacks, including

James Meredith. Meredith claims that he was inspired to apply to the University of Mississippi because of the inaugural address. Still, this was hardly the strong moral rhetoric Kennedy had promised during the 1960 campaign.

President Kennedy also eschewed moral rhetoric on the civil rights issue in his 1961 State of the Union address. He suggested that civil rights was one of the "unfinished and neglected tasks" that cluttered our national household. Rather than advancing a moral commitment, the president's rhetoric assigned a secondary role to African Americans' civil rights. Kennedy further subordinated the issue by claiming that the domestic problems facing the nation "pale when placed beside those which confront us around the world." He again discussed freedom in the context of international issues. Within this context, JFK assigned a religious imperative to freedom abroad by describing liberty as a "blessing." He did not, however, provide a moral imperative for the struggle for freedom at home.[56]

In a special message to the Congress on May 25, 1961, President Kennedy once more subordinated African Americans' struggle for freedom. His speech emphasized freedom but claimed, "The great battleground for the defense and expansion of freedom today is the whole southern half of the globe—Asia, Latin America, Africa, and the Middle East—the lands of the rising peoples."[57] The president ignored the battlegrounds of freedom at home—in Birmingham, Little Rock, Nashville, Selma, and Montgomery. Near the end of the address, Kennedy did make a brief gesture toward domestic civil rights, praising Americans for their willingness to "practice democracy at home, in all States, with all races, to respect each other and to protect the Constitutional rights of all citizens." This constitutional argument, however, nearly ignores the United States' racial problems and is cloaked in a speech that provides moral imperative for freedom abroad but not at home. In the final words of the speech, JFK stated, "It is heartening to know, as I journey abroad, that our country is united in its commitment to freedom—and is ready to do its duty." Kennedy's speech emphasizes a duty, a moral obligation, for promoting freedom abroad, an obligation that is not applied to freedom for all races at home.

Halberstam describes Kennedy's political philosophy, focused on moral duty in international relations, as "American elitism." The goal of this philosophy, Halberstam argues, was "not necessarily to bring the American dream to reality here at home, but to bring it to reality elsewhere in the world. It was heady stuff, defining the American dream and giving it a new sense of purpose, taking American life . . . and giving it a new and grander mission."[58] Kennedy's public rhetoric throughout most of his tenure as president was consistent with this philosophy. His speeches emphasized a moral obligation to promote free-dom internationally, attempting to appeal to Americans' sense of "Manifest Destiny." And in his public messages, domestic civil rights issues were often subordinated to Kennedy's focus on foreign affairs.

I do not wish to take President Kennedy's international politics to task here, nor to argue that civil rights was a strictly domestic issue. Clearly, civil rights was an important international issue for the United States during the Cold War. Political scientist Mark Stern notes that the World War II victory over Nazism—an ideology centered around racism—focused attention on racism in the world's leading democracy. Racial segregation and discrimination against African Americans was an embarrassment and a political liability for the nation in the postwar years. The status of African Americans undercut the United States' moral claim to free world leadership.[59]

That this inconsistency and embarrassment undermined American foreign policy was not lost on President Kennedy. In spite of Kennedy's criticism of his predecessor's approach to civil rights during the 1960 campaign, JFK shared one vision with Dwight Eisenhower, that civil rights was a dominant issue in the international political context. Like Ike, Kennedy discussed civil rights as a serious issue in the Cold War that could be used by the Soviet bloc to attack the American social and political system and to propagandize on behalf of Communism. For example, in the 1961 State of the Union address, JFK claimed, "The denial of constitutional rights to some of our fellow Americans on account of race . . . subjects us to the charge of world opinion that our democracy is not equal to the high promise of our heritage."[60] President Kennedy was especially concerned about civil rights at home, in part, because he was preaching the "freedom doctrine" to people of color—Latin Americans, Africans, Asians—many of whom were acutely aware of the United States' racial problems. Schlesinger suggests that since the distance between African Americans and Africans had narrowed during the 1950s and 1960s, the United States especially was susceptible to criticism from African nations for its mistreatment of African Americans at home.[61] The formation of the American Negro Leadership Conference on Africa in 1962 revealed the increasing identification between blacks in America and Africa and showed that even moderate African Americans saw colonial issues in Africa as civil rights issues, just as many African leaders viewed African Americans' civil rights as important to their relationship with the United States.

President Kennedy became aggravated when images of violence against African Americans damaged the nation's image in the world community and sometimes turned his frustrations on civil rights activists instead of southern racists. In 1961, Kennedy complained that the Freedom Rides damaged the nation's image and hurt him on the eve of important meetings in Vienna with Soviet premier Nikita Khrushchev: he viewed the demonstrations only through the prism of his own political interests.[62] The president and the attorney general asked publicly and privately for a "cooling off" period in the riders' protests, hoping to avoid embarrassment during Cold War dealings.[63] The administration's particular definition of civil rights as an important Cold War issue seemed to gain force in public discourse about the Freedom Rides. During the demonstrations, for instance, a newspaper reporter queried civil rights activist Ralph Abernathy of the Southern Christian Leadership Conference (SCLC): "Reverend Abernathy, President Kennedy is about to meet with Premier Khrushchev. Aren't you afraid of embarrassing him with these demonstrations?" Abernathy, resisting this interpretation of events, replied, "Man, we've been embarrassed all our lives."[64] Kennedy biographer Herbert Parmet argues that African American leaders were unhappy that the president did not intervene to attempt to prevent bloodshed. Parmet also claims, "Neither were the activists happy that the President was then also contemplating the ramifications of the violence upon his forthcoming meetings with De Gaulle, Khrushchev, and Macmillan."[65]

In 1962, during the desegregation of the University of Mississippi, Kennedy once more worried about the international implications of racial violence, though this time he did not become cross with blacks. JFK did not want to be faulted for creating a second Little Rock situation, which would provide the Soviets with fuel for their propaganda machine. Sorensen claims, "The possibility of domestic violence [in Oxford, Mississippi] made him more anxious than usual." However, Kennedy was preoccupied with crucial developments in the Cold War, especially events that ultimately led to the Cuban Missile crisis that October. Violence eventually broke out in Oxford, leaving two dead and hundreds wounded. The president addressed the nation on September 30, indicating that the problem would pass, at the same moment that events were escalating. President Kennedy's speech employed a "whole world is watching" appeal to attempt to persuade local obstructionists to desist and restore order; he informed the citizens of Mississippi that the "eyes of the nation and of all the world are upon you and upon all of us."[66]

Civil rights was an international issue, but the way in which JFK's rhetoric often connected civil rights with international affairs was largely ineffective. Kennedy's argument that whites should end discriminatory practices at home because it made the nation look bad abroad did not have much rhetorical force with southern segregationists, who were much more interested in preserving their way of life (which they believed was moral) than in what foreign countries thought about the United States. Furthermore, the president's rhetorical association of civil rights and the Cold War angered civil rights advocates. Kennedy's rhetoric suggested that civil rights was not a moral issue important in its own right but rather that its importance was wholly dependent upon its connection to international relations. Civil rights leaders—even those who worried that civil rights abuses would damage the United States' position in the Cold War—resented the subordination of their struggle to the Cold War and demanded that the president address the moral rightness of civil rights.

Contrary to Kennedy's hopes, Cold War politics and rhetoric may have actually increased African Americans' confrontational activism. In his 1963 book *Why We Can't Wait,* Martin Luther King, Jr., stated that the black community had seen the nation go to the brink of war and had heard the justifications for this danger expressed in terms of "America's willingness to go to any lengths to preserve freedom."[67] But blacks were disappointed, King observed, that the readiness to take heroic measures in the protection of freedom abroad seemed tragically weak when applied to the defense of liberty at home. King argued that as a consequence, the civil rights movement stepped up its protests in 1963 and planned to engage in massive nonviolent resistance. After the setback in Albany, Georgia, the movement achieved perhaps its most successful protest to date during the spring of 1963 in Birmingham.

Crises in Alabama

Birmingham, Alabama, was the most segregated city in the nation. Extremist white violence against those who spoke up for desegregation kept most of its citizens silent.[68] African Americans had dubbed the city "Bombingham," as eighteen racially motivated bombings had occurred there between 1957 and 1963. On the invitation of local activist and minister Fred Shuttlesworth, King and the SCLC went to Birmingham with the purpose of exposing the extremity of southern racism in order to arouse the conscience of white America and to pressure the White House to provide moral and legislative leadership. Civil rights leaders feared that Kennedy had signaled to the South that it could do as it pleased if it maintained a facade of order. King was troubled greatly by this message and feared that the administration was beating a serious retreat.[69]

Drawing upon the lessons of Albany, King developed a three-part plan called Project C—for Confrontation. First, leaders would activate the entire African American community. Second, they would attack the business community with a focused economic boycott. And third, they would use mass marches and arrests to call attention to their plight. Protesters calculated that this plan would escalate events until a moment of "creative tension" arose, thereby revealing the evils of segregation and forcing local merchants to the negotiating table. The moment of tension should also produce confrontation that would shock most Americans, activists reasoned, since local police commissioner Eugene "Bull" Connor had strong racist sentiments, a short temper, and a penchant for violence. Civil rights leaders believed that if they could succeed in a city that stood as the pinnacle of white racism, their efforts would be enshrined.

The demonstrations in Birmingham commenced in earnest on April 3, with sit-ins at downtown lunch counters, and continued into the middle of May. The moment of "creative tension," however, that the movement was looking for began on May 2, or "D-Day." With many demonstrators jailed, some local blacks reluctant to protest, and the national press losing interest in events, SCLC officials Wyatt Tee Walker and James Bevel mobilized local children into a strategic mass march. King initially questioned the tactic—which Walker claimed would evoke segregationist brutality from Bull Connor—but ultimately endorsed the move, however reluctantly. Waves of teenagers and elementary school children marched out of the Sixteenth Street Baptist Church for City Hall, only to be arrested by Connor's men. Walker sent boys into the outskirts of town to turn in false alarms that would split up city police and firefighting forces. By the end of the day, over five hundred young people were under arrest, but law enforcement officials had not turned violent. On May 3, "Double-D Day," circumstances changed. Near midday, a phalanx of children marched toward Connor's forces, who were stationed near downtown. African American onlookers stood along the perimeter of Ingraham Park, waiting for the children, and Connor ordered the deployment of police dogs to disperse the crowd. The jails were nearly full, and the police chief turned to force. When a ruckus ensued as blacks tried to avoid being bitten by German shepherds, Connor ordered the full K-9 squad into action and called for fire hoses to be turned on the blacks, including the wave of children. The high-pressure water rolled one black woman down the street, blasted some African Americans to the sides of brick buildings, and tore the clothing off the backs of some targets. Police dogs lunged at other blacks, ripping their clothes and breaking their skin. Connor yelled, "I want to see the dogs work."[70] Journalists snapped photographs and rolled their cameras. The student marchers and onlookers retreated to the sanctuary on Sixteenth Street.

Journalist Theodore White claims that the police dogs and fire hoses became "symbols of the African American revolution: When television showed dogs snapping at human beings, when the fire hoses thrashed and flailed at the women and children, whipping up skirts and pounding at bodies with high-pressure streams powerful enough to peel bark off a tree—the entire nation winced."[71] President Kennedy said in private that the pictures of police dogs attacking African Americans in Birmingham made him "sick." But Kennedy did not express his sickness or any sense of moral outrage in public. Instead, he expressed hope that a settlement soon would be reached between the demonstrators and business leaders (negotiations had begun on the evening of May 5, under the direction of Assistant Attorney General for Civil Rights Burke Marshall) and communicated concern about the ramifications of the violence.

The president found the international implications of the protests at Birmingham particularly troubling.[72] For Kennedy the timing was wrong: violence against African Americans broke out at the same time as trouble in Vietnam intensified and just prior to his scheduled meetings with European leaders. Privately, the president ordered members of his staff to urge black leaders to continue negotiations and to halt further protests in order to protect the nation's image abroad. Publicly, JFK expressed his concern about damage to America's credibility abroad. In a press conference on May 8, 1963, Kennedy called the events at Birmingham "a spectacle which was seriously damaging to the reputation of both Birmingham and the country." Later in the press conference, the president repeated that "the situation in Birmingham was damaging to the reputation of Birmingham and the United States," and he called the damage to America's image "very serious."[73]

Civil rights leaders were upset by the president's subordination of their plight to America's image abroad. They wanted a ringing speech embracing the morality of their cause, but instead the president spoke to the international implications. In a sermon at a mass meeting on Friday, May 10, King decried Kennedy in a sarcastic tone: "The United States is concerned about its image. When things started happening down here, Mr. Kennedy got disturbed. For Mr. Kennedy . . . is battling for the minds and the hearts of men in Asia and Africa—some one billion men in the neutralist sector of the world—and they aren't gonna respect the United States of America if she deprives men and women of the basic rights of life because of the color of their skin. Mr. Kennedy *knows* that."[74] Whitney Young, Jr., also criticized JFK. He told newspaper reporters, "Their [the Kennedy administration's] attitude has been: How can we keep people from revolting and demonstrating and embarrassing us?"[75]

While protests embarrassed Kennedy overseas, some of his political rivals attempted to humiliate him at home. During the negotiations between Birmingham's business leaders and civil rights leaders, congressional Republicans introduced legislation to outlaw segregation. Some liberals within the GOP, such as New York Congressman John Lindsay and California Senator Thomas Kuchel, were committed to civil rights, but overall the move seemed calculated to shame JFK during a precarious circumstance. And King hinted that if the president would not raise bond funds to bail demonstrators out of Birmingham's jails, New York Republican governor Nelson Rockefeller might help.[76] Such a move, if made public, certainly would have embarrassed Kennedy in some circles. Rather than remaining quiet during this politically delicate moment for the president, King stepped up his demands. He claimed that the White House, which apparently believed that no federal law had been violated in Birmingham, must take a moral, forthright stand on segregation.

The administration considered a public message in response to the bombing of A. D. King's home at the end of the crisis in Birmingham. The message, which was prepared but not communicated publicly, called civil rights "one of the great moral issues of our time" and claimed that racial discrimination is a problem that "all of us have a moral obligation to put right."[77] Although this statement was never made, the president did make at least one public statement that was more forthright than most of his civil rights messages. In a speech at Vanderbilt University on May 18, one week after a settlement had been brokered in Birmingham, JFK suggested that civil rights activists were acting "in the highest tradition of American freedom."[78] Never before had an American president so resolutely affirmed the efforts of civil rights demonstrators. Although this affirmation was significant and foreshadowed portions of Kennedy's June 11 address, civil rights leaders still demanded stronger moral leadership. Some white Americans, moved by the violence in Alabama, also began to look to the White House for stronger leadership. Columnist Walter Lippman wrote that the drive for desegregation "must become a national movement . . . directed by the Federal Government."[79] The administration realized that events in Birmingham had aroused the nation's conscience and now believed that whites had some idea of what it was like to be black in the South. The international embarrassment and outpouring of national support seemed likely to push the president into more aggressive support of civil rights legislation and into a stronger rhetorical stance than his commencement address at Vanderbilt University.

Burke Marshall claims that Kennedy became convinced as a result of Birmingham that he "had to deal with what was clearly an explosion in the racial problem that could not, would not go away."[80] On May 22, the president announced at a press conference that the White House was considering new civil rights legislation. In a meeting with the Justice Department staff two days later, Robert Kennedy claimed that the administration ought to propose major, sweeping legislation, and he instructed a group to draft a proposed bill. On June 1, JFK met with top administration officials to discuss civil rights measures. The attorney general argued for comprehensive civil rights legislation, including public accommodations provisions. Many staff members replied that Congress would never pass a bill with such provisions. Staff members Lawrence O'Brien and Kenneth O'Donnell supported the inclusion of Title III, which had been stricken from the Civil Rights Act of 1957, but Justice Department officials were reluctant to accept the legal power to initiate civil rights cases afforded by the title. Some members of the staff asked whether Fair Employment Practices Committee provisions should be included. The president believed that the legislation must include some key public accommodations provisions and wondered whether the White House could in good conscience propose a civil rights bill without Title III, in spite of the political and legal difficulties that would be created by the title. He ordered aides to draft legislation, but which provisions would be included in the final proposal remained uncertain. The political scene had changed quickly regarding civil rights, and President Kennedy now needed to formulate a legislative and rhetorical response appropriate to new exigencies—a response that he had believed unachievable or unnecessary just months earlier, and one asynchronous with his own prior understanding of civil rights.

Neither Kennedy nor the nation would be free from further civil rights difficulties as White House officials developed legislation. Civil rights demonstrations continued in Jackson, Mississippi, under the leadership of NAACP official Medgar Evers: an earlier agreement between the city's mayor and local blacks had broken down, and so boycotts, mass marches, and sit-ins resumed. In Tallahassee, Florida, local police officers fired tear gas canisters at African Americans protesting the city's segregated movie theaters, then arrested the demonstrators. And racial tensions rose in Tuscaloosa, Alabama, where two black students planned to enroll at the University of Alabama.

The same month that King announced he would go to Birmingham to lead demonstrations, George Wallace had been inaugurated as the state's governor. During the Birmingham protests, the governor had deployed state troopers to Ingraham Park to engage in maneuvers, and his inflammatory speeches helped incite violent reactions from local segregationists, including the bombing of A. D. King's home and the Gaston Hotel on May 11.[81] Wallace was infamous for his anti-integrationist slogan, "Segregation now! Segregation tomorrow! Segregation forever!" In grand rhetorical style, he had pledged during his gubernatorial campaign to "stand in the schoolhouse door" to keep Alabama's state university lily white. By the end of May, it became clear that he planned to keep his promise. Fearing a repeat of the crisis in Oxford, Mississippi, the Kennedy administration plotted to ensure the peaceful enrollment of James Hood and Vivian Malone.

The Tuscaloosa situation became critical in mid-June, but the desegregation problem there had developed concurrently with events in Birmingham. Robert Kennedy had met with Wallace in Montgomery on April 25 but was unsuccessful in persuading the governor to accept his constitutional duty to abide by court desegregation orders. Wallace emphasized instead his duty to the state of Alabama to preserve the peace and claimed that "you just can't have any peace in Alabama with an integrated school system." Wallace also denied the validity of the Federal District Court's authority to force integration on a "sovereign state" and claimed that he would never "submit voluntarily to any integration in a school system in Alabama."[82] On May 18, President Kennedy met Wallace during a stop in Muscle Shoals following the president's speech at Vanderbilt, but the two did not discuss school desegregation—despite the mounting tension in Tuscaloosa. Around this time, the Justice Department worked to persuade Alabama business leaders to pressure Wallace into a peaceful resolution: most of the business leaders agreed but were certain that Wallace would not change his mind under any form of pressure. The governor continued to announce on statewide television that he intended to keep the peace in Tuscaloosa and that he intended to keep the university segregated. On May 24, Justice Department lawyers sought an injunction to stop Wallace from standing in the schoolhouse door, and U.S. District Court Judge Seybourn Lynne issued the order barring the governor from obstructing the entrance of the two students on June 5. On June 7, more than 750 state troopers arrived at the university, encircled the campus, and promptly instituted a curfew. Wallace demonstrated the sincerity of his desire to keep the peace on June 8, when state troopers arrested Ku Klux Klan leaders headed for Tuscaloosa "to tear the school apart."[83] The attorney general called Wallace on June 8 to confirm his intentions, hoping that the governor might capitulate. Wallace did not yield. The White House was unsure of what exactly Wallace would do and remained anxious about how events in Tuscaloosa would unfold.

The Justice Department had plenty of officials on the scene in Tuscaloosa but did not put together a final plan until the last moment. For example, Robert Kennedy worried whether marshals would need to pick up Wallace and move him aside to enroll the students or whether they could just push him aside. Officials were undecided about whether federal marshals should withdraw Malone and Hood from the registration area if Governor Wallace stood in the schoolhouse door or try to force their way into Foster Auditorium. The Justice Department was also unsure what the state troopers might do: they might step aside peacefully, attempt to maintain public order, abandon their posts if disorder broke out, assist the governor, or form a line between Wallace and federal troops. Deputy Attorney General Nicholas Katzenbach, who arrived on the scene in Alabama on June 9, hoped that things would go smoothly but instructed his marshals to use guns if necessary to protect the two students.[84] Historian Culpepper Clark observes that the Kennedy administration never believed that Wallace would win, but Wallace never acted as though he were going to lose—in part because the governor never made clear what constituted winning.[85] Would he need actually to block Malone and Hood from registering, or would a defiant stand count? Wallace's stand seemed primarily symbolic, but his unpredictable behavior, ranting rhetorical style, and questions about his mental health led the Justice Department to plan for the unexpected.

On Monday, June 10, plans quickened. President Kennedy met in the oval office with the attorney general, Sorensen, Marshall, and O'Brien. The group discussed how to determine if or when the president should federalize the National Guard and how long it would take for federalized troops to arrive on the university campus. JFK and his staff also discussed the specifics of how to approach Governor Wallace at the entry to Foster Auditorium on Tuesday. Two plans were developed. First, Justice Department officials and the two students could simply approach Wallace with the backing of the Guard. This plan would allow the immediate entry of the students but might seem like an unnecessary display of force. Second, they could approach Wallace without federal troops and try to get around him or have marshals push him aside. If the governor persisted, Justice Department officials would take the students to their dormitory rooms and wait for National Guard troops to arrive on Wednesday morning. Then the soldiers, government officials, and students would again attempt to enter the auditorium. This plan would avoid the perception of an excessive show of force but would cause an embarrassing delay. The president advocated the second plan and ordered the attorney general to work out the specific arrangements with his men in Alabama. Robert Kennedy communicated the general plan to his assistants but still worried whether local citizens would turn on the soldiers (as they had in Oxford, Mississippi) and wondered how many troops would be enough to intimidate Wallace into retreat.

The governor of Alabama and the attorney general both took to the airwaves on Monday to state their positions. Wallace's televised address affirmed that he would keep his campaign promise to stand in the schoolhouse door, in spite of federal pressure. He also asked Alabamans to stay away from the university and tried to convince them that he could keep the school segregated and "keep the peace." In his television appearance, Robert Kennedy affirmed that the federal government would enforce the court order to desegregate the University of Alabama. In an important rhetorical reversal, RFK also indicated that the federal government's resolute action was driven by a sense of morality, not by Cold War motives: "It is unfortunate that these pictures go abroad. And I don't think there's any question that it affects our position throughout the world. But that's only a secondary reason for doing what we have to do. The first reason is because it's the right thing to do. And as President Kennedy has said, we're going to do this because it is the right thing to do." The attorney general conveyed that the administration's commitment was steadfast and its plan of action firm.

Behind the scenes, things were less certain. On Tuesday, June 11, Burke Marshall and Nicholas Katzenbach still were debating exactly what would happen during the attempt to register, just hours away. Katzenbach advocated a third plan in which he would attempt to register the students, withdraw if refused by the governor, and then arrange for the students to begin attending classes. Such a plan would avoid any further staged confrontation with Wallace, but as a consequence might enrage the governor and lead to violence. A breakthrough in the Justice Department's planning came when Robert Kennedy learned that, once federalized, a National Guard unit could be on the university campus in several hours, avoiding the impression of delay. Following this breakthrough, RFK decided that only Katzenbach, U.S. Marshal Peyton Norville, and U.S. Attorney Macon Weaver would approach Governor Wallace, in order to spare the black students racial indignities. If Wallace maintained his stand in the schoolhouse door, Katzenbach would take Malone and Hood to their dormitory rooms. Such a move would demonstrate that the federal government was not retreating. Then, the Justice Department triumvirate would attempt to gain entry for the students later in the day, backed by National Guard troops. Still, uncertainties remained. What would Katzenbach say to Wallace upon approaching him? How would Wallace respond? How would citizens and police officers respond to the use of troops?

Secretary of State Dean Rusk signed a cease and desist order for Katzenbach to present to Wallace. Robert Kennedy gave Katzenbach a short pep talk by telephone before he headed toward campus, telling his deputy that Wallace was a second-rate figure to him and that he should use a tone to dismiss the governor as such. RFK's final words were, "Good luck. You'll do well." Upon arriving at Foster Auditorium, Katzenbach approached Wallace and served him with the cease and desist order. The deputy attorney general stated his purpose and asked Wallace for assurance that the students would not be barred entry to the university. Wallace interrupted Katzenbach and read a prepared statement for the pack of journalists gathered on the school's grounds. Katzenbach then decried the governor's "show" and again asked for his assurance that the students would be allowed to register. Wallace then made his symbolic stand by positioning himself in front of the auditorium's door. Justice Department officials followed their plan, which surprised Wallace and university officials, by escorting Hood and Malone to their dorm rooms. RFK, who had been listening to news reports on the situation, contacted Katzenbach by radio. Katzenbach told the attorney general that no violence had occurred but that the president should now federalize the National Guard in order to proceed with their plan to enroll the two students that afternoon.

President Kennedy was meeting with legislative leaders to discuss civil rights legislation when RFK contacted him, but the president soon issued a proclamation ordering the governor to cease and desist from obstructing justice, then Executive Order 11111 to federalize the National Guard.[86] The Army sent General Henry Graham to Tuscaloosa to assume command of military operations there. While officials organized the Guard for its deployment to campus, General Taylor Hardin, a personal friend of Governor Wallace, contacted Graham with an offer to cut a deal. Wallace would step aside peaceably if allowed to make another statement upon the arrival of the Guard. The Justice Department reluctantly agreed. Graham sent an overwhelming numbers of troops to the university to ensure compliance, and officials left for Foster Auditorium. The General, Katzenbach, Norville, Weaver, and four sergeants approached the governor. Graham saluted Wallace (who returned the sign of respect) and stated, "It is my sad duty to ask you to step aside, on order of the President of the United States." Wallace made his second statement, attempting to depict his capitulation as a victory: "Alabama is winning this fight against Federal interference because we are awakening the people to the trend toward military dictatorship in this country." Wallace left the scene quickly and returned to Montgomery by motorcade. Vivian Malone and James Hood entered the University of Alabama through the door Governor Wallace had blocked, registered for the semester, and prepared to attend classes the following day. In spite of the short delay and Wallace's showmanship, the Kennedy administration ultimately got what it wanted: assurance from the governor that the students would be allowed to enter the university and a nonviolent resolution to the situation.

Many scholars have overlooked or underestimated the impact of the University of Alabama crisis on President Kennedy's address to the nation on June 11. For example, Robert Gilbert and Harold Fleming observe that JFK spoke in response to the national situation following Birmingham, but both authors ignore the events in Tuscaloosa in their accounts of Kennedy's development on civil rights.[87] Mark Stern notes that the events in Tuscaloosa provided JFK with an immediate opportunity to speak but emphasizes the impact of the Birmingham protests without indicating how the university desegregation might have shaped the president's perspective and his rhetoric.[88] The events in Birmingham did influence Kennedy's perspective on civil rights and his movement toward moral rhetoric, but the events in Tuscaloosa also were critical. Neither the national outrage following Birmingham nor the White House's consideration of civil rights legislation had broken southern resistance to integrated public facilities or public education. It seemed that the South might try to hold onto Jim Crow through an endless series of standoffs with the federal government. The choreographed, somewhat comic nature of Governor Wallace's stand suggested that southerners would resist integration even when it was clear that they would lose. The outcome of the desegregation crisis in Tuscaloosa demonstrated clearly that civil rights was more than a legal or legislative issue: unlike the crises in Little Rock and Oxford, the state governor probably would have upheld law and order in Tuscaloosa—but the students' right to attend a public educational institution still would have been obstructed. Summoning the memory of the administration's failure at Oxford, the frustrations, wasted time, public furor, and ardently segregationist rhetoric at Tuscaloosa may have offended President Kennedy's moral sensibilities in addition to his political ones. And, by his former aides' accounts, intense personal involvement in the political crisis helped Kennedy's personal sentiments mature. The president also may have realized the truth in his own 1960 campaign statement that a moral argument rooted in the ethos of the presidency would be "more effective than force in ending discrimination."

By June 11, the costs of not speaking out on civil rights became too high. Civil rights activists who turned the moral rhetoric of Kennedy's campaign and his Cold War discourse against him made his relative silence on the moral dimensions of segregation seem conspicuous and unconscionable. The events in Birmingham had activated many Americans' moral concern about civil rights and had shaped the president's thinking about racial problems, as had the situation at Tuscaloosa. The desegregation crisis in Alabama also intensified public criticism of Kennedy's civil rights leadership—especially his rhetorical leadership. For example, in early June, an editorial in *Commonweal* urged the president to "support his legislative efforts with a firm public avowal of the rank injustice of racism" and claimed that he should transcend political issues by making "a straight moral statement against segregation and discrimination." The *Christian Science Monitor* noted that Kennedy was under pressure to provide rhetorical leadership, perhaps in the form of a "fireside chat" on civil rights.[89] Increasingly, his silence on the moral aspects of racism opened President Kennedy to criticism from his liberal supporters. Moreover, silence on the moral issue might keep the South insurgent. Still, making a public moral argument was a complicated enterprise, and some members of the White House staff continued to doubt the wisdom of addressing the nation. The president himself remained apprehensive. What would JFK say and when would he say it? What might be the reactions to his public moralizing? To what sense of collective morality could he appeal? What were the realistic possibilities of a moral argument on civil rights to a nation divided on race? The administration pondered these questions throughout the spring and did not finalize a presidential speech to the nation until the evening of June 11.

Declaring "A Moral Issue"

Although it is clear that Kennedy felt pressure to speak to the moral dimensions of civil rights, confusion surrounds the preparation of the speech itself. Theodore Sorensen, who drafted the message, claims that he "did not start a first draft of the speech until late in the afternoon or complete it until minutes before [the president] went on the air." Robert Drew's film *Crisis,* a documentary that captures the White House decision making during the Tuscaloosa affair, reveals a different story. The film shows that although Sorensen did not begin the first draft until the afternoon of June 11, he did show that draft to the president, who revised it with the help of Burke Marshall and Robert Kennedy. JFK then sent Sorensen back to work on a second draft of the speech. While Sorensen worked on the second draft, the president discussed the speech with his brother. Documents at the Kennedy Library show that several of RFK's suggestions were included in the final message. The president's speech, as delivered, also includes seven paragraphs at the end of the message that did not appear in Sorensen's final draft. President Kennedy apparently extemporized the conclusion.[90]

Although the president's speech was revised until the last minute, the language and approach of the message had been suggested weeks earlier. After Birmingham, some members of the Kennedy administration had begun to realize that the White House's approach to civil rights issues was problematic and did not satisfy civil rights leaders. In a memorandum to the attorney general on May 13, 1963, civil rights adviser Louis Martin emphasized that most African Americans looked to the White House with hope for racial progress and for the redress of civil rights violations. Martin also suggested that racial problems were ready to erupt and claimed, "I believe the Administration should consider seizing the initiative in the current struggle and make some constructive moves which will ease tension and advance the general welfare."[91] During the White House meetings preceding the speech, Robert Kennedy suggested that Sorensen bring in Louis Martin to work on the speech.

By late May, the White House staff began to discuss a proposed presidential message on civil rights and solicited suggestions for the message. The members of the administration who seemed to understand best what the president's rhetoric was missing were Vice President Lyndon Johnson and his staff. Johnson and his aides discussed the president's need to address the moral imperative of integration and equality long before the final decision to speak. For example, in a memorandum to LBJ on May 24, George Reedy, assistant to the vice president, wrote:

It is a belief that the United States—in the person of the President Himself—has not made a real moral commitment to the cause of equal rights and equal opportunity. Both sides realize that the courts are on the Negroes' side . . . [but] the Negroes are uncertain that the moral force of the presidency is on their side and the whites believe that the President is acting out of political expediency. . . . The Negroes are going to be satisfied with nothing less than a convincing demonstration that the President is on their side. The backbone of white resistance is not going to be broken until the segregationists realize that the total moral force of the United States is arrayed against them.[92]

On June 3, 1963, Sorensen placed a telephone call to LBJ to elicit his advice for a possible address. Johnson argued that civil rights leaders "want that moral commitment, and that will do more to satisfy them than your bill. I mean you've got to have your bill too. But . . . he [Kennedy] should stick to the moral issue and he should do it without equivocation."[93] Repeating the thrust of Reedy's memo, Johnson claimed, "Now, I think the Southern whites and the Negroes share one point of view that's identical. They're not certain that the government is on the side of the Negroes." LBJ argued, "What the Negroes are really seeking is moral force and be sure that we're on their side and make them all act like Americans, and until they receive that assurance, unless it's stated dramatically and convincingly, they're not going to pay attention to executive orders and legislative recommendations."

Johnson told Sorensen that a presidential address emphasizing morality also would be an effective way to deal with southerners. Johnson claimed: "The difference is if your President just enforces court decrees the South will feel it's yielded to force. But if he goes down there and looks them in the eye and states the moral issue and the Christian issue . . . these Southerners at least respect his courage—they feel that they're on the losing side of an issue of conscience." Johnson's suggestions influenced Kennedy's rhetoric: Sorensen incorporated many of the vice president's suggestions into the speech text.[94]

On June 3, Assistant Attorney General Norbert Schlei traveled to Johnson's office to discuss the president's approach to the civil rights issue. Schlei summarized the meeting in a memorandum to Robert Kennedy on June 4, 1963. LBJ repeated many of his suggestions to Sorensen, emphasizing that the president should address "the moral principle involved in ending discrimination."[95] Johnson also suggested that the president should emphasize Christian morality, especially the golden rule, and tell his listeners that they "would have to look into their souls, make the necessary moral decision and give the Administration their support in the effort." President Kennedy's June 11 address includes many of the rhetorical suggestions made by Johnson. Schlei even claims that JFK's passionate extemporaneous remarks at the close of his speech were due in part to Johnson's advice.[96]

Attorney General Robert Kennedy also was a key influence on the president's June 11 address. Johnson's suggestions shaped the language of speech, but RFK was key to persuading the president to deliver the speech. Schlesinger claims that when President Kennedy indicated that perhaps the time had come to assert leadership and appeal to the nation, most of his advisers disagreed. O'Donnell and O'Brien did not think the president should get personally involved. Sorensen believed that a peaceful resolution to the immediate crisis at the University of Alabama made a televised speech to the nation unnecessary.[97] Robert Kennedy was the only adviser present at the White House meetings preceding the speech who urged the president to take a moral stand in a public message to the American people.[98] Repeating the suggestions that Lyndon Johnson had provided to the assistant attorney general, Robert Kennedy claimed that the president must take a strong stand "to obtain the confidence of the Negro population in their government and in the white majority."[99]

Moved by his brother's appeals, national events, political considerations, and his conscience, President Kennedy made a last-minute decision to speak to the nation on the evening of June 11. As television cameras were moved into place, the president sat down to address the nation with an incomplete speech text in front of him. The language of his address bore the imprint of Vice President Johnson, the attorney general, and Louis Martin, and it resuscitated themes from Kennedy's own campaign rhetoric. The president spoke about events in Tuscaloosa and Birmingham; he discussed legislative solutions to solve discrimination in places of public accommodation; he addressed the legal, economic, and social aspects of racism. But most importantly, the president's speech drew upon religious and democratic foundations to make a sustained moral argument about civil rights.

The speech begins by pledging a commitment to court orders aimed at ending segregated education: "This afternoon, following a series of threats and defiant statements, the presence of Alabama National Guardsmen was required on the University of Alabama to carry out the final and unequivocal order of the United States District Court of Alabama." Kennedy then praises the southern students for their good conduct: "That they [Vivian Malone and James Hood] were admitted peacefully on the campus is due in good measure to the conduct of the students of the University of Alabama." After listening to the beginning of the address, civil rights activists must have worried that Kennedy planned to repeat his "law and order" refrain. The start of Kennedy's speech echoes his rhetoric during the integration crisis at the University of Mississippi in September of the prior year.

But after this brief flirtation with "law and order" rhetoric, JFK clearly defines civil rights as a moral issue: "I hope that every American, regardless of where he lives, will stop and examine his conscience about this and other related incidents." The president finally made the moral commitment that he had promised yet failed to deliver during his first two years in office. Issuing a moral statement to the American people was a significant step for Kennedy, not only because it was a departure from his preference for pragmatism over idealism but also because of the rhetorical constraints inherent in public moral argument. Although most Americans invest the presidency with priestly power and expect chief executives to provide moral leadership, they often reject presidential preaching. For example, many of Jimmy Carter's speeches failed because they sounded more like moral sermons than political speeches. That Americans expect the president to ascend to the "bully pulpit" yet not to address the public with too much moral force is a paradoxical part of American political culture. Apparently, American political rhetoric can be sermonic but not didactic: presidents must search for the line of demarcation.

In addition, piety has become increasingly private in American political culture.[100] Political rhetors who speak with excessive moral vigor in the public sphere often appear self-righteous rather than uplifting. Public expression of morality was especially dangerous for JFK, since he had vowed to keep part of his moral underpinnings—his Catholic faith—private. Americans expected President Kennedy to provide moral leadership, yet the privatization of morality seriously constrained what he could say: the "public" dimension of public address limited the president's rhetorical possibilities. Kennedy needed to find a way to exhort the citizenry toward civic virtue without canting.

Kennedy's rhetorical situation was especially complicated because he faced a domestic problem: antecedents existed for using crisis rhetoric to address international problems, but it would be difficult to apply those principles to domestic affairs. No counterpart to the commander in chief role exists in the domestic sphere for building presidential ethos. In foreign crisis rhetoric, presidents regularly engage in scapegoating rituals of naming and blaming national enemies—a strategy that would be difficult to apply to the domestic sphere without fracturing the nation. Scapegoating rhetoric would have been particularly problematic for Kennedy, since he needed to forge a political coalition to pass civil rights legislation. In addition, whereas the president can effectively control information about international affairs, at home the news media is better equipped to provide words and images that contradict the president's rhetoric. The media and the public audience can challenge more effectively the president's definition of a domestic situation as a crisis.

Audiences are more likely to accept a rhetor's definition of a problem when that definition reflects and reinforces the dominant ideology. Kennedy's definition of civil rights as a moral problem on June 11 used a vocabulary central to the national ideology: American civil religion. Sociologist Robert Bellah, who stimulated scholarly discussion of civic piety in 1967, defines civil religion as the religious dimension of the political realm through which a people interpret its historical experience in light of transcendent reality.[101] While many scholars have challenged Bellah's definition of American civil religion as elaborate and well-institutionalized, nearly all agree that religious symbolism is a prominent feature of the American political landscape. Roderick Hart notes that American political rhetoric has been characterized, in part, by talk about "God's special love for America, of America's unique responsibility to God, of a New Israel and a Chosen People, of rededicating ourselves to the principles of basic, Christian Americanism."[102] In short, civil religious rhetoric employs mythic appeals—including notions of purpose, founding, and promise—to symbolically construct reality so that specific circumstances are invested with spiritual and moral meaning.

President Kennedy's address employs civil religious appeals immediately after defining civil rights as a moral issue: "This Nation was founded by men of many nations and backgrounds. It was founded on the principle that all men are created equal, and that the rights of every man are diminished when the rights of one man are threatened." Kennedy's words invoke the myth of the United States as a nation founded with a purpose—to serve as the chosen land for the freedom and equality of all men. How a nation conceives of its origins reveals the character of its people: the founding myth is an important part of the American character and of American political rhetoric. Historian Russell Nye notes, "Deep within the American mythology lies the conviction that a new free form of government was introduced into this continent by people chosen of God, in order to found a society in which the individual would possess all that liberty to which God thought him entitled."[103] Periodically, national prophets have found it necessary to remind the people of its origins—to invoke the nation's founding in order to recall the people to its original task.

Kennedy's civil rights address uses the language of the nation's founding document to transform an immediate situation into a timeless urgency. The temporal movement in Kennedy's speech suggests that the audience look to the past for inspiration to overcome struggles in the present. For example, the verb tense in the speech changes quickly from present ("I hope that every American . . . will stop and examine his conscience") to past ("This Nation was founded"). The speech's temporality suggests that the answers to contemporary moral problems lay in political convictions conceived during the very founding of the United States. Kennedy constitutes the modern American conscience as conformity to the ideals of the Declaration of Independence and recalls the people to the nation's founding principles. Kennedy leaves no doubt that the nation's special status as the sacred land for freedom and equality must be made real: "Now the time has come for this Nation to fulfill its promise."

Kennedy also invokes the memory of Abraham Lincoln, a principal figure in American civil religion, to suggest that America has not lived up to the commitments made in its past: "One hundred years of delay have passed since President Lincoln freed the slaves, yet their heirs, their grandsons, are not fully free. They are not yet freed from the bonds of injustice. They are not yet freed from social and economic oppression. And this Nation for all its hopes and boasts, will not be fully free until all its citizens are free." The temporal movement in this passage—past to present to future—is central to Kennedy's argument: national ideals proclaimed in the past are being violated in the present, and the nation will falter in the future unless its citizens change their ways. The president's address depicts the present as a time of trial, testing whether American ideals can meet the challenges of current social problems; the "nation will not be fully free" until African Americans are free. President Kennedy's speech functions as a civil religious ritual that allows people to pass from what Mircea Eliade calls "profane time" into "sacred time."[104] Current events no longer are ahistorical, they must be interpreted in light of the nation's sacred past. By commemorating sacred events from the past, the past is made present and provides the inspiration needed to overcome the nation's present and future obstacles. Kennedy interprets accepted cherished American ideals in a way that suggests an incongruity between words and deeds, between the American promise and the nation's performance.

President Kennedy's address alludes to two potent rhetorical documents— the Emancipation Proclamation and the Declaration of Independence—in a peculiar yet powerful way. The principle that "all men are created equal" was taken by the nation's founding fathers as a "self-evident" statement of natural political rights, yet Kennedy transforms that statement into a code for moral action that Americans must obey. In other words, the president's address transforms a political theory into a moral theory. Kennedy performs a similar rhetorical feat with his interpretation of the Emancipation Proclamation. Lincoln's proclamation freed southern slaves, yet Kennedy uses the document as a sanction for freedom from "the bonds of injustice" and from "social and economic oppression." Kennedy twists President Lincoln's words to transform the Proclamation into a moral decree for kinds of freedom that Lincoln never intended. Kennedy rhetorically converts two statements of the way things are ("all men are created equal"; southern slaves are "henceforward free") into petitions for the way things ought to be. The president's speech functions as what Kenneth Burke calls a secular prayer: the address interprets events through the lens of historic documents in order to coach the attitudes of the American people, to goad them toward moral action.[105]

Although Kennedy clearly suggests that the nation has not fulfilled its promise, he does argue that America has attempted to live up to part of its mission — to promote freedom around the world. About one-third of the way through his speech, Kennedy claims: "We preach freedom around the world, and we mean it, and we cherish our freedom here at home, but are we to say to the world . . . that this is the land of the free except for the Negroes; that we have no second-class citizens except Negroes; that we have no class or caste system, no ghettoes, no master race except with respect to Negroes?" In a speech about domestic affairs, Kennedy also reaffirms the nation's duty to mankind. A central myth in American civil religion is that Americans are a chosen people: the nation has seen itself as the New Jerusalem and the "last hope on earth." According to this myth, America has a duty to ensure freedom at home and to promote it abroad.

The theme of Americans as a chosen people is prevalent in American political discourse and in literary texts. On the occasion of his first inaugural address, for example, George Washington claimed that the "Almighty Being" has entrusted Americans with the "preservation of the sacred fire of liberty." In *White-Jacket,* Herman Melville wrote: "And we Americans are the peculiar, chosen people — the Israel of our time; we bear the ark of the liberties of the world."[106] Americans have interpreted this myth as the duty to serve as a model for the world, "a City upon a Hill." But Americans also have interpreted the myth of the chosen people as sanction for exerting political influence over foreign nations. President Kennedy's civil rights address attempts to put an ideology that has been used to justify jingoism and imperialistic expansionism to work for progressive purposes.

In addition to drawing upon the "myth of America," Kennedy mixes political rhetoric with Christian virtue in order to appeal to the nation's civil religious ideology. Bellah suggests that belief in "the obligation, both collective and individual, to carry out God's will on earth" is a central tenet of American civil religion.[107] Kennedy's speech emphasizes the obligation that both the government and its citizens have to do God's work: "Next week I shall ask the

Congress of the United States to act, to make a commitment. . . . But legislation, I repeat, cannot solve this problem alone. It must be solved in the home of every American in every community across our country." The president also claims that collective action must take place across the nation, not just in the South: the moral problem involves "every American regardless of where he lives." Racial discrimination and segregation were perceived as largely southern problems, a perception that Kennedy challenges with a civil religious interpretation of events: "It is not enough to pin the blame on others, to say this is a problem of one section of the country or another." The president argues, "Difficulties over segregation and discrimination exist in every city, in every State of the Union, producing a rising tide of discontent that threatens the public safety." Kennedy's rhetoric alludes to condemnations of hypocrisy in the Christian Bible: "Let anyone among you who is without sin be the first to throw a stone" and "Why do you see the speck in your neighbor's eye, but do not notice the log in your own eye?"[108] The North, President Kennedy claims, must correct its own problems rather than casting blame at the South.

Historian Hugh Davis Graham argues that "Kennedy's denial that the racial crisis was not sectional, while statesman like, was also politically disingenuous."[109] The president's national address, though, was not "mere rhetoric" designed to be conciliatory toward the South, as Graham suggests. Rather, Kennedy's interpretation of civil rights as a national rather than sectional issue reflected a maturing understanding of racial problems by the White House. On June 1, White House aide Louis Martin advised Kennedy that "the unrest in the South is not confined there" and claimed the administration should be concerned with the possibility of racial unrest in the North.[110] Three days later, during a telephone conversation with Louisiana governor James Davis, the president claimed that America's racial crisis had moved beyond the Mason-Dixon line: "This isn't any more just a Southern matter."[111] Kennedy's June 11 warning about "the fires of frustration and discord" burning in northern cities echoed Whitney Young, Jr.'s warning that incidents in the South were "mild in comparison with those on the verge of taking flame in the tinder-box of racial unrest in Northern cities."[112] In the language of the scriptures, the North needed to take the log out of its own eye before turning to its Southern neighbor.[113]

Throughout the address, Kennedy's definition of America's racial problems establishes a connection between politics and religion, and denies sectional and other purely secular definitions of the nation's difficulties. The president structures his argument as a refutation of alternate interpretations of the civil rights crisis:

"This is not a sectional issue" [refutation].

"This is not even a legal or legislative issue alone" [refutation].

"We are confronted primarily with a moral issue" [definition].

The moral issue is civil religious in its character: "It is as old as the scriptures and is as clear as the American Constitution." Two sacred texts, President Kennedy suggests, tell Americans that racial discrimination is morally wrong; but he focuses exclusively on forging a scriptural decree for equal treatment, providing no evidence for a Constitutional mandate: "The heart of the question is whether all Americans are to be afforded equal rights and equal opportunities, whether we are going to treat our fellow Americans as we want to be treated." The touchstone for the president's moral argument is Christianity's Golden Rule: "In everything do to others as you would have them do to you."[114] Kennedy puts a civic spin on religious virtue by inserting the word "American" into the Christian principle. His address collapses the distinction between the secular and the sacred—a distinction that rarely holds in American political rhetoric—in order to urge white Americans to treat black Americans equally.

The rhetoric of Kennedy's civic version of the Golden Rule is powerful. The president enacts what Celeste Condit suggests is a basic function of public moral argument: he transforms basic human desires into a shared moral code.[115] Part of the force of Kennedy's rhetoric is that in spite of being based on needs and desires, it appears rational. That is, his argument functions as what Chaim Perelman and Lucie Olbrechts-Tyteca call an argument of reciprocity. It aims at giving equal treatment to two situations that are counterparts of each other; it has the rhetorical force of appearing rational because it is quasi-logical.[116] One means of effecting persuasion through an argument of reciprocity is to encourage the audience to transpose its point of view. Kennedy's address invites the audience to participate in a role reversal; the oppressor is encouraged to take the place of the oppressed: "If an American, because his skin is dark, cannot eat in a restaurant open to the public, if he cannot send his children to the best public school available, if he cannot vote for the public officials who represent him, if, in short, he cannot enjoy the full and free life which all of us want, then who among us would be content to have the color of his skin changed and stand in his place?"[117] President Kennedy's rhetorical task was formidable: his potential for rhetorical success seemed to hinge upon his ability to encourage audience members to put themselves in the place of African Americans, yet many racists were unlikely to accept the president's encouragement. The rhetorical process involves the presentation of messages that invite certain responses and discourage others; but the audience is always free to decline any invitation.

To encourage his white audience to apply a civic version of the Golden Rule, to take the perspective of black Americans, Kennedy appeals to a potent myth in American political culture—the myth of the American Dream:

> In short, every American ought to have the right to be treated as he would wish to be treated, as one would wish his children to be treated. But this is not the case. The Negro baby born in America today, regardless of the section of the Nation in which he is born, has about one-half as much chance of completing a high school as a white baby born in the same place on the same day, one-third as much chance of completing college, one-third as much chance of becoming a professional man, twice as much chance of becoming unemployed, about one-seventh as much chance of earning $10,000 a year.[118]

In this passage, Kennedy suggests that African Americans simply want to pursue the same ideal that all Americans dream. Part of the rhetorical force of the president's argument resides in his universalization of human desires and in his ability to symbolize those desires in a myth central to the American ethos.

Clearly, not all members of President Kennedy's immediate audience accepted his reciprocal argument: an argument from reciprocity fails to persuade its hearers when they view the two beings under comparison as essentially different. White racists viewed African Americans as fundamentally different, as "other," and did not accept the notion that blacks wanted to pursue the American dream. Condit notes that for perspective taking to occur, one must feel that the "other" is in some fundamental way the same; some members of Kennedy's audience were unwilling to assent to similarities—an assent required for an argument of reciprocity to persuade.[119] Perhaps as an attempt to cover for this potential problem, Kennedy combines his appeal to the Golden Rule with an argument based on the categorical imperative, "Always act on a maxim which you can will to become a universal law of nature."[120] Perelman and Olbrechts-Tyteca and Condit suggest that the universalization of basic human desires is expressed in both the categorical imperative and the Golden Rule.[121] In fact, only the Golden Rule is based on desire; the categorical imperative is based on reason. The categorical imperative has the potential to persuade audience members who would not participate in the universalization of desires, by appealing only to their sense of reason.

President Kennedy appeals to his audience's sense of reason by outlining a series of moral oughts according to the categorical imperative:

"It ought to be possible . . . for American students of any color to attend any public institution they select."
"It ought to be possible for American consumers of any color to receive equal service in places of public accommodation."
"It ought to be possible for American citizens of any color to register and vote in a free election."

With each of these "oughts," Kennedy presents a case of what Immanuel Kant calls imperfect duty. That is, one can create a maxim that counters Kennedy's argument, but one cannot will it to be universal. It is logically possible to exclude persons of a particular color from attending public institutions, from receiving service in places of public accommodation, and from voting. It is not logical, however, to will such a maxim to be universal: to do so would be to exclude oneself from equal treatment. Kennedy is not satisfied with persuading Americans to accept an imperfect duty; he also formulates a case of perfect moral duty: "It ought to be possible, in short, for every American to enjoy the privileges of being an American without regard to his race or color." It is logically inconsistent to deny the privileges of being an American to any American; to deny those rights to any citizen proves that being an American does not involve any particular privileges. The president combines this argument based on reason with his appeal to Christian virtue: in the sentence immediately following his argument for perfect duty, Kennedy states his civic version of the Golden Rule.

This rational approach to moral argument matched Kennedy's usual manner of personal convictions and his chief speechwriter's affinity for reason. Kennedy's argument for moral duty may be logically sound, yet it seems unlikely that it had much persuasive force with many white racists. At an abstract, philosophical level, President Kennedy's rhetorical strategy seems sensible. His purely rational argument demands that his audience make moral decisions based on its consequences for everyone—a principle that the categorical imperative shares with the Golden Rule. But, unlike the Golden Rule, the categorical imperative does not require the audience to become consubstantial with the "other"; a rational argument has the potential to overcome the weaknesses of a moral argument whose success depends on empathic perspective taking. Yet discrimination was an emotional, cultural, and historical issue: few white racists would be so antiseptically objective as to be converted by the president's formulation of a moral duty through the universalization of reason.

The success of the president's speech, though, did not depend entirely upon his ability to persuade whites to change their racist practices: this was not the only goal of the address, nor may it have been Kennedy's primary goal. Lyndon Johnson's advice prior to the speech suggested that the president did not necessarily need to invent discourse that would alter behavior; rather, he needed to employ discourse that would convince whites—primarily southern whites— that the moral force of the chief executive was on the side of civil rights. Public address that changed segregationists' behavior would alter the rhetorical situation facing the president, but it seemed unlikely that rhetoric would immediately convert white racists. Perhaps the nation's racial situation could be ameliorated by convincing the South that holding out against court orders and local conflicts was meaningless because the moral force of the presidency was against them. Kennedy's speech was a significant departure from Eisenhower's discourse on civil rights and JFK's own prior discourse. This address made it clear that civil rights was not merely a political issue that southern segregationists could try to thwart in a series of local battles. The rhetoric of advocacy and resistance shifted from a political tone to a moral tone.

Kennedy spoke a language of collective symbols and myths on June 11, but this language could not persuade all segregationists to change their personal behaviors. Yet the president did use his rhetorical powers of definition and interpretation: his speech interprets the nation's history and purpose as inconsistent with current practices and formulates a new political vocabulary for talking about civil rights. Immediately following Kennedy's speech, white segregationists could claim that Jim Crow was consonant with national values: Georgia Senator Richard Russell claimed that segregation did not violate "the Constitution or Judaeo-Christian values or common sense and reason."[122] In the long run, however, segregationists would find it difficult to talk about civil rights in that way: Kennedy's speech would make their vocabulary antiquated. Kennedy was not the first to suggest that racial discrimination was a violation of Christian and national principles—Gunnar Myrdal's landmark 1944 book *An American Dilemma,* for example, argued that America needed to live up to its political and religious creed—but Kennedy was the first American president to make a moral argument for civil rights. The president had rhetorical power that civil rights activists did not: whereas activists had to rely on persuasion, Kennedy could use rhetoric to constitute Americans as citizens of a nation in which segregation and discrimination were morally wrong.

Kennedy's moral arguments also appealed to many African Americans, but on a different level. His argument that the nation fulfill its promise and live up to the principles of the Declaration of Independence echoed arguments common in the black rhetorical tradition. President Kennedy's claim that America was founded on the principle that "the rights of every man are diminished when the rights of one man are threatened," for example, echoed Frederick Douglass's claims about the nation's founding principles: "All men by nature are equal, and have inalienable rights, or none have. We beg you to reflect how insecure your own and the liberties of your prosperity would be by the admission of such a rule of construing the rights of men."[123] In the first issue of the *Crisis*, W. E. B. Du Bois claimed that the official organ of the NAACP would stand for "the highest ideals of American democracy, and for reasonable but earnest and persistent attempts to gain these rights and to realize these ideals."[124] Urging the realization of American ideals also is a common theme in African American fiction and poetry—a theme crystallized in Langston Hughes's poem "Let America Be America Again":

> *O, let America be America again—*
> *The land that never has been yet—*
> *And yet must be—the land where every man is free. . . .*
> *O, yes,*
> *I say it plain,*
> *America never was America to me,*
> *And yet I swear this oath—*
> *America will be!*[125]

Praising American ideals, condemning America's hypocrisy, and urging the nation to fulfill its promise was central to African American rhetoric.

Kennedy's pairing of political principle with Christian morality also tapped into a common theme in African American discourse: many prominent black orators and writers had combined Christian and civic appeals in their protest rhetoric. For example, in his "What to the Slave Is the Fourth of July" address, Frederick Douglass goaded Americans toward Christian virtue and urged them to uphold the principles embedded in the Declaration of Independence.[126] Author and activist James Weldon Johnson urged Americans to end racial discrimination "because it is contrary to the spirit of democracy and Christianity."[127] During Kennedy's own era, Martin Luther King, Jr., appealed powerfully to civic piety and the myth of America in his sermonic rhetoric. In his April,

1963, "Letter from Birmingham City Jail," King claimed: "I have no fear about the outcome of our struggle in Birmingham, even if our motives are at present misunderstood. We will reach the goal of freedom in Birmingham and all over the nation, because the goal of America is freedom. Abuse and scorned though we may be, our destiny is tied up with America's destiny. . . . We will win our freedom because the sacred heritage of our nation and the eternal will of God are embodied in our echoing demands." King argued that civil rights activists were "standing up for what is best in the American dream and for the most sacred values in our Judaeo-Christian heritage" and would bring the nation "back to those great wells of democracy which were dug deep by the founding fathers in their formulation of the Constitution and the Declaration of Independence."[128]

President Kennedy, then, spoke the language of African American protest rhetoric as he spoke the language of American civil religion. Kennedy's moral argument had both national and racial appeal. His ethical vocabulary was familiar to audiences versed in American civil religious discourse and to audiences versed in the rhetoric of African American protest. The president's address shifted the terms of the civil rights debate on a national level and fortified civil rights activists' stance on the moral high ground. His speech changed the relationship between himself and civil rights activists and between the presidency and issues of race.

Response and Aftermath

Many American newspapers and magazines applauded Kennedy's speech. His declaration that civil rights was a moral issue received strong praise, suggesting that JFK had found a moral vocabulary that appealed to the nation. Several periodicals called the address the most important message Kennedy ever had delivered.[129] For example, the *New Yorker* magazine claimed: "The President's proclamation of a state of 'moral crisis' is surely the most important one he has ever made and perhaps the most important one he ever will make. For the first time in history, the government has championed complete equality for the Negro as a matter of right; for the first time, it has acknowledged a moral obligation to seek equality, as a matter of right, by political means."[130]

The *New York Times* noted that Kennedy's speech was a strong departure from his earlier civil rights rhetoric, especially his speech during the Oxford crisis: "Last night's address could not have been in greater contrast to what he said last fall. He left the lofty realms of the law and talked about the moral issues involved in treating human beings differently because of the color of their skin. Few Kennedy speeches have been so personal or so committed." The *St. Petersburg Times* claimed that the president spoke with "grace and understanding," and the *Nashville Tennessean* reported that Kennedy's moral appeal had "put the race issue in its proper perspective." The *St. Louis Post-Dispatch* indicated that the speech was more than just the best of the president's rhetorical career; rather, it was one of the most moving messages of the civil rights movement: "President Kennedy's moving appeal to the conscience of America should be regarded as one of the major achievements of the civil rights struggle." *Time* magazine agreed that the speech was "possibly the most important that Kennedy has delivered" but tempered its praise of the president's national address by indicating that it was long overdue.[131]

The most common criticism of Kennedy's address was that his forthright rhetoric and moral argument were belated. *Newsweek,* which called the speech "an unprecedented plea for a basic change in American society itself," claimed that it was "long awaited and much postponed." The *Milwaukee Journal* asserted, "If there can be any criticism of what the president said it is only that it should have been said sooner." Many periodicals implied that recent events in the struggle for civil rights had forced Kennedy to act and indicated that—in the minds of his critics—his words were overdue. The *New Yorker,* however, disagreed with critics of the president's timing. Writer Richard Rovere reported that some Americans would criticize JFK for not acting until forced by events but indicated sympathy with the president's view: Kennedy had always supported civil rights, Rovere argued, but he had been uncertain of the possibility for legislative action until June 1963. The *New York Daily News* also claimed that Kennedy had always backed civil rights, but reporter Ted Lewis was not so lenient in his coverage: he asked bluntly "why it took so long" for JFK to provide moral leadership. The *Daily Standard* of Celina, Ohio, was even more critical, claiming that the president's speech revealed his "unwillingness to speak or act unless prodded by a groundswell of public opinion." An editorial in the newspaper claimed, "He should be a leader, molding new thoughts and ideas to be relayed to the citizens of the nation."[132]

Most liberal publications congratulated Kennedy for his moral appeal—still noting that it was overdue—but emphasized that the president must do more. The *New Republic,* for example, claimed that while the president deserved a salute for declaring that civil rights is a moral issue, his commitment must be embraced by all who serve under him. The magazine also demanded that

Kennedy continue his rhetorical leadership, including trips to the South to speak out about the morality of civil rights. The *Nation* praised Kennedy for calling constitutional privileges morally right but criticized him for describing civil rights as an end in itself rather than addressing the root causes of racial inequalities. The *Progressive* called the president's message to the nation a "landmark speech" that stood in stark contrast "to the cool summons to law and order that had characterized most of his previous utterances on race relations." The magazine's account of the speech came after JFK had delivered his civil rights message to Congress, however, and the *Progressive* used Kennedy's words as a benchmark against which to measure his legislative proposals. The magazine criticized the president's legislative initiatives, noting, "Mr. Kennedy's half-a-loaf program was all the more disappointing because he had sounded, in his address to the nation, like a man aroused, a leader committed to bringing moral passion and political power to the struggle ahead."[133]

Many African Americans were impressed with Kennedy's speech and also hoped that the president would continue to bring his moral passion and political power to the civil rights issues. But blacks' attention quickly turned to another event that drained much of the hope Kennedy had aroused. Just hours after JFK's address, Byron de la Beckwith murdered Medgar Evers, whose family had waited up past midnight to hear his reaction to the president's speech. The black press devoted most of its attention in the following days and weeks to the Evers murder and funeral: the *Crisis, Pittsburgh Courier,* and *Chicago Defender* dedicated most of their pages to Evers's death, neglecting the president's address entirely. Kennedy's message still received considerable attention from African Americans. Overall, civil rights leaders lauded his moral argument even more vigorously than the mainstream white press. In a telegram to the president on June 12, King claimed, "I have just listened to your speech to the nation. It was one of the most eloquent, profound, and unequivocal pleas for justice and the freedom of all men ever made by a president. You spoke passionately to the moral issue involved in the integration struggle." NAACP executive secretary Roy Wilkins called the president's speech "a clear, resolute exposition of basic Americanism and a call to all our citizens to rally in support of the high traditions of our nation's dedication to human rights." Jackie Robinson, still seen by many blacks as an influential civil rights leader, called JFK's speech "one of the finest declarations ever issued in the cause of human rights." Two prominent African American newspapers claimed that the address was one of the most impressive in the history of the presidency. The *Norfolk Journal & Guide* declared that the president's address was "the greatest civil rights pronouncement since Lincoln." The *Philadelphia Afro-American* praised his discussion of civil rights as "a burning moral issue" and called the message "unquestionably the greatest speech ever made by a Chief Executive."[134]

Perhaps the most significant outcome of President Kennedy's speech among African Americans was that civil rights leaders altered their plans for the August March on Washington for Jobs and Freedom. In a telephone conversation the day after Kennedy's address, King told his friend and supporter Stanley Levison that the speech meant the march would be aimed at Congress rather than at the president, and Levison agreed. This agreement was a significant shift from their plans of just over a week earlier. In telephone conversations on June 1 and 2, King and Levison had discussed how civil rights activists might "frighten the president [so] that he would have to do something." King advocated a mass march on the nation's capital, an idea that Bayard Rustin and A. Philip Randolph had been developing seriously since January, in order to force JFK into a more forthright stance. Rustin and Randolph also had hoped that the March would pressure the president into stronger support for civil rights. But President Kennedy's address on June 11 brought him into the mainstream civil rights movement: his language and arguments echoed those articulated by many moderate civil rights leaders, and he made the moral commitment activists had urged. The March on Washington, therefore, was transformed into a celebration of values expressed by activists and the president and into a demonstration urging Congress to pass the administration's civil rights bill. However, despite JFK's argument for legislation in his nationwide address, many civil rights leaders were skeptical of its chances in Congress. King and Wyatt Walker were deeply pleased by Kennedy's June 11 statement, but neither had high hopes for the passage of his proposed legislation. Walker expressed his doubts publicly on television and called for "strong executive action" to prevent further incidents like those in Birmingham and assassinations like that of Medgar Evers. The president's speech helped avert the march's focus on the White House but did not prevent those involved in the march from urging him to move beyond his admirable yet singular statement.[135]

Still other African Americans were not so moved by Kennedy's address that they eased their demands on the administration at all. For example, on June 12, three thousand anti-segregation picketers stationed themselves outside Robert Kennedy's office door at the Justice Department. The attorney general argued unsuccessfully before the crowd that demonstrations were unnecessary since the administration was on their side, as evidenced by the president's televised speech the previous evening.[136] President Kennedy's speech had not squelched protests as many white newspaper and magazine writers seemed to hope. Civil rights demonstrations still commenced in Danville, Kansas City, Harlem, Chicago, and Philadelphia—some of them turning violent. Some southern critics of Kennedy's speech claimed that the president was in fact responsible for stimulating African American protest. In a public response to JFK's address on June 12, Senator Richard Russell (D-Georgia) argued: "I was . . . shocked to hear the President justify, if not encourage, the present wave of mass demonstrations." Russell called the speech "propaganda" that "appealed eloquently to the emotions but completely disregarded reason, human experience, and true equality under the Constitution."[137] Senator Russell's response may have appealed to some moderate whites—in addition to his usual audience of ardent segregationists—who were frightened by the civil rights demonstrations that began during the weeks following the president's message.

Internationally, Kennedy's address received significant attention, especially considering the gravity of concurrent events. On June 10, the president had delivered a speech on international peace at American University that aimed to redefine attitudes toward the Cold War, and the Profumo affair in Great Britain also captured international media attention. English-language periodicals generally gave Kennedy's moral statement positive reviews. For example, the *New Statesman* praised JFK for his "unequivocal support" of African Americans' civil rights and for asking his countrymen "to see life through the eyes of the oppressed one-tenth of a nation." The *New Statesman* claimed that the president went beyond common themes of equality and that his words "were those of an otherwise prudent politician who has crossed a moral divide." The *Spectator* reported: "It was an extraordinary speech, if only because no other President before him had ever used nouns like 'conscience' or adjectives like 'moral' about this issue before." The *Manchester Guardian Weekly* stated that until June 11, Kennedy had seemed unable or unwilling to provide strong leadership, and thus identified his speech as a turning point. The *Weekly* claimed, however, that JFK would need to provide sustained rhetorical leadership to truly improve civil rights: "He has found his voice: he will now have to speak out not once but again and again." Some British periodicals also implied that since Kennedy had "struggled to catch up" with the civil rights movement, perhaps he should follow some of his countrymen's advice to stay home and provide moral leadership rather than fly to Europe for meetings with foreign leaders.[138]

Overall, then, evaluators of Kennedy's speech esteemed its moral argument and the president's shift away from "law and order" rhetoric with regard to issues of race. The address helped redefine the relationship between the president and the civil rights movement and had a material impact on the March on Washington. The primary behest issued by concerned journalists was that JFK continue his moral, rhetorical leadership, and the primary criticism leveraged against Kennedy was that he should have spoken this vigorous moral appeal sooner. Commentary regarding the perceived timing of the June 11 address deserves our close attention. Kennedy's moral appeal had long seemed overdue to many African Americans and liberal whites. Eisenhower's refusal to address the moral imperative of school desegregation coupled with candidate Kennedy's call for moral leadership made a statement by the nation's president feel imperative; yet JFK deferred for over two years. Kennedy's speech clearly seemed overdue to some Americans, but why was it too late according to some critics?

Interestingly, polling data suggests that only a minority percentage of Americans believed the president was not moving fast enough on civil rights. A Gallup poll in May, 1962, found that only 11 percent of respondents claimed Kennedy was moving too slowly on racial integration: 32 percent indicated that he was moving too quickly, and 35 percent indicated that he was moving at about the right pace. A November, 1962, poll found that only 12 percent of respondents claimed JFK was moving too slowly on racial integration: 42 percent indicated that he was moving too quickly, and 31 percent indicated that the president was moving at about the right pace. A poll eight months later in July, 1963, indicated little change in public opinion: 14 percent of respondents claimed Kennedy was moving too slowly on racial integration; 41 percent indicated that he was moving too quickly; and 31 percent indicated that he was moving at about the right pace. While these polls do not focus on the timing of Kennedy's rhetorical leadership, they do suggest that most citizens did not believe that his civil rights leadership in general was too slow. Some Americans, then, may have found JFK's June 11 address admirable without thinking it late or too late. The notion that the message came "too late" suggests that President Kennedy spoke after a critical moment beyond which some significant event or events could not be forestalled.[139]

Some Americans, or at least some journalists, worried that the president's message came too late to forestall racial demonstrations and African Americans' loss of faith in political processes and institutions.[140] Several periodicals expressed apprehension that by waiting so long to speak out, JFK would find himself unable to abate growing impatience among African Americans. Implicit in many of these accounts was a fear that black protesters might turn violent. In an opinion essay published the day of Kennedy's speech, Walter Lippman claimed that the nation had passed a "point of no return" on racial issues; any attempt by the president to redress civil rights grievances would only be met by swelling discontent.[141] Soon after the president's speech, *Newsweek* claimed: "The question for history, as the flames of an angry summer danced higher, was whether Mr. Kennedy has spoken soon enough."[142] The timing of rhetorical leadership was crucial, some journalists implied, not merely because it was overdue but because the president's failure to provide moral, rhetorical leadership might have turbulent consequences. *Time* and *Newsweek* both paired their coverage of President Kennedy's speech with accounts of increasing militancy and impatience within what they called "the Negro Revolution."

Some African Americans also claimed that the timing of Kennedy's speech was more than overdue. The *Philadelphia Afro-American* conducted a survey soon after the address to gauge the reaction of the "black man on the street" to the president's message. Many praised his moral appeal as courageous, but a significant number of blacks said that his message came "too late."[143] For some African Americans, JFK's speech came too late to head off their loss of faith in the federal government. Some civil rights activists remained unconvinced that Kennedy was firmly on their side, given the timing of his moral appeal. SNCC members, for example, planned to speak out against the president at the March on Washington—despite other leaders' intentions to focus instead on Congress. SNCC Chairman John Lewis's prepared speech for the march claimed that the administration's civil rights bill was "too little and too late." Lewis was prepared to indict the federal government for moving too slowly and planned to reveal SNCC's suspicion of political processes and institutions: "We will not wait for the President, the Justice Department, nor Congress but we will take matters into our own hands."[144] The time for waiting had passed, Lewis planned to assert, suggesting that JFK's rhetoric and proposals had in fact come after a point of no return. Although Lewis personally lauded Kennedy's address, many within SNCC believed that it was a token statement that had come too late.[145] Other organizers of the March on Washington objected to Lewis's prepared statement, however, and prevented him from criticizing the White House. The speech that Lewis actually delivered did not criticize the president and instead fit into an event that made Kennedy's speech seem like a timely herald of civil rights progress in America.

Yet reactions to the timing of the president's speech were complex and not uniformly critical. Some Americans, including African Americans, apparently believed that Kennedy did not deliver his address too late. For instance, in its issue the week after JFK's speech, the *Norfolk Journal & Guide* reprinted a full speech text and claimed that the president's moral appeal was "one of the most important and timely civil rights pronouncements in the nation's history." *Washington Post* writer Chalmers Roberts also indicated that Kennedy's speech was indeed timely, claiming that he had "seized upon a moment of vast national concern to appeal to the mind and conscience of the American people."[146] Citizens' perceptions of the timing of historical events involving civil rights differed drastically, and Americans interpreted Kennedy's rhetorical intervention in these events as timely, belated, and too late—all at the same moment. The notion of timing has historical, epistemological, and rhetorical components: it involves events, knowledge of events, and how people depict events. The understanding and depiction of racial issues in 1963 differed between citizens, and citizens referred to different historical events. We cannot make a singular, unqualified claim about the appropriateness of the timing of Kennedy's address—from either a contemporary or a historical perspective. To say that Kennedy's speech was timely in a rhetorical sense, that he effectively appealed to what classical rhetoricians call *kairos,* would mean that his speech came at an opportune moment within historical events and depicted the timing of those events in a way that advanced his purpose. But Kennedy's address seemed overdue or too late to some audiences, and his rhetorical depiction of the present as a sacred moment, a civil-religiously important "now," was unpersuasive with some of his listeners. JFK's moral appeal did come too late to head off the so-called Negro Revolution, though the nation may not have listened had he articulated it sooner. And although his address frames events in a way that emphasizes the urgency of the present, it does not specify why the immediate present is more urgent than the immediate past nor indicate how a moral issue can be influenced by a seemingly amoral factor like time. To judge Kennedy's speech as either timely or untimely would be to simplify the timing of his address and the notion of *kairos.* The rhetorical timing of the president's address was simultaneously opportune, inopportune, and misopportune.

Conclusion

President Kennedy's civil rights message of June 11, 1963, is a significant episode in American public address, especially with regard to race and rights. The speech met African Americans' demands for a moral commitment from the president, which had been urged during the Eisenhower administration and which Kennedy himself had promised during the 1960 campaign. Kennedy spoke out in large part because the costs of remaining silent became high—personally, politically, and rhetorically. Pressure from civil rights activists helped propel him into action, as did critical events in Birmingham and Tuscaloosa. Still, his speech demonstrated rhetorical courage, as a public moral argument was a risky endeavor and its outcomes were unknown. Moreover, JFK's own moral understanding of civil rights developed in 1963 and became especially keen by spring. The speech itself relies upon civil religious appeals and ethical reasoning to define civil rights as a primarily moral issue and to construct a sense of moral urgency. His address appeals to Christian virtue, rationality, and the American ideology to urge citizens to end discrimination in their daily lives and to urge legislators to pass a civil rights act. The address also puts the moral authority of the presidency firmly behind civil rights progress, thereby communicating that the backbone of resistance to racial integration and equality of opportunity will be broken.

Kennedy's civil rights address is a complicated instance of crisis rhetoric. The speech defines the nation's racial problem as a "crisis," a rhetorical strategy that suggests the failure of normal politics to deal with an issue. And Kennedy's discourse did represent a departure from his normal approach to civil rights and the normal approach to racial issues exercised by previous presidents: it emphasizes the moral dimensions of racial issues and downplays the legal dimensions. In another sense, though, Kennedy's speech both was and was not crisis rhetoric. By defining civil rights as a "crisis" the president implied the failure of normal political institutions to handle the nation's race problem, yet Kennedy argued that a return to traditional political principles would solve the problem. The president urged Americans to take timely action in response to the nation's crisis, and at the same time he urged the citizenry to consider its action as a response consonant with timeless American principles. Kennedy's term "moral crisis" itself is paradoxical. The word "moral" suggests an argument from principle, while "crisis" implies an argument from circumstance. The president's address is a peculiar mix of the particular and transcendent: it speaks to an immediate audience during particular circumstances and to a universal audience about timeless themes.

Kennedy appealed to American civil religion as the foundation of his moral argument: it provided an acceptable set of commonplaces for moral rhetoric in the public sphere. He exhorted Americans toward civic virtue without preaching, in the pejorative sense of the word. The president appealed to notions of promise and destiny to construct the solution to racial discrimination as moral realization rather than moral change. That is, Kennedy did not suggest—as did Harry Truman—that the nation needed to develop new concepts of civil rights. Rather, he advanced the traditional reformist argument for fulfillment. Kennedy described the American struggle for civil rights as the story of a nation that would eventually live up to its divinely sanctioned purpose. JFK's address added the ethos and rhetorical powers of the presidency to this particular narrative of equality—the narrative that Celeste Condit and John Lucaites note has become the dominant interpretation of the history of U.S. race relations.[147] Kennedy suggested that America is not a land of revolution but rather that the nation needs to rededicate itself periodically to its original purpose. The rhetorical timing of the president's civil religious discourse also framed historical events as a sacred present requiring immediate action from the American citizenry in order to demonstrate its commitment to its hallowed national duty regarding civil rights.

Historians, rhetoricians, political scientists, and biographers still discuss another sense of timing related to Kennedy's speech—its timeliness as a rhetorical intervention during a crucial historical moment. Theodore Sorensen claims that by speaking out on June 11, Kennedy placed himself at the head of the civil rights revolution. By June 11, Sorensen argues, the country was just listening for a presidential message on civil rights when it had not been listening during the prior weeks and months. Sorensen also suggests that JFK's message represented the fulfillment of a historical and rhetorical development, that it completed his prior, progressive rhetorical and political action on civil rights.[148] The president's speech effectively directed itself toward *kairos*, Sorensen suggests, because it came at just the right moment: Kennedy did not pledge his power and prestige suddenly but rather only when the nation was ready to hear his message, which stands as a timely fulfillment of his civil rights commitments as president. Arthur Schlesinger also asserts that Kennedy's moral argument was a timely instance of rhetorical action. Schlesinger argues against contemporary critics who indicted JFK for not delivering it sooner, claiming that "the timing was a vindication of his approach to mass education." Like Sorensen, he claims that Kennedy had prepared the ground for the speech since becoming president, yet "did not call for change in advance of the moment."[149] The speech was delivered at the appropriate moment, Schlesinger claims, as the events in Birmingham had given the president the nation's ear: had Kennedy delivered his civil rights message earlier, it would not have received significant or favorable national attention. Rhetorical critics Steven Goldzwig and George

Dionisopoulos claim that JFK's speech was a timely response to the historical moment, since the events at Tuscaloosa presented him with "a golden opportunity to make his case." Historian Carl Brauer argues that June 11 was "an excellent moment" for the president to address the nation on civil rights, and political scientist Mark Stern asserts that Kennedy effectively "seized the opportunity" provided by Governor Wallace and the events in Birmingham to deliver his speech. Even political scientist Bruce Miroff, one of Kennedy's sternest critics with regard to civil rights, argues that the speech was "timely" and "appropriate."[150]

Yet none of these writers describes in detail why prior critical moments in the civil rights movement did not constitute opportune moments for Kennedy to address the nation. Neither do they explain fully why waiting for this moment of heightened conscience was the timely thing to do. Each suggests that events had sufficiently raised the national conscience by mid-June and that waiting to address the public at that moment was a timely decision. Such claims require a careful, complex account of historical events, public knowledge, and public discourse. Goldzwig and Dionisopoulos provide a detailed account of the development of historical events and of Kennedy's discourse yet do not explore the ways in which the president's speech might have been untimely. Schlesinger points to the flat reception that met Kennedy's civil rights message on February 28 as evidence that June 11 was the right time to make a public moral statement. Yet he does not acknowledge that the June 11 speech was a more vigorous, sustained ethical argument that drew upon a familiar moral vocabulary: these important variables clearly account for much of its rhetorical force. Claims that President Kennedy's speech was timely also require a complicated understanding of what constitutes timely rhetorical leadership, an understanding missing from existing written accounts.

We can question the existing explanations of Kennedy's speech as timely on existential grounds—that is, whether or not June 11 represented a uniquely critical moment that made presidential discourse particularly fitting. For instance, the violence against protesters during the 1961 Freedom Rides was more brutal than against demonstrators in Birmingham. Arguably, the Freedom Rides received media attention equal to the Birmingham crisis and aroused similar levels of national and international outrage. Why was it not timely for Kennedy to speak out then? But perhaps more important, we can question existing accounts of JFK's speech as directing itself toward *kairos* from a uniquely rhetorical perspective. Why should waiting for national sentiment to mature before speaking out be judged unequivocally as timely? Or, is what some identify as a timely spoken response necessarily an optimum form of rhetorical leadership? By waiting for what some considered to be the opportune moment, Kennedy let pass a critical moment in some protesters' relationship to the national government: as such, his speech was in another sense too late. But Kennedy's own understanding of civil rights as a moral issue (presumably a requirement for making a public moral argument) only recently had developed. In classical rhetorical theory, the concept of *kairos* involves epistemology, not only discourse. That is, in a sense JFK's speech can be judged as timely because it was only at that moment that he had achieved knowledge of race as a moral issue. Still, we can interrogate the timeliness of Kennedy's civil rights message, or any rhetorical act, with other crucial questions. To what extent can we judge a speaker who waits for the opportune moment to be courageous? Might a speech judged as "ahead of its time" during its own era be considered timely at a later historical moment? These questions—in addition to others that probe the very notion of speaking at the opportune moment—should lead us to interrogate simple, unambiguous evaluations of the timing of rhetorical action.

Finally, despite any shortcomings in timing, moral understanding, or argument, Kennedy's speech clearly marked the beginning of a new public vocabulary on civil rights. Lyndon Johnson maintained the moral commitment in his presidential rhetoric that Kennedy had established, providing the mainstream civil rights movement with the moral high ground throughout the 1960s. In addition, as a consequence of Kennedy's rhetoric, the vocabulary of "law and order" would no longer stand without question both as a pretext for keeping peace and for resistance to racial integration. JFK's moral rhetoric was important, because afterward the same vocabulary used to advocate civil rights could not be used for resistance—unlike earlier civil rights discourse rooted in law and order. The shift to a moral vocabulary gave activists an effective language of protest and helped incapacitate the voices of racial discrimination. Segregationists could debate the relationship between legality and morality, but moral advocacy of segregation was not a viable argument nationally.

On November 22, John F. Kennedy was felled by an assassin's bullet, stunning the nation. Many African Americans worried that Vice President Johnson would end the civil rights progress JFK had begun. As Johnson himself acknowledged in his memoirs, "Just when the blacks had their hope for equality and justice raised, after centuries of misery and despair, they awoke one morning to discover that their future was in the hands of a President born in the South."[151] Johnson was a southern politician—in the worst sense of the word, according to some critics—who had weakened previous pieces of civil rights legislation, and most blacks did not believe that his attitude toward racial progress would be nearly as strong as President Kennedy's recent moral commitment, however overdue or motivated by expediency.

Yet the progress begun in June, 1963, did not end with the Kennedy assassination. LBJ worked vigorously to help ensure the passage of Kennedy's legislative proposal, which ultimately became the Civil Rights Act of 1964. Johnson also spoke out regularly on civil rights issues, claiming, for example, that "we must bring equal justice to all our citizens."[152] But Lyndon B. Johnson's greatest moment of rhetorical leadership on civil rights came during the drive for voting rights in Selma, Alabama, in the spring of 1965. Civil rights leaders who were pleasantly surprised to hear Jack Kennedy call civil rights a "moral issue" must have been shocked when a southern president exclaimed the rallying cry of their movement, "We shall overcome," before Congress, the nation, and the world on March 15, 1965.

CHAPTER FIVE

Lyndon Johnson Overcomes

Although Lyndon Johnson demonstrated his political determination by guiding the Civil Rights Act of 1964 into law, skeptics wondered whether LBJ would still support racial equality after he had paid his homage to the Kennedy legacy with a legislative offering. Would the president-by-inheritance propose legislation to address inequalities not covered by the public accommodations measure? Would he use executive orders to end discrimination in domains covered by his power as chief executive? And, finally, would Johnson take a strong rhetorical stand on civil rights: could he use public discourse effectively to induce the people and the Congress to accept racial equality in law, in principle, and in reality? Now that his honeymoon with the citizenry and the legislature had ended, Johnson would need to exhibit rhetorical skills he seemed to lack in order to make racial progress. LBJ's homespun stories about race told in interpersonal situations were often touching, though sometimes corny, but he would need additional communicative abilities to talk to the public. Johnson did not possess the refined fluency of his predecessor, and his nineteenth-century conception of rhetorical leadership often prevented him from using his gifts for narrative and expressiveness. His speeches were often flat and hackneyed, and comprehensive presidential leadership on racial equality would require eloquence.

Yet in his televised voting rights address of March 15, 1965, President Johnson was eloquent. Communication scholar Roderick Hart claims: "He linked his intellect with his words and then with his feelings and urged his suspicious, sometimes hostile listeners to throw off their old ways and to reach for something new and better. . . . In his speech, LBJ found new ways of linking familiar nationalistic myths with untried domestic policies, thereby allowing his listeners some comfort as they contemplated doing uncomfortable things."[1] This speech was perhaps Johnson's "most moving public address, conveying the natural eloquence that he so often took care to shield."[2] Like Harry Truman, President Johnson seemed to exhibit uncharacteristic eloquence on the occasion of a major civil rights speech. In the wake of demonstrations in Selma, Alabama, he urged the passage of a voting rights bill aimed at securing the franchise for African Americans living in the South. Johnson drew upon his personal experience, referred to the nation's historic principles, and appealed to Americans' sense of morality and sanctified purpose. LBJ made an important contribution to presidential rhetoric by enacting and promoting a tradition of civil religious appeal in presidential discourse on civil rights and affirming that racial equality in America will be realized. His speech reached a surprising climax when he articulated the anthem of the civil rights movement, "We shall overcome."

LBJ's voting rights speech was surprising and unusual in other ways too; he departed from his typical approach to rhetoric. Johnson habitually focused on the urgencies of the moment, and his rhetoric was often shortsighted. Critics of the Civil Rights Act of 1964 charged that the president had legislated in haste, through rhetorical appeals to temporarily aroused emotions. Some opponents of the voting rights bill worried that 1965 would bring a reprise. The bill did move through Congress quickly, in part because of Johnson's rhetorical emphasis on timing. He claimed that "the time for waiting is gone" and warned that if legislators did not pass the voting rights act promptly, "they would fall victim to the harsh judgment of history." Besides prodding from the president, a sense of urgency following the Selma demonstrations influenced legislators: many senators and congressmen claimed that the protests helped create "an irresistible public pressure" for swift action on the voting rights bill.[3] LBJ's speech on March 15 capitalized on the nation's aroused emotions and urged Congress to act immediately. Depending on one's perspective, his discursive involvement in the voting rights campaign seemed to be crisis rhetoric at its finest or its worst: Johnson seized an opportune moment and used rhetoric to finesse the situation, using public disgust over the police violence against African Americans to pass legislation. LBJ's critics decried him as an opportunist, but in a sense, the president's speech was opportune and timely.

In this chapter, I contend that Johnson's response to the voting rights crisis was unusually eloquent and timely. He departed from his usual approach to rhetoric in two important ways. In this case, the legislation had been under consideration for some time and was nearly finished when the crisis came. Furthermore, President Johnson not only was ready to speak to the immediate tactical issue of voting rights but had already formulated his own under-standing of voting rights as a moral and historical issue. My argument in the chapter has four parts. First, the existing body of scholarship on Lyndon Johnson needs modification. Nearly all of the relevant scholarly literature iden-tifies President Johnson as a shortsighted rhetor who spoke before he should have and whose own discourse created most of his political problems. Close attention to the voting rights address shows that Johnson's rhetoric was not always myopic. Second, Johnson planned carefully his voting rights strategy; he considered both the legislative and rhetorical implications of speaking pub-licly about the voting rights bill. The president also directed his rhetorical ap-peals toward what Greek rhetoricians called *kairos*—a timely response to a given situation. Third, LBJ's timely response was a complicated proposition. Johnson's speech was a timely response because it reshaped time itself not by taking the immediate case outward to an extended time and space but instead by focus-ing all of America's history and ideals inward to bring them to bear on the immediate situation. Fourth, although Johnson's speech was tactically timely, it was too little and too late for the rising militancy within the civil rights movement. LBJ's voting rights address was timely, timeless, and, ironically, out of time—all at the same moment.

To advance these claims, the chapter is divided into four sections: (1) a dis-cussion of Johnson's attitudes and approach toward civil rights, especially important given his lengthy political experience with racial issues; (2) an investigation of the context in which the president's speech was delivered—focusing on three historical constraints that influenced and were modified by the address; (3) a close reading of LBJ's voting rights message; (4) an examina-tion of the responses to Johnson's speech, with close attention to how the address resonated with activists in the civil rights movement.

LBJ, Racial Politics, and Racial Equality

Born and raised in the Texas Hill Country in 1908, Lyndon Johnson had few occasions to interact with African Americans as a child. Few blacks lived in Johnson City, and not many had reason to pass through the area. Overt racism was not a part of Johnson's family background or early social environment, though his parents and neighbors may have held some racist sentiments. Lady Bird Johnson suggests that her husband's infrequent interaction with African Americans as a boy may have been a blessing, as it meant that "he did not grow up absorbing the attitudes of his parents and neighbors toward blacks."[4] LBJ's parents may have had racial biases, but his father once walked off the floor of the Texas House to show his opposition to a bill that excluded African Americans from voting in the Democratic primary.[5] He also opposed the campaign of racial terror committed against blacks by white supremacists. Sam Johnson once denounced the Ku Klux Klan before a session of the Texas House of Representatives, at the risk of endangering himself and his family. Later, LBJ often described the Klan's threat against his father's stand as a formative moment in his own attitudes toward racism: "The Ku Klux Klan was at its height when my father was in the Texas Legislature. . . . They threatened him. . . . Men were called upon and told they'd be tarred and feathered, and a good many of them, friends of ours, were. I was only a fifteen-year-old boy in the middle of all of this, and I was fearful that my Daddy would be taken out and tarred and feathered."[6] Johnson viewed the episode as an affront to community and as indicative of white supremacists' irrationality. Whether or not this experience influenced his racial attitudes as a boy or young man, journalist Leonard Baker observes, "There is nothing to indicate Lyndon Johnson ever harbored personal prejudices against the Negro or member of any minority."[7] Instead, LBJ seemed to inherit his family's deep sympathy for the downtrodden, which ultimately shaped his attitudes toward racial minorities. Still, if Johnson did not mature with a strong racial prejudice, neither did he develop a sense of the injustice being done to African Americans and other minorities.[8] Even his experiences teaching in a Mexican-American community in Cotulla, Texas—which Johnson often identified as a critical moment in his developing compassion for racial minorities—only appealed to his sympathies for the economically disadvantaged and did not develop in the young man an understanding of the peculiarly racial dimensions of minorities' socioeconomic problems.

Johnson's first regular interaction with African Americans was during his tenure as director of the Texas branch of the National Youth Administration (NYA), from July, 1935, to February, 1937. LBJ impressed administration officials, including blacks such as Mary McLeod Bethune and Beatrice Denmark, because of his reputation for treating African Americans fairly. For instance, Johnson once met with local black leaders in the basement of an African American Methodist church, informing them that he was eager to assist jobless black youth. He also met with the presidents of several African American colleges in Texas to encourage greater involvement in the NYA by black youth, and he later traveled to Washington to plead successfully for increased funds for black colleges.[9] In addition, LBJ supported specific programs for African American youth, including domestic training projects and vocational training camps for young black women and a Civilian Conservation Corps (CCC) camp for young black men. Although he generally provided equal opportunities to African Americans, Johnson still maintained a segregated NYA administration. LBJ's office did not hire blacks for paid supervisory positions, despite the persistent urging of national officials, especially Bethune: his only concession was to appoint a symbolic "black advisory council" with no decision-making power. Johnson claimed that harmony between the races existed in Texas, an uneasy peace that would be broken by violating its "social customs."[10] Historian Monroe Billington observes that LBJ was interested in helping blacks economically but not in altering traditional social structure.[11]

Despite this potential blemish, which is not an especially conservative one, given the era, historians generally agree that Johnson's conduct exhibited his genuine concern for blacks. One should keep in mind, however, that the NYA was more progressive on race than most New Deal agencies. National director Aubrey Williams aimed to make his administration a model of racial fairness, and LBJ's equal treatment was in part a consequence of Williams's directives. Yet local administrators across the South usually attempted to undermine directives from the national administration with regard to race, and so Johnson's equal treatment was the product of some limited racial understanding or motivated his politically ambitious desire to please his superiors— or perhaps both.[12] Even if Johnson's fairly progressive treatment of blacks did not reflect a preexisting progressive attitude on race, his experiences working with African Americans seemed to arouse some heartfelt concern about race during this formative experience in LBJ's nascent political career. His experiences at this early stage also stimulated Johnson's ability to finesse the politics of a potentially controversial action. LBJ tried to keep all news of NYA projects for African Americans from reaching the pages of white newspapers. Biographer Paul Conkin claims, "In a sense, he pleased Washington with his positive steps but without in any way harming his reputation in Texas, a strategy that he used over and over again on issues concerning race."[13]

Johnson's record on race in his next political office, U.S. congressman from the tenth district of Texas, was mixed at best. LBJ exercised some progressive action between 1937 and 1948, but few would argue that his racial understanding matured during this period. Moreover, Johnson engaged in political conduct that seemed to betray some African Americans' belief that he cared about their plight. LBJ's accomplishments included successful lobbying for a public housing project that helped blacks and Mexican Americans. While serving in the House, Johnson called President Roosevelt to complain that racial minorities in Texas were not receiving benefits under the 1938 Agricultural Administration Act (AAA)—a move that ultimately insured their inclusion in federal benefits. A Farm Security Administration official also claimed that LBJ "was the first man in Congress from the South ever to go to bat for the Negro farmer."[14] These actions helped LBJ gain a reputation as someone concerned about minorities and helped him win support among many of his district's black citizens: he became known as a friend to the poor—white or black. Political scientist Mark Stern claims that Johnson's "basic fairness in dealing with race-related issues gave him a following among blacks in his home area and throughout Texas."[15] Yet his advocacy for minority tenants and black farmers cannot be judged as a political cunning: both actions held few, if any, political benefits, since many of the racial minorities in his district could not afford the poll tax required to vote. In fact, his advocacy could have brought him political damage if news had circulated among Johnson's white constituents back home.[16] Above all, LBJ's intervention on behalf of minorities indicated his general commitment to equal opportunity and fair play, his cursory understanding of racial injustice and inequality, and his unwillingness to upset local racial customs. The housing project that Johnson secured for Austin was segregated, and he did not challenge the basic inequity in pay between black and white farmers under the AAA.

Johnson's efforts to secure housing and agricultural benefits may have won him some support among some Texas minorities, but his voting record in the House did not endear him to many African Americans. Johnson voted against antilynching legislation in 1938 and 1940; anti-poll tax measures in 1942, 1943, and 1945; Fair Employment Practices Committee legislation in 1946; and an anti-discrimination clause to the federal school lunch program in 1946. In fact, LBJ opposed every proposed civil rights bill during his congressional terms. His rhetorical justifications for opposition included the "states' rights" arguments common to the oratory of his southern colleagues in the legislature. When explaining his stand to African American supporters and other civil rights advocates, Johnson claimed that he would work for civil rights measures when there was a chance of passing them. His favorite line of argument was, "One heroic stand and I'd be back home, defeated, unable to do good for anyone, much less the blacks or underprivileged."[17] Some blacks had faith that Johnson actually would support civil rights legislation when it became politically feasible, while others—especially members of civil rights groups—believed that LBJ was an opportunist with conservative personal sentiments on race.[18]

Johnson also disappointed some African Americans by associating with southern white supremacists during his tenure as a congressman, though his closest southern colleagues, including mentor Sam Rayburn, were not ardent racists. Moreover, despite his associations, Johnson was not an heir to the southern rhetorical tradition on race. For example, journalist Robert Mann notes: "In his congressional campaigns, he had never played on racial fears to win votes. He had paid perfunctory lip service to segregation but had not made the issue a central theme. And unlike some southern members of the Congress, he made no speeches to the House about the dangers that civil rights and racial integration posed to the Republic—a practice then widely known as 'talking Nigra.'"[19] Although Johnson did not join in this expected southern rhetorical practice, neither did he protest against his colleagues' white supremacist remarks. Such a move would have been an act of principled courage, but LBJ was too focused on his political future to risk offending congressmen who later might help his career.

Johnson furthered his bright political career in 1948 by campaigning successfully for the U.S. Senate. His record on race during his early Senate years was hardly more shining than during his time in the House. In fact, even LBJ's campaign included vocal opposition to President Truman's proposal for civil rights legislation. The company that Johnson kept on Capitol Hill was also racially suspect: he allied himself with John Stennis of Mississippi, Lister Hill of Alabama, Strom Thurmond of South Carolina, Walter George and Richard Russell of Georgia, and Harry Byrd of Virginia—senators who Johnson believed would help him attain Senate influence and national prominence. Indeed, LBJ's first speech on the Senate floor bore the mark of this southern influence. On March 9, 1949, he spoke in favor of upholding the right to filibuster, southerners' favorite tool for killing civil rights legislation. Though LBJ's ostensible argument was based on the right of free speech, as were the speeches of his fellow southerners, he also made the connection between the filibuster and current civil rights measures clear: he exclaimed, "We cannot legislate love."[20] In subsequent congressional sessions, Johnson strongly opposed federal anti-poll tax and antilynching legislation, stating the common states' rights refrain that racial issues should be handled at the local level. Many African Americans in Texas lashed out at Johnson for his stance on civil rights measures, yet the senator enjoyed political benefit among many whites back home for his anti-civil rights stance. In private, LBJ told African Americans that he supported equal opportunity. Historian Robert Dallek argues that as a senator, Johnson genuinely wanted to improve the lives of blacks but did not see the path to this advance through civil rights laws.[21] Despite his legislative stance in the Senate, LBJ did not seem to have the personal bitterness toward blacks that his southern colleagues felt: in the same year he denounced civil rights legislation and efforts to limit senators' right to filibuster, Johnson offered his seat to an African American woman during a bus trip in New York City—a gesture that Richard Russell, and probably many other whites, never would have extended.[22]

Johnson differed from his southern associates on other racial matters too. LBJ took a moderate, conciliatory tone toward the Supreme Court's *Brown* ruling in 1954, though he claimed it was based on "criteria other than law and equity."[23] He emphasized that the South should try to get past the decision, though, and not cry over "spilt milk." Soon after being elected majority leader in 1955, Johnson surprisingly proposed a constitutional amendment to abolish the poll tax as part of his "Program with a Heart." One of LBJ's most significant departures from the South came in March of 1956, when he refused to sign the Southern Manifesto, or "Declaration of Constitutional Principles," which challenged the Supreme Court's right to mandate school desegregation and urged massive resistance. Johnson was one of only three southern senators (the others were Estes Kefauver and Albert Gore, Sr., of Tennessee) who did not sign the manifesto. Senator Richard Neuberger (D-Oregon) called LBJ's refusal to sign the symbol of southern defiance a courageous act of political valor. Johnson himself, however, did not depict his action as courageous support for civil rights: soon after the manifesto was presented in Congress, he told journalists, "I am not a civil rights advocate."[24] And although LBJ did not sign it, neither did he denounce the declaration or the attitudes of its signers. He instead took the southern stance of emphasizing a local solution to school integration. Moreover, southern senators, including Russell, Johnson's mentor, did not object to his refusal to sign the manifesto; rather they accepted and reiterated LBJ's explanation that he needed to demonstrate a broader vision as majority leader and that adding his name to the declaration would have eliminated his chance to be named the Democratic Party's presidential nominee. Johnson departed from his southern associates on some racial issues but usually in ways they could understand or rationalize. Still, his stance on the Southern Manifesto helped initiate Johnson's commitment to civil rights, though mildly, by convincing him to look beyond the partisan, parochial concerns that shaped his early action on most racial matters.

In 1957, LBJ moved a little farther away from his southern origins. As majority leader he engineered a compromise on civil rights legislation that ultimately became the Civil Rights Act of 1957. Johnson appeased the segregation-ist-states' rights bloc by eliminating Title III, which authorized the attorney general to file injunctions against obstructions of civil rights, and by adding a jury trial amendment to Title IV—thereby forestalling a potentially deadly fili-buster. Critics claimed that the new bill was a mere shell of the original legisla-tion, a toothless voting measure. The compromise was also a blow to President Eisenhower's leadership but a victory for Johnson's. The pundits and the pub-lic were astonished at his ability to craft a compromise believed to be impos-sible: LBJ amassed political capital and praise and became known as a leader with astonishing legislative skill. Johnson's legislative accomplishment also prepared the way for his presidential ambitions by garnering national atten-tion and demonstrating that he was not a narrow sectionalist. His own politi-cal ambitions and other politicians' expectations for his future moved LBJ farther away from a southern position on civil rights.[25] Conkin claims that despite his personal and political journey on civil rights, Johnson still was not immune to racial stereotypes by 1957, and he still indulged in crude jokes about African Americans.[26] But by 1957, it seems clear that LBJ was prepared to embrace black voting rights and the Supreme Court's rulings on school desegregation—a major step forward from his past and away from his peers from Dixie.[27] Johnson demonstrated how far he had come, even if motivated primarily by political desire, later in the year when he muted his criticism of Eisenhower during the Little Rock crisis: he did not denounce the president vigorously, unlike his southern associates. LBJ offered the mildest of southern responses, stating that he believed no troops from either side should be stationed outside Central High and that local residents should respect the law.[28] Johnson sounded more like moderate politicians than he did Strom Thurmond, Harry Byrd, or Richard Russell.

Johnson's most significant split with Dixie legislators came in 1959 and 1960. In 1959, LBJ proposed a mild civil rights bill, critics charged, to keep race from becoming an election issue and to preclude meaningful civil rights legislation. But then he promised to take up civil rights proposals from the floor by Feb-ruary 15, 1960—a move that appalled most southerners. Surprisingly, on Feb-ruary 15 Johnson did more than keep his word: he effectively bypassed the Senate Judiciary Committee and House Rules Committee (which probably would have diluted any Senate-passed bill) by asking for civil rights amendments to an unrelated military housing bill. Russell and his segregationist colleagues viewed Johnson's move as sneaky, underhanded, and unforgivable. Illinois Republican Everett Dirksen added the Eisenhower administration's recent civil rights bill as an amendment to the housing bill, and LBJ started round-the-clock sessions to debate it—hoping to prevent a filibuster. Ultimately, Johnson's tactic failed, and he was forced to broker another compromise.[29] The Senate waited for the House civil rights bill, a watered-down version of the White House proposal, and passed it with some amendments. The bill satisfied no legislator completely, but again the process helped LBJ gain political capital: many praised his ability to break legislative gridlock. Journalist Tom Wicker claims that Johnson supported the bill only to win recognition as a truly national leader, but Congress of Racial Equality activist Floyd McKissick argues that LBJ was sincere in his desire to pass civil rights legislation, though few believed him in his sincerity at the time.[30] In any case, Johnson made a clear break with the Dixie bloc in the Senate and seemed to have shed any reluctance to support civil rights initiatives.

By the 1960 presidential election, though, few African Americans saw LBJ as supportive of their cause. But NAACP executive secretary Roy Wilkins believed that Johnson was the better friend of civil rights among the candidates. Wilkins felt that the senator from Texas had "a deep, inner determination . . . that stemmed from his intimate knowledge of the damage racial discrimination was doing not only to the South but to the whole country."[31] Most blacks, however, regarded LBJ as a halfhearted newcomer to the civil rights debate and opposed his unsuccessful campaign for the Democratic presidential nomination and his subsequent nomination by Kennedy as the party's vice presidential candidate.[32] For example, CORE chairman James Farmer opposed JFK's naming Johnson as his running mate, considering the move "a disaster, because of his southern background and his voting record on civil rights." Conkin claims that blacks had good reason to be skeptical of Johnson: although he was not opposed to all civil rights measures as before, he still needed to develop the moral passion necessary to support Kennedy's campaign promises on civil rights.[33] Presidential scholars and Johnson's friends and colleagues still debate whether or not LBJ had a deep-seated passion for civil rights at this point in his career. What seems clear is that LBJ tried to convince some African American leaders that he had a strong commitment to their cause, telling them, "I'll do more for you in four years than anyone else has done for you in one hundred years."[34] Johnson also spoke out vigorously in support of the Democrats' strong civil rights plank during the 1960 campaign, even before southern audiences.

Most of Johnson's critics—and most scholars—claim that LBJ's most significant transformation on civil rights occurred during his vice presidency, despite his general stagnation during that period. Kennedy named Johnson chairman of the President's Committee on Equal Employment Opportunity (PCEEO), which made reasonable equal employment progress through voluntary cooperation by businesses. Mann claims that while chairing the committee, LBJ seemed to become an all-out civil rights liberal.[35] He hired Hobart Taylor, Jr., an African American from Houston, to become executive director of the PCEEO. He spoke at National Urban League's Equal Opportunity Day dinner. CORE leader James Farmer changed his attitude toward LBJ, as did *Chicago Defender* editor Louis Martin: both praised the vice president's leadership of the equal employment committee. Conkin argues that Johnson's tendency to throw himself into a job fully and to identify with his constituents and absorb their outlook made him develop a personal commitment to civil rights.[36] In actuality, Johnson sometimes seemed distracted or uninterested during PCEEO meetings and became detached from the committee after Robert F. Kennedy castigated him for not moving quickly enough. Still, LBJ's regular contact with blatant forms of racial discrimination led him to speak about civil rights in a more personal way, which former skeptics interpreted as expressive of his private, heartfelt commitment. Interpersonally, Johnson began to tell stories about the discrimination confronted by his African American employees; he seemed stirred by their situation and determined to end senseless bigotry.[37] Publicly, Johnson began to deliver major speeches on civil rights. For example, in 1963 he delivered civil rights addresses in Detroit, Boston, Cleveland, Gettysburg, and Washington, D.C. In June, 1963, LBJ voiced his support for an FEPC measure in the Kennedy administration's civil rights bill, and word soon spread on Capitol Hill that Johnson would not help cut a deal on the bill, that the administration supported fair employment legislation. Baker claims that the vice president's firm support for strong civil rights legislation demonstrated that his "commitment to civil rights was complete."[38] Some critics claimed (and still claim) that LBJ supported civil rights for practical reasons related to his national constituency as vice president; others have argued that Johnson genuinely had overcome his former prejudices to support civil rights. The vice presidency clearly provided LBJ with new opportunities to expand his understanding of the moral dimensions of civil rights, and nothing in his vice presidential papers indicates that his speeches and actions on civil rights were merely gestures.[39]

As president, Johnson became even more committed to civil rights publicly, and his personal understanding seemed strong. LBJ made the civil rights bill a legislative priority soon after the Kennedy assassination, and his speech to Congress on November 27, 1963, urging immediate passage of the measure, comforted many blacks. African American entertainer Dick Gregory claimed that after the speech, "twenty million of us unpacked."[40] Johnson talked with black leaders by telephone and in person upon assuming the presidency, asking for their support and assistance in making the legislative dream a reality. Through these meetings, Johnson convinced civil rights leaders that his convictions were real and vigorous.[41] Martin Luther King, Jr., told *U.S. News & World Report* that he was "impressed by the President's awareness and depth of understanding." King also asserted, "We will proceed on the basis that we have in the White House a man who is deeply committed to help us." National Urban League president Whitney Young, Jr., claimed that Johnson "has deep convictions" on racial issues, and Roy Wilkins told the *New York Times,* "We have very great faith in the President's attitude on civil rights."[42]

Although African Americans leaders did not see LBJ's civil rights advocacy as motivated by expediency, some scholars of the Johnson presidency claim that he supported civil rights measures for political reasons. Eric Goldman argues that LBJ could not have won the 1964 election if he alienated African Americans and the urban liberal interests by refusing to support civil rights legislation. In order to show to the nation that he was not a conservative southerner and to create the impression of himself as a liberal, broadly national leader, Johnson supported civil rights.[43] However, while advocacy of civil rights legislation could gain some votes from African Americans and whites outside the South, such a stance risked loosing the white southern vote and the southern support he needed in Congress. Bruce Altschuler suggests that LBJ supported civil rights legislation to provide reassurance to the nation that there would be no dramatic break with Kennedy's policies.[44] Yet Johnson's civil rights advocacy went further than JFK's support: he was unwilling to compromise on Title III of the civil rights bill or on its FEPC provision. Scholars also argue that LBJ's support for civil rights rested on his desire to be regarded by history as a great president.[45] Many of Johnson's private conversations indicate that he often thought about the historical implications of his presidential actions, but his belief that civil rights advocacy made for a great president might have shaped his personal beliefs about race in a positive way. Moreover, a political commitment to civil rights or personal motivation to be well-regarded by history does not exclude LBJ from feeling a personal commitment. Nicholas Katzenbach, whom Johnson named attorney general, claims, "President Johnson believed deeply in racial equality. He believed it I think as a moral principle, and he believed it as a political principle."[46] As with most presidents,

Johnson's political involvement with racial issues and his sense of what the presidency required of him influenced his personal attitudes toward civil rights.

Authors have heralded Lyndon Johnson as "the greatest human rights and civil rights President America has ever known," noting that he "had overcome his racist past to become a powerful and effective advocate of civil rights."[47] Although he may never have fully divested himself of southern racial attitudes, his attitudes toward African Americans were similar to those held by many liberal reformers of his time.[48] Unlike most of his predecessors, LBJ's political career had afforded numerous opportunities to confront civil rights issues and to develop some level of personal understanding of African Americans' problems. By the time Johnson became president, most who knew him conceded that for all his earthy language, barnyard metaphors, capacity for cruelty, posturing, and political scheming, "he seemed to have an almost total lack of bias toward African Americans."[49]

But few blacks knew Lyndon Johnson: civil rights leaders who had met with LBJ believed in his commitment to their cause, but this belief was not widespread—even by the time of the Selma protests in 1965. Many of the protesters at Selma believed that Johnson revealed his insincerity by not protecting them from violence; they believed his numerous speeches on civil rights were mere words. Robert Caro's biography of LBJ begins with an insightful commentary on the Selma crisis and Johnson's relationship to the mainstream civil rights movement. Caro writes that by the time the demonstrations reached their climax on March 7, 1965, "Very few of the tens of thousands—hundreds of thousands—of men and women, black and white, in the American civil rights movement believed Lyndon Johnson was wholeheartedly on their side."[50]

Legislative Development and Historical Urgencies

For all his legislative acumen, his ability to discern the potential consequences of a particular stand, and his concern with how his actions might be viewed by history, LBJ sometimes seemed unable to think through the long-term implications of his rhetoric. Scholars often describe President Johnson as a shortsighted rhetor who tried to muster public support for his programs—including civil rights legislation—before he had fully developed his policies.[51] Authors note that Johnson spoke prematurely, spoke in language that aroused expectations beyond what he could achieve, and spoke without considering carefully the relationship between rhetoric and policy.[52] Some protesters at Selma might have felt that Johnson spoke too late in response to civil rights problems, but scholars claim he regularly spoke too soon, before he had developed thorough policy responses to political crises. Both protesters and scholars might agree that LBJ's words were "mere" rhetoric—protesters claiming that his words were not heartfelt and scholars claiming that they reflected the urgencies of the moment rather than thoughtful political analysis. Yet analysis of the historical context leading up to President Johnson's voting rights address on March 15, 1965, suggests a different, more complex understanding than most scholarly accounts of Johnson's rhetorical habits. The events preceding the president's speech show that LBJ prepared his legislation before the crisis came, and Johnson's own understanding of civil rights as a moral and legislative issue seemed to develop during this time. Throughout 1964 and 1965, careful debate and detailed policy discussions of the voting rights bill preceded discussions of public rhetoric. In contrast to what most scholars would predict, the White House spent more time developing the legislative proposal to ensure voting rights rather than developing a rhetorical campaign to sell it to the public. In fact, the public, protesters, and legislators criticized Johnson for spending too much time developing legislation and for not speaking soon enough in response to the violence at Selma. Eventually, President Johnson spoke, and his voting rights message did respond to the urgencies of the moment, but it responded carefully. His speech was timely, in one sense, but LBJ did not let events force him to announce the voting rights bill prematurely.

Voting Rights Proposals

By the end of 1964, the Johnson administration had begun working on legislation that would guarantee African Americans the right to vote. Historian David Garrow notes, however, that some confusion exists about the timing of the Johnson administration's plans to push for new voting rights legislation. In his memoirs of the presidency, LBJ claims that he had directed Attorney General Nicholas Katzenbach to begin drafting a voting rights bill soon after the 1964 election. In contrast, biographer and former presidential advisor Eric Goldman claims that Johnson did not intend to bring a voting rights proposal before the Congress in 1965. Instead, Goldman suggests, the president wanted to give the South time to "digest" the Civil Rights Act of 1964, and he feared losing congressional support for the rest of his legislative plans. Doris Kearns, author and White House Fellow during the Johnson administration, corroborates Goldman's claims, stating: "Johnson's sense of timing told him that after the struggle over the Civil Rights Act of 1964, 1965 was not a propitious year to press for more civil rights proposals."[53]

Documents at the Lyndon B. Johnson Library, however, suggest that at least by December of 1964 LBJ had shown his desire to move forward with voting rights legislation in 1965.[54] In a memorandum to Bill Moyers on December 30, 1964, presidential aide Lee White wrote: "If I understood our conversation of the other day correctly, the President has indicated a desire to move forward early next year with a legislative proposal authorizing a commission to appoint federal officers to serve as registrars for the purpose of registering individuals for federal elections."[55] White opposed moving forward on voting rights legislation in 1965, though, and recommended that the administration wait until 1966. In his memo to Moyers, White wrote: "Certainly I have absolutely no problem with the desirability of such legislation, but I do have a problem about the timing and the approach." White suggested that LBJ should call attention to the importance of voting registration in a speech and identify 1965 as a year of testing whether the nation would need federal legislation in 1966. But other administration officials and presidential advisers disagreed. In July, 1964, before the signing of the Civil Rights Act of 1964 into law, a presidential task force on civil rights had recommended further legislative action as soon as possible to guarantee voting rights in the South.[56] A December memorandum from Matthew Reese, director of operations for the Democratic National Committee, urged the federal government to eliminate "antiquated election laws and practices" that prevent many Americans, including African Americans, from voting. Reese emphasized the urgent need for legislative action to secure voting rights: "And *now* is the time!"[57]

Archival documents at the Johnson Library also corroborate President Johnson's later claim that he had instructed the Justice Department to begin drafting voting rights proposals soon after the election. Harold Greene, chief of the Civil Rights Division's Appeals and Research Section, sent a memorandum to Katzenbach, which he then forwarded to the president, that outlined three major proposals.[58] It is important to note that the Justice Department proposed voting rights solutions as early as December 28, 1964, the date of the memorandum, and that the department did not confine its suggestions to legislation.

The memo makes three suggestions for solving the voting rights problem, and ranks them in order of preference: (1) a constitutional amendment prohibiting states from imposing any voting qualification or disqualification other than age, residency, a felony conviction, or commitment to a mental institution; (2) legislation vesting in a federal commission the power to conduct registration for federal elections; and (3) legislation granting to an agency of the federal government the power to assume direct control of registration for voting in both federal and state elections in any area where the percentage of potential Negro registrants actually registered is low. Greene called the constitutional amendment approach "the most drastic but probably the most effective of all the alternatives." His memorandum also notes, however, that the ratification process was cumbersome and that the constitutional amendment could be blocked by the legislatures of just thirteen states.

Although he continued to confer with the Justice Department, President Johnson did not publicly state his intention to submit voting rights legislation until his State of the Union address on January 4, 1965. In that speech, Johnson stated, "I propose that we eliminate every remaining obstacle to the right and opportunity to vote."[59] LBJ also claimed in the address that within six weeks he would send messages to the Congress with detailed proposals in each area of domestic concern—including civil rights. Johnson made his intent clear but did not specify the exact nature of the proposed legislation.[60] On January 11, the Justice Department informed Johnson that they were drafting legislation "to implement the President's State of the Union Message remarks with respect to the elimination of barriers to the right to vote."[61] The draft legislation included a constitutional amendment and legislation to provide for federal registrars to register persons for voting in federal elections. The Justice Department already had completed a draft of the proposed constitutional amendment on January 8, but the January 11 report was the first mention that the administration planned to move forward with legislation that provided for federal registrars.[62]

Throughout January and February, the Justice Department continued to work on both legislation and a constitutional amendment behind closed doors. On February 6, Press Secretary George Reedy announced that the president would make a strong recommendation to Congress on voting rights legislation in the near future, but he did not specify the precise nature of that legislation.[63] The Justice Department continued to draft voting rights legislation throughout February and early March. By late February, the Justice Department scrapped the constitutional amendment approach and instead focused on legislation that would abolish literacy tests and use federal registrars to ensure enfranchisement.[64] The Justice Department had supported the amendment, but it had been opposed in closed-door meetings with the NAACP and Republican members of Congress. In a meeting with the president and vice president on February 9, Martin Luther King, Jr., also had suggested that legislation should focus on abolishing literacy tests and on providing for federal registrars.[65] On March 4, Lee White sent a memorandum to Johnson that claimed, "There is general agreement that the Constitutional amendment approach would require too much time and thus we have concentrated on a statute."[66]

On March 5, the Justice Department completed the draft legislation. The bill outlined a "trigger formula" aimed at eliminating the use of literacy tests and other tests aimed at blocking black voter registration. The proposal also outlined the use of federal registrars in local elections. Talk of constitutionality dominated discussion about the legislation. The Justice Department found it difficult to draft a measure that would effectively guarantee enfranchisement without disrupting normal federal-state relationships. If the administration fought for legislation that pushed the limits of constitutionality, the Supreme Court might strike it down later. But if the White House did not push the limits, voting rights legislation might become a merely symbolic act that failed to improve African Americans' access to the ballot box. Despite several attempts, no federal legislation had effectively increased black ballots since Reconstruction. The administration also worried that the measure would smack of Reconstruction—where national politicians manipulated the local franchise for their own political purposes.[67] Johnson's southern ethos provided him some latitude in his civil rights dealings with the South, but the president still needed to produce legislation that would be enforced by the same local officials who preached nullification. Members of the Johnson administration discussed the legislation with select members of Congress to ensure constitutionality and palatability before the bill was formally introduced to Congress. The administration moved slowly and carefully on the proposed legislation. They realized that it was an important bill with significant ramifications, and, therefore, did not want to act hastily. On Sunday, March 7, however, violence against civil rights demonstrators in Selma, Alabama, changed everything.

Voting Rights Campaign

Even as the Johnson administration explored its legislative options, Selma, Alabama, had been a point of tension on civil rights for several months. In late December of 1964, King and the Southern Christian Leadership Conference began to plan a voting rights campaign in Selma. Hugh Graham notes that King chose Selma because it promised to provide three key ingredients necessary for a successful protest.[68] First, Selma was a clear case of blatant racial disenfranchisement. In 1960, the population of Dallas County (of which Selma was the county seat) was 58 percent African American, but of the county's registered voters only 2 percent were listed as black. Second, Selma demonstrated the ineffectiveness of the Civil Rights Acts of 1957, 1960, and 1964. In spite of a sustained voting drive between 1962 and 1964, African Americans were successful in only 93 of 795 attempts to register to vote. Finally, the protests at Birmingham demonstrated that to arouse national support King needed defiant, vicious southern officials to play their role. He found such officials in Alabama governor George Wallace and in Dallas County sheriff Jim Clark—who had an uncontrolled temper, armed his deputies with electric cattle prods, and wore a button on his lapel proclaiming when he thought segregation would end: "Never."

King launched the Selma voting rights campaign with a speech at Brown's Chapel African Methodist Episcopal Church on January 2, 1965. On Monday, January 18, King led four hundred African Americans in the first march to the courthouse in Selma to attempt to register to vote. Sheriff Clark confronted the protesters, made them wait in a back alley, and then refused to allow them to register. On Tuesday, January 19, protesters again attempted to register. They again were herded into an alley. This time, however, Clark responded violently when protesters were slow to move off the courthouse sidewalk. The *New York Times* reported that Sheriff Clark grabbed Amelia Boynton, a local black leader, by her collar and dragged her half a block into a patrol car. This incident sparked national media coverage that raised the nation's conscience. Marches and attempts to register to vote continued throughout January and February, as did scenes of arrests and beatings by local law officials.

By early March, 1965, the tempers of local law officials continued to rise, and their ability and willingness to restrain themselves diminished. On March 7, the Selma campaign reached its climax. On that Sunday morning, marchers moved out from Brown's chapel toward the Edmund Pettus Bridge. When they reached the crest of the bridge, the marchers encountered a line of about fifty Alabama state troopers backed by several dozen of Sheriff Clark's posse, some on horseback. Major John Cloud ordered the marchers to stop. They did. The SCLC's Hosea Williams asked, "May we have a word with the major?" Cloud replied that there was no word to be had and demanded that the protesters turn around and return to the chapel within the next two minutes. After one minute passed with the protesters standing their ground, Cloud issued the order, "Troopers, advance."

The law officers rushed forward and assaulted the protesters with nightsticks, whips, electric cattle prods, and tear gas. The troopers knocked the demonstrators to the ground, beat them, and pushed them backward toward Brown's Chapel. The troopers also blocked ambulances from crossing the bridge to reach the scene of the attack. Estimates of the total injured ranged from ninety to one hundred. The injuries included broken ribs, wrists, teeth, and severe head gashes. John Lewis, chairman of the Student Nonviolent Coordinating Committee, sustained a fractured skull. Amelia Boynton was knocked unconscious by a combination of blows and tear gas. The news media quickly circulated images of the violence and bloodshed around the nation. Around 9:00 P.M. on March 7, ABC-TV interrupted its evening movie, *Judgment at Nuremberg*, to present footage of the assault at the Pettus Bridge. On Monday morning, every major newspaper carried headlines about the violence at Selma. Photographs in the *New York Times* and *Washington Post* showed graphic scenes of police beating protesters with nightsticks. Writers soon called the day "Bloody Sunday." The American people were sickened and outraged.

Response to the President and Protesters

Across the nation American citizens and their legislative representatives responded to the events in Selma and to the White House's response to the events in Selma. Senators and congressmen began to express their concerns soon after the first blows by Alabama police landed on protesters. On February 3, New York Senator Jacob Javits claimed that the arrests of and violence against protesters were shocking, because they were simply seeking the right to vote, "the most basic right guaranteed by the Constitution."[69] Javits quickly contacted the Justice Department and expressed his concern about the protests in Selma. At the same time that Javits expressed his concerns, a group of House members organized a visit to Selma for February 5 to see whether or not new voting rights legislation was necessary. Upon their return from Selma, the congressmen told reporters that their trip convinced them of the need for new voting rights legislation: they urged President Johnson to present legislation immediately that would establish federal voting registrars, eliminate literacy tests, and abolish the poll tax.[70] On February 23, a group of thirty-one congressional Republicans issued a statement criticizing the administration's refusal to announce publicly precisely what voting rights proposals it would make to the Congress. The legislators asked, "How long will Congress and the American people be asked to wait while this Administration studies and re-studies . . . new federal legislation? The need is apparent. The time is now." Congressional demands continued following the violence on "Bloody Sunday." Minnesota senator Walter Mondale claimed that the Selma outrage "makes passage of legislation to guarantee Southern Negroes the right to vote an absolute imperative for Congress this year."[71] Fifty members of Congress denounced the attack against the marchers and pressed for new voting rights legislation.

The outcries against the violence and perceived presidential inaction were not limited to members of Congress. After "Bloody Sunday," sympathy marches were organized in Chicago, New York, Detroit, and Boston. Demonstrations also were held in the nation's capital. Approximately six hundred picketers marched outside the White House to protest what they believed to be inaction by the president. SNCC protesters staged a sit-in at the Justice Department. A group of national religious leaders staged a demonstration in Lafayette Park to protest President Johnson's failure to act or issue a strong public statement. Scores of demonstrators marched in front of the White House chanting, "LBJ, just you wait . . . see what happens in '68." Others carried placards that read, "LBJ open your eyes, see the sickness of the South, see the horrors of your homeland." President Johnson himself later claimed, "Everywhere I looked I was being denounced for my 'unbelievable lack of action.'"[72] Protesters even found their way into the president's home. On Thursday, March 11, a group of twelve demonstrators entered the White House on a regular tour and staged a sit-in in a first floor hallway. Although most demonstrators emphasized the need for new voting rights legislation, they also wanted Johnson to use federal troops to intervene to protect the civil rights activists in Selma.

Nearly all persons who denounced the events at Selma and what they perceived as presidential inaction—including members of Congress—looked to the president for a rhetorical response. The circumstances following Selma clearly constituted a rhetorical situation. That is, in Lloyd Bitzer's terminology, it "invited discourse capable of participating with the situation and thereby altering its reality."[73] At the same time, the situation demanded legislative action—more than "mere" rhetoric in the form of a presidential address. Again, most Americans looked to the president, not the Congress, for a response. Members of Congress reinforced the public's response by also turning to the president for legislative solutions. In the situation facing President Johnson, speech and legislation were bound closely. In order for Johnson to make an appropriate rhetorical response, his legislative proposal needed to be complete. It was not. While the American people and their elected representatives were chastising the president and waiting for a response in the wake of the events at Selma, the White House was putting the finishing touches on the legislation, especially a carefully constructed "trigger formula" that would prove both effective and constitutional.

Johnson, therefore, appeared to be caught in a presidential dilemma. The public created rhetorical space for LBJ to speak on an issue that he believed in strongly. Many Americans demanded the voting rights legislation that he had been waiting to propose.[74] In other words, the time was right for the president to speak and to act. At the same time, however, the voting rights legislation was not finished. The president realized that speaking prematurely could constrain unnecessarily his administration's legislative options. President Johnson told reporters in a press conference on March 13 that he had seen no purpose in making a public statement before the voting rights proposal was ready.[75] Johnson felt that the White House needed to move quickly, but he also believed that "it was equally important that [the administration] move in the right direction."[76] The legislation needed to be effective and constitutional. Johnson also believed that sending federal troops to Selma too soon would destroy the chances for passing that legislation. To LBJ, each of the situational constraints—legislative proposal, protests, and public response—was closely connected to the others.

"We Shall Overcome"

Initially, President Johnson did not plan to give a public speech before a joint session of the Congress to propose the voting rights bill. By the end of February, White House aide Horace Busby had drafted the first message to accompany the legislation—a written message to be sent to Congress with the bill, which was the only voting rights message being prepared at that time.[77] By March 12, members of the administration sent memoranda to the president that suggested a public message on voting rights was under consideration, but still no speech had been drafted.[78] Sometime after March 12, Lee White and Harry McPherson drafted short messages on voting rights—though it is not clear whether their drafts were designed to be released as written messages, spoken at a press conference, or delivered to the nation.[79] In any case, Johnson did not decide to make a speech to the Congress and the nation until the evening of March 14, during a meeting with the congressional leadership.[80] During this meeting, LBJ reviewed the situation at Selma and the administration's efforts on the voting rights bill. The conversation initially centered around legislative concerns. Senate Majority Leader Mike Mansfield, Senate Minority Leader Everett Dirksen, and Ohio congressman William McCulloch suggested dates for sending the voting rights bill to Congress. Then, Speaker of the House John McCormack shifted the discussion toward rhetorical concerns, suggesting that the president deliver a voting rights message before a joint session of the Congress. Dirksen claimed that a public speech would circumvent the Congress, and Mansfield also opposed a speech before a joint session. LBJ argued that the public did not know what the White House was doing in response to Selma and suggested that a speech would show the American people that "we are doing everything we can to solve this." Vice President Hubert Humphrey agreed, saying that the president should give a televised message to articulate publicly "what this government is doing." House Majority Leader Carl Albert also supported a public speech, claiming, "I don't think it would be a sign of panic. I think it would help." McCormack agreed, claiming that a speech "would show the world that action is being taken." Attorney General Katzenbach stated that a speech "would put the problem and the solution before the country." By the end of the meeting, the congressional leadership unanimously advised that Johnson address a joint session of the Congress.

Johnson's decision to give a speech was marked by intertwined legislative and rhetorical concerns: the president wanted to respond effectively to the national situation following Selma, a situation that demanded both a legislative and spoken response. Whereas most scholars suggest that Johnson usually spoke without careful consideration to the relationship between rhetoric and policy, Johnson was closely attuned to this relationship following Selma. Johnson's rhetorical calculations were careful because he worried that a presidential address on voting rights might negatively affect the legislative process. A speech that informed the public about the provisions of the voting rights bill would relieve public pressure on the executive and, therefore, would be a timely response to the rhetorical situation facing the president. This type of rhetorical response, however, would complicate the legislative situation. By outlining the specific provisions of his bill and urging Congress to pass it, Johnson would constrain the legislative options available to the Congress and possibly increase resistance. But a response that would leave open legislative options and encourage deliberation—such as a written message, the administration's original plan—would not bring rhetorical satisfaction. Finally, Johnson decided that he needed to respond to the urgencies of the rhetorical situation. Johnson later claimed, "I felt I had to reassure the people that we were moving as far and as fast as we could. I knew this reassurance would not be provided by the cold words of a written message." Near midnight on March 14, LBJ instructed presidential speechwriter Richard Goodwin to draft the address. In his memoirs, President Johnson recaps the instructions he provided to Goodwin: "I wanted to use every ounce of moral persuasion the Presidency held. I wanted no hedging, no equivocation. And I wanted to talk from my own heart, from my own experience."[81] The voting rights address was revised until the moment of its delivery at 9:02 P.M., March 15, 1965—eight days after the violence against the Selma protesters.[82]

President Johnson's speech was a timely, fitting response to the rhetorical situation. That is, considered historically and rhetorically, the speech directed itself toward *kairos,* or fitness for the occasion. Johnson's rhetoric provided a sense of closure to events that led the public to demand new voting rights legislation. Public opinion had been behind voting rights measures before violence erupted in Selma. A January 9, 1965, Lou Harris public opinion poll suggested that 95 percent of the American public believed that voting rights legislation should be enacted.[83] Public opinion may have been on the side of voting rights, but active public support for immediate legislative action did not mature until Selma. The civil rights movement had succeeded in transforming African Americans' social conditions—including the denial of the right to vote—into a perceived social problem before Selma. Actually solving the problem of disfranchisement, however, seemed to require an additional step. Many activists believed that an event like Selma was necessary to move from public acknowledgment of the problem and a mere desire for a solution to active public pressure for an immediate solution. The chief function of the Selma demonstrations was to translate public opinion about what should be into overwhelming public pressure that demanded federal voting rights legislation.

LBJ realized, however, that active public support could fade quickly. Mass mediated images of law officials beating protesters had aroused the nation's emotions, but those images soon would stop, since Johnson promised to send in federal troops to protect the demonstrators if further violence occurred. The president needed to act quickly if he were to manipulate the urgencies of the situation. In his memoirs, Johnson claimed: "I knew that it would probably not take long for these aroused emotions to melt away. It was important to move at once if we were to achieve anything permanent from this transitory mood."[84] LBJ's public appeals for legislative action attempted to bring public opinion to bear on the Congress while public support was at its peak. He also capitalized on the emotions of the members of Congress, many of whom were genuinely moved by the events at Selma. In the wake of the demonstrations at Selma, the time was right to propose publicly the administration's voting rights bill.

The language of Johnson's speech, not just its moment of delivery, also appealed to the urgencies of the moment. President Johnson claimed that there must be "no delay, no hesitation" in passing the voting rights bill. Speaking with conviction in his voice, he also claimed, "And we ought not and we cannot and we must not wait another eight months before we get a bill. We have already waited a hundred years and more, and the time for waiting is gone."[85] He was interrupted by applause. Then, LBJ made his intentions plain: "So I ask you to join me in working long hours—nights and weekends, if necessary—to pass this bill." In these passages, and throughout the speech, Johnson argued from expediency. He suggested that in light of current circumstances, Congress must act, and it must act immediately.

The timing of Johnson's speech was more complex, however, than merely appealing to the urgencies of the moment. President Johnson did attempt to respond to and capitalize on the exigencies of the immediate situation. Passage of the voting rights bill depended upon it. But to use only an argument from circumstance—that is, to appeal only to urgency and expediency—would be shortsighted given LBJ's broader purposes. Lyndon Johnson wanted to be the president to end all racial inequality, bigotry, and injustice. Argument from circumstance would be too grounded in the sensed urgencies of the moment, which eventually would fade. Appeals to expediency often prove effective in attaining instant success but represent a problematic rhetorical strategy for achieving broader, long-term goals. A purely expedient argument on civil rights could effectively manage the immediate circumstances for immediate political purposes, but would only subsume momentary conflicts rather than transcend the lasting frictions that have characterized race relations in the United States.

Arguments from circumstance did prove powerful, and members of Congress employed them during hearings on the voting rights bill. For example, in the first hearing in the House, Emmanuel Celler, chairman of the Judiciary Committee, claimed: "Recent events in Alabama, involving murder, savage brutality, and violence by local police, state troopers, and posses have so aroused the nation as to make action by this Congress necessary and speedy. . . . The climate of public opinion throughout the nation has so changed because of the Alabama outrages, as to make assured passage of this solid bill—a bill that would have been inconceivable a year ago."[86] President Johnson, though, did not want to look forced into action by civil rights activists, which would be the implicit meaning of argument from circumstance. During Johnson's March 14 meeting with the White House staff and congressional leadership, Dirksen told the president, "Don't panic now. This is a deliberate government. Don't let these people say, 'We scared him into it.'" LBJ replied, "I wouldn't think about that."[87] Johnson recognized that if he argued only from circumstance, he risked projecting the appearance that he could only respond to civil rights crises, rather than provide strong leadership.

An argument from circumstance also could prove problematic because, while it might effectively manage the urgencies of the moment, it would not provide assurance that the proposed action was in accordance with higher principles—assurance that Americans typically demand. In his March 15 address, President Johnson used rhetorical appeals that allowed him to benefit from the exigencies of the moment but also avoided the pitfalls of an argument based only on circumstance. Johnson's speech gave a broader philosophical meaning to the urgencies of the immediate situation by placing them within a larger context of events. In this way, Johnson's speech engaged time on another level. Johnson's voting rights address used rhetorical appeals to American civil religion, the religious dimension through which the nation interprets its historical experience, in order to influence the perceived timing of events in the world in which it was delivered.[88] These appeals contextualized the current civil rights struggle as part of a larger, transhistorical struggle for the United States to fulfill its divine promise and to do God's will on earth. To experience LBJ's speech is to be instructed to experience events in American history—including the immediate situation following Selma—as part of a transcendent reality. Johnson's March 15 address rehearsed key values and myths in the American civil religion—including freedom, equality, the myth of origin, and the myth of America as chosen people—in order to assign a divine meaning to the particular struggle confronting the nation at that historical moment. Analysis of the key terms in Johnson's speech reveals how he contextualized the situation following Selma as part of the American civil religion.

Selma is a pivotal term in Johnson's speech: it is the term that marks the movement from the immediate present to a more mythic time. In the third paragraph of the address, LBJ claims that Selma is part of "man's unending search for freedom." Later, Johnson claims that Selma is part of a larger effort in which "Americans are struggling for the fruits of freedom," again associating Selma with freedom. Johnson's speech also associates Selma with the terms "equality" and "equal rights." He claims that at Selma, men and women "peacefully protested the denial of their rights as Americans" and calls the demonstrations at Selma a protest against "the long denial of equal rights of millions of Americans." President Johnson also argues that in Selma and across the nation, "the promise of equality" has not been fully kept, and he identifies Selma as part of a larger "battle for equality."

Through a clustering of terms, Lyndon Johnson's speech contextualizes the events at Selma as part of a larger struggle for freedom and equality. Johnson's speech also gives Selma a broader historical meaning by associating the terms "freedom" and "equality" with the terms "purpose" and "promise." For example, in the eighth paragraph of the speech, Johnson claims that the issue of equal rights represents a challenge to "the values and the purposes" of the United States. Later in the address, Johnson articulates a similar theme, drawing upon the civil religious myth of America's origin: "This was the first nation in the history of the world to be founded with a purpose. The great phrases of that purpose still sound in every American heart, North and South: 'All men are created equal' . . . 'give me liberty or give me death.' . . . Those words are a promise to every citizen." That promise, LBJ later suggests, rests upon a citizen's right "to be treated as a man equal in opportunity to all others." Johnson emphasizes in his address that the pledge of equality has not been fulfilled: "A century has passed, more than a hundred years, since equality was promised. And yet the Negro is not equal. A century has passed since the day of the promise. And the promise is unkept."

By associating the terms "freedom" and "equality" with the terms "purpose" and "promise," Lyndon Johnson's speech assigns a civil religious meaning to the current civil rights struggle. The speech's clustering of terms draws upon America's myth of origin ("founded with a purpose"), alludes to key texts in the American civil religion (the Declaration of Independence and Emancipation Proclamation), and alludes to a key figure (Abraham Lincoln). The rhetorical timing in the speech is also central to the clustering of freedom and equality with purpose and promise. This associational cluster facilitates a movement from the past to the present. In Johnson's speech, promise and purpose are referred to in the past tense, but LBJ uses those terms to move toward the present. The temporal movement in the speech suggests that the promise and purpose were declared in America's mythic past and that the present civil rights struggle for freedom and equality is a time of trial, a testing of whether current political and social institutions can fulfill the American promise and live up to the nation's purpose. Johnson's speech blurs past-present time distinctions. Within Johnson's speech, current circumstances are part of transcendent reality, and events from the past have entered into the present. The mythical time of America's past reappears in the present, and, therefore, becomes timeless. Past and present are interconnected: each makes sense only with reference to the other. By reintroducing the past into the present, LBJ suggests that the American promise and purpose are eternal.

The temporal movement and the civil religious terminology in President Johnson's speech project a peculiar view of time on to the world in which it was delivered. Johnson's address responds to events such as Selma, events without inherent religious meaning. LBJ assigns to those events a civil religious meaning and suggests a sense of continuity between America's mythic past and the present. Johnson's speech invites its audience to see contemporary events as a sign of the reintegration of sacred time into the present. For example, LBJ refers to previous events in American history where the sacred reappeared and indicates that it has happened again in 1965. By reenacting and commemorating sacred events from the past, Johnson gives those events a sense of presence. For example, he claims: "At times history and fate meet at a single time in a single place to shape a turning point in man's unending search for freedom. So it was in Lexington and Concord. So it was a century ago at Appomattox. So it was last week in Selma, Alabama." In the fifth paragraph, President Johnson also suggests a sacred dimension to the present: "There is cause for hope and for faith in our democracy in what is happening tonight." In the eighth paragraph, Johnson presents his most dramatic statement about the reintegration of sacred time into the present: "In our time we have come to live with moments of great crisis. Our lives have been marked with debate about great issues; issues of war and peace, issues of prosperity and depression. But rarely in any time does an issue lay bare the secret heart of America itself. Rarely are we met with a challenge, not to our growth or abundance, our welfare or our security, but rather to the values and the purposes and the meaning of our beloved Nation. The issue of equal rights for American Negroes is such an issue." Lyndon Johnson also ends his speech with words that reintroduce the sacred into the present. LBJ claims, "God will not favor everything that we do. It is rather our duty to divine His will. But I cannot help believing that He truly understands and that He really favors the undertaking that we begin here tonight."

Johnson's speech invites its audience to view the world in a different way. By using terminology that assigns a civil religious quality to current events, and by blurring the distinction between the mythical past and the present, LBJ argues that the historical present is best understood not as a merely secular time but rather as a sacred time. To experience Johnson's speech is to be directed to understand current events from a sacred, civil religious perspective. If Americans do not view current events from that perspective, LBJ suggests, then they will not see the broader meaning or understand what must be done. Rather than merely emphasizing the urgencies of the moment, Johnson's speech underscores the importance of broader historical understanding within a civil religious frame.

Within the expanded context of Johnson's speech, the consequences of not understanding the world from a sacred perspective are severe. If America fails to fulfill its promise and do God's will, the nation will have faltered. In the ninth paragraph of the speech, LBJ claims, "And should we defeat every enemy, and should we double our wealth and conquer the stars, and still be unequal to this issue, then we will have failed as a people and as a nation." In the next paragraph, President Johnson emphasizes the failure in biblical terms. Quoting from Luke 9:25, he claims, "For with a country as with a person, 'What is a man profited, if he shall gain the whole world and lose his own soul?'" Later in the address, Johnson claims that to deny equal rights to a person because of his or her color "is to deny America."

In this civil religious view of the world, Lyndon Johnson plays the role of the nation's prophet/priest. The delivery of his speech enhances this role. The tone of his voice, his speaking rate, and his vocal emphasis give him the persona of a preacher—not that of a hellfire-and-brimstone evangelical, but rather of a reflective, dignified minister. American civil religion provides a powerful set of commonplaces for political rhetors. LBJ uses that rhetorical power to recall the nation to its original task. Rather than merely responding to the crises of the moment, priest/President Johnson reinterprets America's civil religious tradition to place current events in their "proper" context. He argues that America's destiny and the nation's civil rights policies must be interpreted in the light of divine will.

Response and Aftermath

Johnson's voting rights speech received considerable attention from the public and the media. The address was viewed by an audience of seventy million.[89] Scores of Americans, including everyday citizens and opinion leaders, wrote to the president, expressing their reactions to his words: most of the responses were positive. For example, labor leader George Meany lauded the president's speech in a telegram: "The AFL-CIO strongly commends your firm stand and ringing declaration."[90] In a letter to LBJ dated March 15, Supreme Court Chief Justice Earl Warren wrote: "Your address before Congress was magnificent. It must have thrilled every American, as it did me, to see and hear our President so forthrightly pledge his faith and his action to make a reality of the principle of equality before the law. . . . And there need be no doubt of this—you *will* overcome."[91] Warren's letter held special meaning, perhaps implying in advance that the Supreme Court would uphold the constitutionality of the White House's voting rights legislation, if passed. To the other Americans who wrote to the president to commend his address, the White House staff sent a reply of gratitude and, in many cases, a printed version of Johnson's speech.

Scores of newspapers reprinted either full-text or abridged versions of Johnson's speech, and white-owned periodicals—even those often skeptical of LBJ—praised his address. The *Christian Science Monitor* called the speech "a landmark" and "one of the most uncompromising and powerful speeches of his career." *Newsweek* contended, "The words were the strongest ever spoken by a U.S. President on the agonizing problem of race." The magazine stated that Johnson's speech was an "extraordinary testament." *Time* reported that "Johnson was never more powerful" than in his March 15 address to Congress and the nation. The *New Republic,* usually critical of LBJ on foreign and domestic affairs, claimed that the voting rights speech was "a moving performance" and "the best we ever heard him give." And the *Nation,* another magazine often reserved in its praise for the president, reported that Johnson's radio and television address "was splendid."[92]

Many periodicals commended LBJ's address on the grounds that it revealed his personal sincerity, sensitivity, and commitment with regard to civil rights—which some writers thought Johnson had not possessed until this speech. The *New York Times* reported, "No other President had made the issue of equality for Negroes so frankly a moral cause for himself and all Americans."[93] An editorial in the *Christian Science Monitor* praised Johnson's "sensitive portrayal of Negro attitudes and aspirations."[94] The *New Republic* commended Johnson's speech as filled with "passion and genuine eloquence," and the *Nation* claimed, "No one who heard the President can doubt his sincerity when he spoke of the 'crippling legacy of bigotry and injustice.'"[95] In addition to acclaiming Johnson for his sincerity, newspapers and magazines found LBJ's affirmation of African American protest efforts especially admirable. The *New York Times* reported that "[n]o other American President had so completely identified himself with the cause of the Negro," and *Newsweek* stated that LBJ's speech had "identified him more closely than any other U.S. President with the cause of the marching

Negro."[96] The *Times* lauded Johnson on its editorial page for having "hailed the Negro as 'the real hero' in the struggle to make freedom secure and meaningful for all Americans."[97] The *New Republic* was uncharacteristically congratulatory, claiming, "It took guts to come out and say 'the real hero of the struggle is the American Negro.'"[98] As with the Birmingham protests, the media had used words and images to depict the protesters at Selma as courageous; yet LBJ's ringing affirmation of the movement surpassed Kennedy's guarded endorsement.

The images of protests and violence in Selma were transmitted abroad, but archival documents do not indicate that the White House was exceedingly concerned with addressing the international implications of civil rights on March 15. Still, the executive branch attempted to gain maximum international propaganda value from LBJ's speech. The United States Information Agency made a twelve-minute color documentary film about the speech and distributed it overseas.[99] Johnson's address also received favorable coverage in the international press, especially in English-language periodicals. The *New Statesman* claimed that LBJ had delivered a "remarkable address," and the *Spectator* praised the president's "splendid" performance and "flat and downright" position on civil rights. The *Manchester Guardian Weekly* called Johnson's speech "the most powerful and persuasive pleas for equal rights for Negroes that has been made by any President." The *Guardian*, like many American periodicals, also praised President Johnson for affirming the civil rights movement, for having "the courage to admit that it was the fortitude and persistence of the Negroes themselves which have largely been responsible for stimulating the Government to act."[100] Several international periodicals reprinted excerpts from the voting rights speech, and the White House worked to ensure more extensive distribution. For example, the federal government planned to have ambassadors in Central and South America distribute print copies to Latin American presidents.[101] LBJ's message had the potential to demonstrate the United States' commitment to civil rights and to repair the damages done to the nation's image by the pictures of violence against its minority citizens, especially in Africa where officials and organizations, such as the Organization of African States, often accepted American presidents' verbal assurances on civil rights.[102]

At home, most civil rights leaders were moved by President Johnson's words and overwhelmingly praised the president's voting rights address. Tears actually came to the eyes of Martin Luther King, Jr., when Johnson proclaimed, "We shall overcome." In a telegram to the president on March 16, King wrote:

"Your speech to the joint session of Congress last night was the most moving eloquent unequivocal and passionate plea for human rights ever made by any president of this nation. You evidenced amazing understanding of the depth and dimensions of the problems that we face in our struggle, your tone was sincere throughout and your persuasive power was never more forceful." In his speech following the march from Selma to Montgomery, King called Johnson's voting rights message "one of the most passionate pleas for human rights ever made by a president of our nation." Roy Wilkins claimed that LBJ's speech was a "moment at the summit in the life of our nation." SNCC chairman John Lewis congratulated the president in a letter, calling his speech "historic, eloquent and more than inspiring for all of us who seek to make the principles of democracy a living reality." And March on Washington organizer A. Philip Randolph claimed that LBJ's address was a "wonderful message" that exhibited "the highest order of moral and political statesmanship."[103]

African American newspapers also lauded LBJ's speech. The *Kansas City Call* stated that the address "cut through to the heart of the matter" facing the nation: "It was as if all the heartbreak, all the hope of the Negro and of the nation had been crammed into the speech."[104] An editorial in the *Call* called Johnson's speech a "stirring address" in which he "made it clear to the South and the nation that he meant business." The author argued that LBJ's address had "been acclaimed everywhere as the strongest speech on human rights ever made by a president."[105] Many blacks did celebrate the president's speech: the publisher of the *Norfolk Journal & Guide* and *Philadelphia Afro-American* reprinted the text of Johnson's address in their March 27 issues upon the demand of their readers. An editorial in the March 27 issue of the *Guide* also called the address "the greatest speech Lyndon Baines Johnson had ever made."[106] Many African Americans seemed to applaud Johnson's speech, in part, because they felt it revealed a personal commitment to their cause. The *Afro-American* called the message a "sincere and moving address."[107] An editorial in the *Guide* noted, "President Johnson went before the nation—indeed, before the whole world—and bared not his soul but his heart" and claimed that the speech expressed LBJ's "moving sincerity and intimacy."[108] Jackie Robinson also praised what he took to be President Johnson's personal sincerity, calling the message a "historic and obviously heartfelt address." Robinson wrote, "He was eloquent as he outlined his personal views about the rights of all Americans."[109] The *Pittsburgh Courier* claimed, "No one who heard the address can deny the sincerity of the man. Here is a Southerner who has broken the bonds of Southern tradition and [shown] all the world that he is great because he has a big heart."[110]

The *Amsterdam News* reported that the words "we shall overcome" "rang with gripping sincerity from the lips of a determined, emotionally-moved President Lyndon Baines Johnson," and claimed that his words expressed a "touching sincerity . . . that flowed from him like the poetry of a democracy."[111]

Other African Americans lauded LBJ's speech because they claimed it had put the full force of the government behind civil rights. The *Norfolk Journal & Guide* reported, "President Johnson this week swung the full weight of the federal government behind a drive to make good the promise of equality."[112] An editorial in the *Kansas City Call* observed, "It was gratifying to hear the President of the United States throw the entire weight of the federal government behind the civil rights movement."[113] These two newspapers made a mistake by equating the president with the federal government, but their comments indicate the importance of a president's rhetorical commitment for many African Americans during this time. Blacks had praised John Kennedy's June 11, 1963, speech for putting the force of the presidency and the federal government behind civil rights, yet it still seemed important in 1965 for President Johnson to reenact that commitment. And LBJ articulated a stronger affirmation of the civil rights movement in his March 15 address than Kennedy ever had spoken. In 1963, critics had claimed that JFK tacitly praised demonstrators: Johnson's speech in 1965 explicitly identified activists as the heroes of the civil rights struggle. The strategy of moderate civil rights leaders had been to raise the conscience of the nation to effect legislative change, and Johnson's voting rights message confirmed their success. LBJ claimed: "He [the African American] has called upon us to make good the promise of America. And who among us can say that we would have made the same progress were it not for his persistent bravery, and his faith in American democracy." Many blacks commended Johnson for his strong endorsement. The *Norfolk Journal & Guide* praised Johnson for having endowed the civil rights movement "with the influence and prestige of the office of the President of the United States."[114] C. T. Vivian, affiliates director of the SCLC, claimed that LBJ's speech was "a victory like none other, it was an affirmation of the movement."[115]

The praise accorded President Johnson's speech by civil rights leaders also was owing, in part, to his combination of moral and democratic language. As with John F. Kennedy's speech of June 11, 1963, the civil religious appeals in LBJ's speech of March 15, 1965, resonated with many African Americans. Prominent civil rights leaders long had argued that America should live up to its promise and purpose. For example, in his landmark "I Have a Dream" speech, King argued that the American promise of freedom and equality was a "sacred obligation" that must be honored, and he urged, "Now is the time to make real the promises of democracy." In this address, King also claimed, "Five score years ago, a great American, in whose symbolic shadow we stand, signed the Emancipation Proclamation. . . . But one hundred years later, the Negro still is not free."[116] On March 15, Lyndon Johnson reiterated King's rhetoric nearly verbatim: "But a century had passed, more than a hundred years, since the Negro was freed. And he is not fully free tonight. It was more than a hundred years ago that Abraham Lincoln . . . signed the Emancipation Proclamation, but emancipation is a proclamation and not a fact." Johnson repeated arguments that African American activists had long advanced, and his speech tapped into the religio-political discourse of the civil rights movement. That is, Johnson's address not only adopted the familiar language of American civil religion but simultaneously appropriated the discursive tactics and strategies used by civil rights activists. Civil religious themes were common in previous presidents' discourse on civil rights, but themes of law and order often dominated presidential rhetoric on racial issues. Like many within the movement and President Kennedy before him, Johnson instead elevated moral and spiritual concerns over legal and political issues. Furthermore, his address articulated values that already had been established by civil rights activists like King. LBJ's value appeals and the mythic timing of his speech spoke to audiences steeped in the nation's civil religious tradition, to audiences affected by the civil rights movement's religious reform rhetoric, and to the activists that actually articulated that religious reform rhetoric.

John Lewis observes, however, that "not everyone was so moved" by Johnson's March 15 speech. In his autobiography, Lewis claims, "I was not surprised to hear Jim Forman [SNCC's militant executive secretary] attack the speech. The President's reference to our anthem was a 'tinkling empty symbolism,' Forman told one reporter."[117] LBJ's speech was timely in that he celebrated the mainstream civil rights movement at its peak, but the address also came too late. Whereas moderate civil rights leaders believed that the Selma protests and Johnson's response were an affirmation of their attitudes, many members of SNCC had decided that appeals to the national conscience were useless. These militant blacks viewed the Selma protests as a confirmation of their attitudes: protests that raised the nation's conscience did not change the distribution of economic and political power in the South. Many SNCC members also believed that African Americans should lead their own movement. They objected to the SCLC's and NAACP's approach to civil rights protest, which depended upon intervention by the white establishment.

Lyndon Johnson's address also praised nonviolent protests at the exact moment that some African Americans called into question nonviolence as both a tactic and a philosophy. The idea of not retaliating against physical violence was losing support. Forman expressed doubts about the value of nonviolent protest and thus decried LBJ's affirmation of that method of protest. Even Lewis, who praised Johnson's speech, shared the more militant African Americans' frustrations, "I could understand people not wanting to be beaten anymore. . . . Black capacity to believe that [a white person] would really open his heart, really open his life to nonviolent appeal was running out."[118] SNCC protesters picketed the White House to protest the president's failure to send federal troops to Alabama to protect civil rights workers. When the protests at Selma ended, SNCC's basic demand still was unmet: their request for day-to-day protection by a special corps of federal agents to protect constitutional rights and prevent violence had been denied.

Johnson's address seemed a timely response because it responded to the problem of disfranchisement at the same moment that King's voting rights campaign made the problem more salient for many Americans. His speech adopted the discourse of the mainstream movement and validated its efforts. However, some African Americans began to reject the SCLC and its leaders at the same moment. After the failed march on "Bloody Sunday," King planned a second attempt to march from Selma to Montgomery. The Johnson administration pressured King to cancel. Judge Frank Johnson had refused to issue an injunction against state authorities without a hearing; he wanted King's march canceled until after that hearing. The White House informed King they would not support a violation of the judge's ruling. Johnson sent Assistant Attorney General John Doar and LeRoy Collins, director of the Community Relations Service, to Selma to persuade King to call off the march. Collins worked out an arrangement with King and Sheriff Clark whereby protesters would be allowed to march toward the Pettus Bridge, then turn around once they reached the line of police. King did not inform the marchers about the agreement, and on Tuesday, March 9, he led them toward the bridge. To the surprise of the marchers, King turned them around to avoid defying Judge Johnson's ruling and Lyndon Johnson's wishes. King's move angered members of SNCC, who found it ironic that the marchers returned to Brown's Chapel while singing the protest song, "Ain't Gonna Let Nobody Turn Me Round." After King bowed down to federal authority, Forman and most other SNCC workers refused to participate in the final, federally protected march from Selma to Montgomery. The Selma campaign reinforced the young militants' doubts about

King (to whom they referred mockingly as "de Lawd"), the federal government, and coalition politics. Johnson effectively managed one of the constraints in the rhetorical situation, SCLC's campaign and its ideology, just as that constraint was being questioned by other African American activists.

Selma was an overall success for King and Johnson, yet from SNCC's point of view, it was a failure. The Selma protests, however successful at raising the nation's conscience, interfered with SNCC's efforts to develop self-sufficient, local African American leadership. In his autobiography, Forman argues that the SCLC-style protests "tended to 'psych off' local protest and make people feel like they had accomplished something—changed something, somehow—when, in fact, nothing had been changed. In 1965 the Selma-to-Montgomery March would confirm this feeling once and for all."[119] Many members of SNCC believed that the SCLC raised community expectations but then left without making improvements for permanent change. SNCC activist Mary King notes that in contrast to the SCLC's approach, "SNCC favored the patient, low-key creation of community organizations that could carry on a long-term struggle 'for the duration.'"[120] SNCC members had organized voter registration projects in southern Alabama for two years before the Selma protests. They would continue to work after King left and LBJ signed the voting rights act into law.

While most protesters marched straight from Selma to Montgomery on March 21, singing and responding to the cheers of onlookers, SNCC activist Stokely Carmichael planned to pick up where King—and Johnson—left off. Carmichael, who later changed his name to Kwame Turé, claims: "I wasn't very enthusiastic about the march itself. But it was a *fait accompli*. . . . Consequently, I marched along with the other marchers, but I wasn't considering myself part of the march. When it entered Lowndes County I would seek out all the people from Lowndes County who came to the march. I would write down their names, record their addresses, and tell them, 'Listen, we're going to stay in Lowndes County. We're not just going to pass through,' and they'd be excited to hear that."[121] Carmichael returned to Lowndes County, Alabama, on March 26. He, Cleveland Sellers, and a few SNCC coworkers traveled door-to-door in Lowndes County to organize local African Americans into a politically powerful organization.

President Johnson's voting rights message did not resonate with the militant members of SNCC, nor did it appeal to African Americans living in urban areas such as Los Angeles and Detroit. Blacks living outside the South were not prevented from voting but still were unequal. Johnson's voting rights speech appealed to a mythic America, but blacks living in the North and on the West

Coast had found this myth to be false. Four days after the voting rights bill was signed into law, violence erupted in the Watts area of Los Angeles. When the rioting and looting ended, at least thirty-four people had been killed and whole blocks of buildings had been burned to the ground. Shouts of "Burn, Baby, Burn" had supplanted cries for "Freedom Now." Johnson's "We Shall Overcome" rhetoric was wholly inadequate for the blacks living in the ghetto, nor would civil rights legislation solve their problems. Paul Williams, a Watts resident, later claimed, "When Johnson signed the civil rights bill . . . nobody even thought about it in Watts. You were too worried about getting your head beat in by your buddy next door to worry about civil rights. It had nothing to do with us."[122]

In retrospect, the assumptions of the Johnson administration's voting rights strategy were shortsighted, even though the administration attempted to look beyond the urgencies of the moment during the development of its voting rights legislation and public address. The White House failed to look beyond the problems of southern blacks to see the problems facing African Americans in the ghettos. The administration's voting rights strategy was idealistic but naive. The White House assumed that securing the right to vote for African Americans also would bring with it comprehensive political power. President Johnson's voting rights speech proposed only a legislative solution to a much broader problem of race and class. Though it would have been difficult for Johnson to appeal to or appease black militants, he might have made a positive contribution to civil rights discourse by hinting at the broader economic, social, and political problems surrounding racial inequality.

Johnson's voting rights address was a high-water mark of American liberalism, but it also signaled the beginning of the end. Selma was the last major white-and-black-together civil rights protest to be effective on a national level. The racial violence that began in Watts soon would spread to cities like Detroit, Chicago, Newark, and Cleveland. Nineteen sixty-five also signaled the end of liberal civil rights legislation. Journalist Milton Viorst claims that the Voting Rights Act of 1965 "was the last of the great civil rights bills of the 1960s and, though only a few then recognized it, brought the revolution to an end."[123]

Conclusion

The existing research on Lyndon Johnson and civil rights does not capture the full complexity of the president's voting rights address. A quote from former

White House aide Joseph Califano, Jr., summarizes well the scholarly assessments of Johnson's speech: "LBJ seized upon the awakening public sentiment to unveil his tough Voting Rights Act and press Congress to pass it." Similarly, Conkin claims that Johnson's March 15 speech was "almost perfectly composed for the occasion" and calls Johnson's timing "perfect."[124] The timing of President Johnson's speech was more complex, however, than writers have made it seem. The Selma crisis brought out the best Lyndon Johnson from his worst habits. Johnson was ready for the crisis, had indeed prepared the ground; he seized the moment and used it to embrace civil rights. But, ironically, President Johnson's speech also saw the maturation of riots and black separatism at just the moment when black moderates had achieved "civil rights." LBJ's landmark speech and the passage of the legislation were juxtaposed by increasing militancy and violence in northern and western urban ghettos.

Rhetorical analysis of President Johnson's voting rights address shows that a timely response to one element of the situation may be untimely for another element. Johnson's speech was timely for achieving civil rights. Even those who had criticized LBJ soon after the violence on Bloody Sunday seemed willing to concede that the president's hesitation was warranted. The *Kansas City Call* wrote, "Those who have said that President Johnson was slow in taking a stand on the Selma situation must have the feeling now that what the chief executive said Monday night was worth waiting for." Other blacks called the speech a timely, fitting response: a journalist for the *Norfolk Journal & Guide* claimed, "The occasion demanded a supreme effort. . . . President Johnson rose to the occasion." Civil rights leaders also praised the president's speech, which was an affirmation of their efforts and helped them achieve their goals. In a letter to LBJ in the summer of 1965, King wrote: "I am convinced that you will go down in history as the president who issued the second and final Emancipation Proclamation."[125] The president's speech also reshaped time itself. Johnson brought America's history and ideals to bear on the immediate situation. LBJ's speech was untimely, however, for the militancy and separatism that were to come. The rhetorical situation facing Lyndon Johnson was complex. The voting rights bill was overdue, yet Americans only now were ready to support it. Americans' present discriminatory actions had a long history in the South, yet they were inconsistent with national ideals conceived in the past. Civil rights activists had raised the nation's conscience for a brief moment to achieve their goals. Militant blacks looked beyond the aroused expectations of the moment; they acted as if Johnson's speech and the Voting Rights Act did not matter. In his voting rights address, President Johnson proclaimed, "We Shall Overcome" as a response to a rhetorical conundrum of audiences, exigencies, and constraints, and the speech was preoccupied with issues of time and timing.

Lyndon Johnson directed his rhetoric toward *kairos,* or a timely response to the situation. However, as it was for President Kennedy in June of 1963, Johnson's attempt to forge a timely response was a complicated endeavor. In explaining the concept of *kairos,* the anonymous author of the *Dissoi Logoi* claims that "everything done at the right time is seemly and everything done at the wrong time is disgraceful." The treatise suggests, however, that seemingly "right" and "wrong" times can coexist: "Death is bad for those who die, but good for undertakers and gravediggers."[126] Death, the author implies, is a complicated business. So, too, is rhetoric. Rhetorical situations are filled with complexities; elements of a situation often are in tension with one another. Multiple audiences to a message can pull a rhetor in separate directions, competing exigencies can suggest divergent responses, and rival constraints can shape a discourse in disparate ways. Formulating a timely response to a complex rhetorical situation, then, is a difficult task.

The tensions that circumscribed civil rights, black power, and American liberalism in the 1960s were especially complex. The American people often responded to the protest rhetoric of moderate civil rights activists, who—to make a point to white liberals—often juxtaposed their labors against the efforts of more militant African Americans, who often juxtaposed their labors against the efforts of moderate activists to make a point to urban African Americans. In addressing "civil rights," many rhetors during the sixties, including Johnson, focused on a certain set of exigencies, audiences, and constraints while ignoring others. Yet those exigencies, audiences, constraints, and often overlooked forces eventually fractured the civil rights movement and pointed out the flaws in the liberal consensus. American liberals' failure to deal with racial problems was not just a problem of ideology but also of an inability to read the complexity of interlocking rhetorical situations. Indeed, racially inscribed rhetorical situations are especially complicated. In speaking to issues of race, the rhetorical terminologies involved often are in tension with one another—freedom and equality, equality of opportunity and equality of condition, rights and needs. Discourse about racial matters often treats racial groups and their interests as monolithic, whereas these audiences and interests are diverse and sometimes in tension. To comprehend the problems and possibilities of discourse circumscribed by the dynamics of race relations, one must understand the ambiguity of multiple rhetorical situations.

Close attention to Lyndon Johnson's voting rights address reminds us that the civil rights movement was more than the public organizing tradition represented by King and that public discourse about civil rights often has overlooked that complexity. The civil rights movement of popular memory is the movement that organized the March on Washington and the Selma protests. Although these events gained public attention and elicited rhetorical and legislative responses from the federal government, they also signaled the beginning of the end of the civil rights movement. Johnson's speech should remind us that popular rhetoric of protest about racial issues does not always reflect the range of interests and problems facing many racial minorities. In responding to the issues made salient by large-scale public events, political leaders overlook the multiple dimensions of the problem of race in America.

Johnson's voting rights message is a complicated instance of presidential rhetoric. LBJ seemed to deviate from his worst habits by considering the legislation carefully before speaking and by thinking through the popular and political effects of his discourse. Johnson's address also reveals the complexity of rhetorical timing and rhetorical situations. While black moderates and white liberals praised the address, black militants denounced the speech or acted as if it had nothing to do with them. LBJ managed the constraints imposed by the Selma protests to respond to the exigence of African American disfranchisement. But the president was managing a constraint that SNCC and other militant blacks were leaving behind. Johnson's identification with King was also a timely reminder to the militants why they were rebelling against black moderates and white liberals. The voting rights message appropriated a discourse voiced by activists like King, which ensured success with one audience and failure with another. Lyndon Johnson spoke about a problem he had given close attention, and he attempted to address the disparate elements of an urgent, complicated, and ambiguous rhetorical situation: his message was timely, yet in another sense too late.

Whether Johnson could have delivered a different speech on March 15, 1965—one that might have assuaged the tensions revealed by racial riots—is uncertain. First, LBJ's own understanding of civil rights at that moment may have prevented him from giving a different speech. During the winter and spring of 1965, the White House focused on issues of discrimination in public life and on the South as the locus of civil rights problems. Ramsey Clark, who succeeded Nicholas Katzenbach as Johnson's attorney general, later claimed: "We had looked at the civil rights problem as basically a Southern problem, but we were approaching a year when half the blacks of the nation would be out of the South, and in fact the civil rights problems of the urban ghettos exceeded any that we were dealing with in the South."[127] Second, the dominant public understanding of civil rights in 1965 might have deterred Johnson from delivering a different speech. Many Americans only then seemed ready to accept voting rights: a presidential discussion of broader race initiatives might have sounded queer or inopportune. Opinion polls conducted soon after the Selma protests suggest that most citizens believed civil rights reform was moving at about the right pace or too quickly; very few indicated that the administration should take more vigorous action.[128] Furthermore, LBJ's previous rhetoric that focused on immediate urgencies may have conditioned the public to attend only to an immediate tactical issue—which in March of 1965 was voting rights legislation. Third, during the time of Johnson's speech, many African Americans' understanding of racial issues was confined to "civil rights." The discontent of urban blacks was different and relatively unarticulated. How could the president appeal to the discontent of a people he had not heard? The focus on "civil rights" by most moderate, mainstream African American leaders (with whom Johnson was familiar) and their reticence toward the concerns of urban blacks may have kept the president from delivering a different speech.

Whether LBJ should have delivered a different speech is also uncertain. To address the concerns of more militant blacks and those who participated in urban riots, Johnson might have needed to abandon the language that helped make his voting rights message so successful. Abandoning the language of civil religion could have cost LBJ the public and congressional support needed to pass voting rights legislation, which ultimately improved many African Americans' station. And even if Johnson could have spoken the language of urban and militant African Americans, it seems unlikely that they would have found his language meaningful. Militants like Malcolm X often claimed that President Johnson was duplicitous, that his rhetoric masked his true motives. Any effort to speak to the problems that ultimately produced race riots might have sounded patronizing to some blacks and thus might have angered them. Robert Kennedy's initial difficulties in communicating his apparently deep concern and thoughtful understanding of racial problems to militant and urban blacks is instructive. If someone like Kennedy initially created backlash when communicating with militant and urban blacks in 1968, should someone like LBJ have tried to communicate with them in 1965?

In general, President Johnson delivered the right speech on March 15, 1965, given the rhetorical situation he faced. LBJ's speech was focused, unusually eloquent, and affirmed the efforts of African American protesters. Perhaps, however, Johnson should have located the voting rights act within a broader context for improving racial problems: rather than making specific claims about the next wave of civil rights legislation, he might have emphasized additional racial problems that needed attention. After the riots in Watts, one local resident claimed the violence was a victory because it made the world pay attention to urban blacks' problems.[129] Perhaps LBJ just needed to give attention to those concerns rather than radically alter the language of his address to reach some urban African Americans. But in the end, Lyndon Johnson's most eloquent civil rights address may have been doomed to incomplete success by the failure of other presidents to speak out sooner about broader racial problems.

CHAPTER SIX

Presidential Rhetoric
and the Civil Rights Era

Soon after Lyndon Johnson uttered the words "we shall overcome," the civil rights movement languished. Organizations committed to dismantling America's racial hierarchy became estranged from each other, and many severed their ties with American liberalism. And despite his efforts on behalf of voting rights legislation, LBJ quickly became a figure of widespread criticism. The president's policy in Vietnam led members of the Student Nonviolent Coordinating Committee to speak out against him just one month after the voting rights address; in January of 1966, SNCC made a formal statement denouncing the administration. Even Martin Luther King, Jr., formally condemned the White House's Vietnam policy in a speech at New York's Riverside Church on April 4, 1967. Johnson's efforts to advance civil rights after the voting rights campaign also were viewed with suspicion or were decried. For example, some blacks initially praised LBJ's commencement address at Howard University on June 4, 1965, as a landmark of progress but then denounced the speech upon discovering its roots. Presidential speechwriters had grounded Johnson's call for "affirmative action" in Daniel Patrick Moynihan's report, "The Negro Family: The Case for National Action," a document that civil rights advocates called fuel for a new racism, given its emphasis on black inadequacies rather than white racism as the central cause of ghetto pathology.

Urban riots tore the country apart throughout the middle and late 1960s, inhibiting racial unity and fueling many white Americans' racial fears. Efforts to advance civil rights were tempered by racial anxieties: fair housing legislation was defeated in 1966 in part because whites were shocked by racial violence and afraid that their neighborhoods would be overrun and devalued by black residents. When the fair housing measure did become law in 1968, it was accompanied by an anti-rioting provision aimed at curbing the urban African American rebellion. Gallup polls suggested that a majority of Americans believed that the nation was moving too quickly on civil rights, and the term "white backlash" became part of the nation's political vocabulary, indicating that many whites had altered their attitudes toward civil rights reform.[1]

The presidential campaign of 1968 helped foment these racial fears and reactions, as two candidates strove to pit whites against blacks for political gain. Although Robert Kennedy's candidacy had been a symbol of hope for many civil rights advocates, black and white, his death from an assassin's bullet on June 6 eliminated hope that the next president would engage in vigorous rhetorical and political action to heal the nation's racial wounds. Instead, the country seemed destined for a presidency that would use rhetoric to increase racial tension. George Wallace's third-party candidacy riled up voters by appealing to their visceral reactions to urban violence and their sense that the federal government had given blacks too much. Perhaps more alarming was the Republican Party candidate's appropriation of Wallace's rhetoric. Richard Nixon's "Southern Strategy" was to win the southern white vote—and thereby the election—by redefining liberalism as an elitist ideology that harmed whites by ignoring the interests of working-class whites, raising blacks' expectations, giving minorities preferential treatment, and failing to curb racial violence. Nixon promised southerners a go-slow approach on race, avowing to oppose open housing legislation, voting rights measures, court-ordered busing, and virtually any other civil rights initiative.[2] Journalists Rowland Evans and Robert Novak observe that Nixon's strategy was conceived out of electoral necessity but eventually took on "the trappings of grand political doctrine."[3] As such, Nixon not only articulated the visceral, yet often unspoken, racial sentiments of some Americans but endowed them with a sense of legitimacy. Moreover, Spiro Agnew's especially vitriolic and divisive race-baiting rhetoric gave even racial extremists a spokesperson in mainstream national politics.

The 1968 election introduced a new kind of civil rights rhetoric—or perhaps more accurately, the campaign amplified and extended a traditional southern rhetoric embodied in the locution "states' rights." The political vocabularies of Wallace and Nixon contained phrases like "law and order," "property rights," "neighborhood schools," "welfare cheats," and "hard-core unemployed," which were code words for ideas that many would find objectionable if stated in plain language: police repression of black urban dwellers, maintenance of all-white neighborhoods and all-white schools, and neglect of the poor, black underclass. These racial code words functioned as what Celeste Condit and John Lucaites call ideographs: culturally-biased, abstract words or phrases that serve a constitutional value for a group of people and serve as motivations or justifications for public action.[4] Part of the rhetorical effectiveness of such code words resides in their flexibility as cultural signifiers; that is, they can take on multiple cultural meanings, depending on the context. When opponents attack a term like "neighborhood schools" as a code word for segregation, users of the term may reply that the phrase merely emphasizes the positive value of children attending school in the areas in which they live. Yet before a racist audience, the term is understood clearly to mean segregated education. Code words are troublesome because they make political discussion slippery by shifting the very terminology of public argument: conversations marked by code words develop a subtext that is difficult to bring to the surface. Indeed, symbols like "law and order" draw their intensity from the associations they repress.[5] In addition, code words are troublesome because for some listeners, the positive denotative associations of a cultural value like "neighborhood schools" may cross over and reinforce the validity of a racist value like segregated schools. That is, if veiled verbal cues can effectively express unseemly messages without social penalty, they can endow an offensive subtext with political and cultural legitimacy.

Code-word civil rights rhetoric did not end with the presidential campaign but rather extended into Richard Nixon's presidency: terms like "forced integration" and "bloc vote" were mainstays of his presidential rhetoric. However, White House and Justice Department rhetoric held that racial discrimination was morally and socially wrong and must be eliminated.[6] Yet the administration's rhetoric seemed intended to deceive, as Nixon did not have a consistent civil rights program congruent with this discourse.[7] Furthermore, Vice President Agnew's speeches were a heavy counterweight to any pro-civil rights discourse by the administration: in the South, Agnew lambasted civil rights leaders and engaged in self-consciously divisive rhetoric on race, saying things the president could not for political gain. In calmer rhetoric, Nixon articulated his own opposition to busing as a means of ending de facto school segregation, most notably in his written statement on school desegregation of March 24, 1970. In this document, the president articulated support for the *Brown* decision but opposition to busing, claiming that the Supreme Court had not settled the issue of de facto segregation; he also called the drive to achieve multiracial schools "a tragically futile effort" and posed "mobility" as an alternate, superior value to "racial balance."[8] In his public speeches on desegregation, Nixon subsequently used the code word "quality education" to mean de facto segregated education.[9]

Above all, Nixon believed that positive, inspiring civil rights rhetoric would bring him little benefit. Viewing rhetoric on race from a narrowly political point of view, he used public statements to gain political power or electoral votes rather than to urge the nation to move toward what Martin Luther King, Jr., called a "beloved community." The president's narrowly instrumental view of civil rights rhetoric is revealed in a private comment to a White House aide: "The NAACP would say my rhetoric was poor even if I gave the Sermon on the Mount."[10] This comment captures part of Nixon's attitude toward civil rights rhetoric—that articulating a positive racial message was futile since African Americans still would oppose him. Nixon's personal feelings did not arouse in him a strong desire to speak out about civil rights either: presidential aide John Ehrlichman claims that the president believed blacks' genetic inferiority kept them down, and historian Stephen Ambrose argues that Nixon had a "meanness of spirit" on issues of race.[11] Neither did the counsel of his advisers move Nixon to words. Speechwriter Patrick Buchanan urged the president to use the race issue to wedge apart the Democratic coalition and to cement a "New Majority." And in his January 16, 1970, memorandum to President Nixon, Moynihan called for a period of "benign neglect" on civil rights, arguing that too much racial rhetoric had stirred racial anxieties. Perhaps Nixon worried that discourse on race might exacerbate racial problems, but primarily he tried to avoid being associated with an explosive issue that his staff manipulated in order to weaken American liberalism.

By the end of his tenure in the White House, drawn short by Watergate, Richard Nixon had said very little to encourage the nation to overcome its racist attitudes and practices. In a few radio addresses, Nixon briefly suggested that the nation should strive for racial justice and that future generations should see equal opportunity as a birthright. Yet he usually overstated the progress the nation had made, provided little justification for moving forward on civil rights, and failed to sketch what an unprejudiced America might look like. For example, in a speech broadcast on February 2, 1973, Nixon simply stated, "We are closer today than ever before to the realization of a truly just society."[12] Viewing civil rights discourse merely as "hokey rhetoric about equality," President Nixon refused to provide rhetorical leadership on the nation's most pressing social problem.[13] As such, he brought the era of modern presidential leadership on civil rights through words to an end. That era had been slow in developing, but the nation had moved from Franklin Roosevelt's trepidation and overall silence to Lyndon Johnson's vigorous advocacy. Even the middle-man of this era, Dwight Eisenhower, saw the value of rhetorical leadership on civil rights, though he usually did not provide it. Transformations in the civil rights movement, blacks' demands, political culture, attitudes on race, and presidential rhetoric (which now often polarized the races) changed the nature of political discourse on race for the worse. Moreover, Americans no longer looked to the president for rhetorical leadership on race.

Significant Episodes in Civil Rights Rhetoric

I began this book by discussing the overture to leadership established by Franklin D. Roosevelt and have suggested that Richard M. Nixon brought the modern era of presidential civil rights rhetoric to a close: examining the advent and decline of presidential discourse on race might indicate under what kinds of circumstances and what kinds of presidents rhetorical advocacy occurs. In addition, I have analyzed four significant speeches on civil rights by modern American presidents: Harry S. Truman's 1947 speech to the annual convention of the NAACP, Dwight D. Eisenhower's national address on the desegregation crisis in Little Rock, John F. Kennedy's speech after the successful desegregation of the University of Alabama at Tuscaloosa, and Lyndon B. Johnson's voting rights address of 1965. By locating each speech within a personal and presidential context and within in a set of historical circumstances, we can better understand the interaction between president-orators, their civil rights rhetoric, and history. By carefully analyzing presidents' language, arguments, evidence, ethos, style, and value appeals, we can better understand the meanings and capacity for influence of their civil rights rhetoric. And by comparing and contrasting individual episodes of presidential rhetoric on race, we can see emerging patterns in civil rights rhetoric, the development of competing discourses, and the initiation of a theme and its abandonment by a successor. Each president made an important rhetorical contribution to an era marked by an urgency for the nation's leader to speak out on civil rights. Each of the speeches analyzed here also revealed the possibilities and limitations of presidential discourse on race.

Harry Truman's address to the NAACP convention on June 29, 1947, is a clear example of a speech that presented a promising line of rhetoric that later presidents did not develop. Truman introduced the idea that the nation needed to move beyond its old conceptions of civil rights to develop new concepts, in cooperation with other nations—a notion that seemed ahead of its time and was a significant departure from dominant civil rights rhetoric. Later presidents (especially Kennedy and Johnson), however, focused exclusively on urging the nation to live up to "sacred" ideals of freedom and equality conceived in the past. Even President Truman himself failed to develop his idea fully, instead reducing the notion of "equality" to mean only "equality of opportunity." Truman's suggestion of forging an international concept of civil rights was bold but had the capacity to conflict with the United States' Cold War motives. Still, he did not reduce the international implications of civil rights to a mere image problem that might harm the nation's global leadership.

The NAACP speech was also a departure from his presidential predecessors' approach to racial issues and an important stage in his own treatment of civil rights. Although Truman likely was motivated by political concerns, the speech also reflected his matured understanding of civil rights as an important political and social problem. He seemed to suppress his personal racial sentiments and biases readily in order to make a strong statement about an issue he believed the nation's president should support, a public issue he had come to champion despite his personal prejudice. Furthermore, the address was an important departure because it represented the first moment an American president defined civil rights as a national crisis. Truman's definition helped make civil rights an issue appropriately within the realm of presidential rhetoric. African Americans now expected the president to speak out, and subsequent presidents would find it difficult to remain silent on racial matters. Truman's 1947 NAACP address also made a lasting mark on political discourse by introducing several commonplaces for presidential civil rights rhetoric—including the apparent disparity between historic principles and present deeds, the disparity between Cold War ideals and domestic accomplishments, and the urgency for immediate action on civil rights demanded by immediate circumstances and revered national principles.

Dwight Eisenhower's address of September 24, 1957, is an important instance of civil rights rhetoric of a different kind. Rather than providing rhetorical leadership at a moment of no particular urgency, Eisenhower responded to a critical and violent series of events. The speech was a significant rhetorical moment: many of his predecessors had not addressed the public about the use of federal troops to quell racial violence—including Franklin Roosevelt, who kept quiet during the military's involvement in the Detroit race riots. Unlike previous presidents, Ike gave the nation a detailed explanation for his actions, though he scarcely addressed the problem of school desegregation in general.

The brouhaha in Little Rock represented a challenge to Eisenhower's leadership and rhetoric and thus influenced his decision to speak and the nature of his appeals. Just two months before the desegregation of Central High School, he had indicated that no circumstances would compel him to send federal troops to occupy school grounds. Eisenhower's argument for dispatching troops to Little Rock in September focused on public duty, principle, the law, the moderate nature of the local school district's desegregation plan, and the international implications of the crisis.

President Eisenhower's speech was powerful in its confirmation of the federal district court's ruling in Arkansas, its argument that lawful enactment of the Supreme Court's rulings on desegregated education is possible in the South, and its consistency in expressing Ike's commitment to gradual progress and states' rights. Nonetheless, Ike became the victim of his own politics and rhetoric: his address to the nation shows he did not fully understand the limitations of his approach and beliefs in regard to civil rights. Eisenhower miscommunicated the level of southern resistance to desegregation and did not denounce forcefully the behavior of local citizens as racist. He undermined the moral legitimacy of the *Brown* decision by claiming that "our personal opinions . . . have no bearing on enforcement" of the law. In addition, by focusing on the law (as interpreted by the Supreme Court) and the chief executive's duty of enforcement, Eisenhower neglected the importance of educating the public to accept the principle behind the law. Ike's focus on the law also ultimately frustrated his effort to advance an argument for moderation and gradualism in school desegregation.

Whereas John F. Kennedy's speech during the desegregation crisis in Oxford, Mississippi, repeated some of Eisenhower's mistakes, his address on June 11, 1963, was a clear departure from his own civil rights rhetoric and that of his predecessors. The speech met African Americans' demands for a moral commitment by the president, which blacks had urged during the Eisenhower administration—and which Kennedy had promised in his campaign rhetoric. On June 11, for the first time in the nation's history, the president made a sustained moral argument for black civil rights. Kennedy spoke out in part because the costs of remaining silent became too high: pressure applied by civil rights activists propelled him to speak, as did critical events in Birmingham and Tuscaloosa, Alabama. JFK's moral understanding of civil rights also developed in 1963 and became especially keen by June. Although it was overdue and too late in a sense, Kennedy's speech still demonstrated rhetorical courage, as a public moral argument was a risky endeavor with uncertain outcomes.

Kennedy relied upon civil religious appeals and ethical reasoning to define civil rights as a primarily moral issue and to construct a sense of moral urgency for individual and legislative action. JFK subordinated the legal arguments featured in his earlier civil rights rhetoric, emphasizing instead a moral imperative. His moral argument was a bit stale, though, as he urged the nation to live up to traditional principles rather than suggesting that perhaps the nation's past failures required developing new concepts of civil rights. Kennedy did demonstrate, however, that the events at the University of Alabama did not represent just another episode in an endless series of local battles against the desegregation of public education but rather a moral victory against segregation. He made clear that the moral strength of the office of the presidency was on the side of civil rights and established that the forces of segregation would now be compelled to fight an ethical battle in which the nation's president declared them to be on the losing side.

Lyndon B. Johnson's televised address before a joint session of Congress on March 15, 1965, employed a similar moral discourse as Kennedy's ethical appeal—which LBJ had shaped. Johnson appealed to national history, principles, and myths to urge the nation to enact voting rights legislation and to conquer its racism. He drew upon a peculiarly American discourse of civic virtue in order to endow current events with hallowed and historical significance. LBJ apparently still believed in the rhetorical principles he had communicated to Kennedy speechwriter Theodore Sorensen in 1963: arguments grounded in the Golden Rule, Christian morality, and national virtue would appeal to most of the nation, validate the campaign for civil rights and weaken the forces of bigotry. Moreover, Johnson's dramatic claim, "We shall overcome," gave new voice to the rallying cry of the civil rights movement and left many southerners speechless. Never before had a U.S. president so closely identified his office with African Americans or endorsed their struggle so clearly and emphatically.

LBJ's speech was a departure in another way too. Close attention to the voting rights address shows that it was not as shortsighted as much of his previous rhetoric. Johnson planned his civil rights strategy carefully in 1965, considering the legislative and rhetorical implications of speaking about the voting rights bill. The president attempted to craft a conscientious, timely response to the civil rights exigency facing the nation. His timely response, however, was a complicated proposition: the speech came at an opportune moment and reshaped time itself by focusing the nation's history and ideals inward to bring it to bear on the immediate circumstance. Yet while Johnson's speech was a tactically timely response to the voting rights urgency hastened by the Selma demonstrations, it was too little and too late for the new militancy within the civil rights movement. The Selma crisis brought Lyndon Johnson out of his poor rhetorical and political habits. He was ready for the crisis and had prepared the ground; LBJ seized the moment and used it to usher in expanded civil rights. But Johnson's speech also saw the maturation of race riots and black separatism at just the moment when black moderates and white liberals had achieved "civil rights," at just the moment when it seemed that the nation might indeed overcome its racial dilemma.

Presidential Discourse on Race

The four speeches analyzed in this book are diverse: each is a distinctive discursive response to a peculiar rhetorical situation by a particular orator-president. Yet each address also represents a moment in an unfolding presidential discourse on civil rights. Although each speech is unique, each also affected the citizenry's understanding of where the American presidency stood on issues of race. Each of the four chief executives influenced the nature of what was sayable about civil rights, and Presidents Truman, Kennedy, and Johnson expanded the range of presidential discourse on race. Truman claimed that civil rights represented a crisis; Kennedy declared that the crisis was a moral one; Lyndon Johnson proclaimed that the nation would overcome that crisis. Each president also influenced the nature of what other presidents would say, by setting precedent or illustrating successful or ineffective rhetorical strategies. For instance, after Truman's address to the NAACP, it became common for presidents to send more than perfunctory messages to civil rights organizations. The acclaim accorded Kennedy's civil religious discourse on June 11, 1963, influenced Johnson's use of similar appeals. Each president also increased civil rights advocates' appetite for eloquent discourse: activists seemed anxious to hear civil rights rhetoric equal to or greater than that of the previous chief executive. Most of the modern presidents met expectations: African Americans—and some whites too—declared that Truman, Kennedy, and Johnson each had delivered the greatest civil rights address by an American president, though each address was a unique moment of rhetorical action.

Although Presidents Truman, Eisenhower, Kennedy, and Johnson governed in peculiar circumstances, we should not overlook the similarities of the rhetorical situations they confronted. For example, Kennedy's civil rights rhetoric in 1961 and 1962 was similar to that of his immediate predecessor not because he used Eisenhower's rhetoric as a model (in fact, he thought Ike's approach had been a failure) but rather because JFK faced similar exigencies, audiences, and constraints. Some authors suggest that Kennedy might not have delivered his celebrated moral appeal had the University of Alabama desegregation not passed peacefully: in other words, Kennedy responded differently to a different situation. Still, the situation during the spring of 1963 was different in another way: JFK himself had changed, as his personal understanding of civil rights had recently matured. Exigencies, audiences, and constraints influence presidents' civil rights rhetoric, but also important are a president's personal and public convictions regarding civil rights and his conception of the office of the presidency. Harry Truman's experience is instructive here. Truman did not face a rhetorical situation substantially different from those that confronted his predecessors, nor did he have strong personal convictions on race. But his public convictions and his belief that the U.S. president should provide civil rights leadership moved him to speak out.

The remainder of this chapter will explore the commonalities and differences—for reasons including rhetorical situation, personality, and duty—in the presidential speeches on civil rights that I have examined in the previous chapters. I will analyze the vocabularies presidents used to discuss civil rights, the common themes and rhetorical strategies in presidents' civil rights rhetoric. In addition, I will discuss how presidents used rhetoric to manage civil rights crises, the timing of presidential discourse, the complex nature of presidents' rhetorical leadership on civil rights, and the relationship between presidential rhetoric and broader social discourses on race. My aim is to make conclusions based on the four case studies and to discuss the implications of modern presidents' use of discourse to address one of the United States' most pressing, persistent social problems.

The most common vocabulary that modern presidents used to address civil rights is a constitutional one. Truman, Eisenhower, Kennedy, and Johnson each appealed to the U.S. Constitution as a document that could transcend national differences of opinion about racial equality. A constitutional vocabulary involves two types of implicit value appeals—an appeal to the value of the Constitution in and of itself and an appeal to the value of the principles that the Constitution expresses. Both appeals can be activated at the same moment (indeed affirming constitutional values can help affirm the Constitution as a value), but rhetors often emphasize one over the other. President Eisenhower used a vocabulary that treated the Constitution—as interpreted by the U.S. Supreme Court—as a value in itself. The Constitution was an especially important value for Ike, of course, because he had sworn a presidential oath to uphold it. Yet Eisenhower refused to discuss the value of the desegregationist principles that the Supreme Court had interpreted the Constitution to embody. Presidents Kennedy and Johnson, in contrast, appealed to principles they presumed the Constitution to embody. JFK and LBJ claimed to support civil rights measures because they were rooted in "color blind" constitutional values like equal rights and equal treatment. President Truman supported the principles underlying the Constitution, like Kennedy and Johnson, but he also advocated moving beyond those principles to develop new concepts of civil rights.

The differences between these constitutional vocabularies is significant. Kenneth Burke argues that the chief problem of positive law—which Eisenhower's civil rights discourse implicitly endorses—is that it looks only to the Constitution itself, not to any doctrine specifying the nature of its underlying doctrines, the "Constitution-Behind-the-Constitution."[14] Eisenhower's civil rights rhetoric did not articulate underlying constitutional doctrines that form the grounds by which the public evaluates the judiciousness of a policy. Ike's rhetoric could uphold order, understood as obedience to the Constitution itself, but could not bring about the acceptance of civil rights rulings. Truman focused primarily on the underlying reasons for supporting civil rights, but his advocacy of moving beyond constitutional principles might have seemed too liberal—or "unconstitutional," in an extralegal sense—to some listeners. Kennedy and Johnson articulated the doctrines underlying civil rights as they affirmed the Constitution as a value. Their vocabulary made progress on racial issues seem safe by allying pro-civil rights values with the nation's fundamental political instrument. The vocabulary used by JFK and LBJ appealed to principles of natural law in which the Constitution was rooted, and thereby provided doctrines that might encourage the acceptance of civil rights—or, at least, demonstrate clearly where the president stood on civil rights, thereby helping to maintain order. Moreover, this kind of constitutional vocabulary afforded the rhetorical advantage that it could be connected to a shared moral vocabulary.

As presidents came to understand that they needed to articulate a moral argument to satisfy African Americans' demands and to defeat the forces of resistance, they also came to understand the difficultly of locating a moral vocabulary with widespread rhetorical force. How could the president urge moral action without pontificating? On what ethical grounds could the president indict segregationists, who had their own moral vocabulary? How could the president make morality, often considered private, a public issue? What moral grounding might have nearly universal appeal to a nation of diverse people? For Presidents Kennedy and Johnson, the discourse of American civil religion served as a shared moral vocabulary. Civil religion, which pairs political principles with Christian morality, is a familiar part of the American ideology; its language permeates canonical texts such as Lincoln's Gettysburg address, the pledge of allegiance, and "America the Beautiful." As such, Kennedy's and Johnson's language of civic-sacred purpose, promise, and duty stirred many American citizens—especially many African Americans, who had long urged the nation to live up to its divine purpose and to enact its consecrated values.[15]

The vocabulary of American civil religion can provide a shared moral code and reinforce citizens' commitment to pro-civil rights abstractions like freedom and equality. Sacvan Bercovitch claims, however, that such discourse can also become a "ritual of consensus" that restricts debates about political reform to the meaning of America and rules out alternatives to the system.[16] In other words, a political conversation rooted in a civil religious vocabulary might become a celebration of historic national principles rather than a means of discovering new principles to advance reform, such as new concepts of civil rights. Kennedy's and Johnson's civil religious rhetoric on race suggested that a system of Enlightenment-era values could help solve America's racial problems— which had changed radically since the late eighteenth century—by protecting citizens' inalienable rights. Among the speeches I have analyzed here, Harry Truman's address to the NAACP is, in one sense, the most progressive. Truman argued rightly that the nation had changed since its founding: while it could draw upon the wisdom of the past, the United States needed to formulate more mature concepts of civil rights that drew upon the wisdom of the present. A moral vocabulary for civil rights that remains potent, yet resists the limitations of civil religion, might sound something like a domestic version of Franklin Roosevelt's expression of the "Four Freedoms"—a vocabulary that appeals to national, moral ideals (such as freedom), while removing those ideals from a nationalistic frame, locating them instead in a global context. Such a rhetoric also might reexamine the very concepts of freedom, equality, and civil rights in light of new national circumstances, perhaps suggesting that the nation has not lived up to its principles because the country has not adequately defined the meaning of those principles.

As a concept central to American civil religion and an idea central to discussions of race, the term "equality" has been featured in modern presidents' discourse on race, often in conjunction with the concepts of freedom and individual rights. Yet in its usage and associations, "equality" meant something different in each presidents' rhetoric. In his speech to the NAACP, President Truman claimed that "each man must be guaranteed equality of opportunity" if each person is to live in freedom and emphasized that each citizen should have an equal right to a decent home, an education, adequate medical care, a worthwhile job, the ballot box, and a fair trial. Truman's understanding of equality centered around equal access to aspects of the good life, unimpeded by discriminatory barriers, including racial insult, racial intimidation, and racial violence. Eisenhower's Little Rock address attended only to issues of equality in public education—and even then, only in an extremely abbreviated manner. Ike claimed that the Supreme Court had found that "separate educational facilities for the races are inherently unequal," but he did not claim that access to a public education should be an equal right. To Eisenhower, equality seemed to be a legal issue alone: he did not articulate a concept of equal rights. Instead, he discussed "individual freedoms" and "lawfully-protected rights." In contrast, President Kennedy did articulate a concept of equal rights. In his June 11, 1963, speech, Kennedy claimed that all citizens should "be afforded equal rights and equal opportunities" and should have "an equal chance to develop their talents." JFK also claimed that the denial of equal rights had restricted the freedom of African Americans to enjoy a full life, and he affirmed the notion that all "men are created equal." President Johnson also emphasized equal rights and opportunities in his "We Shall Overcome" address; he focused on the "right to be treated as a man equal in opportunity to all others." He claimed that every citizen has an equal right to share in national freedom, especially through the right to vote. Contradicting Eisenhower's statement in the Little Rock address that the basis of rights and freedom depends upon federal enforcement, LBJ stated that equal rights depend upon democratic processes and "the force of moral rights," not the force of arms. Near the end of his speech, Johnson extended the notion of equality expressed by his predecessors, claiming that equal rights were a privilege, not just a legal right.

The rhetoric of equality uttered by each president is distinct, though among the three Democratic presidents, there is a sense of development. The lone Republican president had an undeveloped sense of equality. Eisenhower's expressed notion of equality is distinct because he conceived of the situation at Little Rock as a legal contest, a problem of enforcement. His political beliefs and his implicit rhetorical theory of the presidency kept him from speaking about the broader issues of equality involved in the desegregation of public education. Ike did not endorse the Court's ruling that separate facilities are unequal, nor did he affirm Truman's moderate claim that African Americans had an equal right to receive a decent education. Because he did not articulate even a conservative concept of equality, Eisenhower failed to provide citizens with an underlying reason to abide by the *Brown* ruling.[17] Presidents Truman and Kennedy shared a similar concept of equality: equal rights and equal opportunities unrestricted by racial discrimination. Both focused on immediate acts of overt discrimination that prevented racial minorities from exercising equal rights rather than the legacy of racial discrimination that might prevent them from having equal opportunities. JFK claimed that not everyone has equal talent, ability, or motivation but everyone should have the equal right to develop his or her talent, ability, and motivation. Neither Truman nor Kennedy spoke about the history of racist practices and attitudes that impacted African Americans' talents, abilities, and motivations. For both, the principle that "all men are created equal" seemed to mean equal opportunity, not that all people are entitled to equal social and material conditions regardless of their abilities — even when those abilities have been influenced by racial discrimination.[18] Kennedy moved beyond Truman's focus on the threat of violence that prevented equal opportunity, however, devoting attention to the system of Jim Crow laws that maintained unequal opportunities. Lyndon Johnson's rhetoric of equality went even further. He proclaimed boldly in his voting rights address that African Americans are not fully free or equal. LBJ asserted that in addition to discriminatory practices, poverty, poor health, and poor education kept many African Americans from sharing equal opportunities. Johnson suggested that true equality meant opening the "gates to opportunity" and "giving all our people, black and white, the help that they need to walk through those gates."

The notion of equality expressed in modern presidents' civil rights rhetoric, then, generally meant legal rights, equal opportunity, or equal rights. Rarely did presidents utter the term "equality" without an adjoining term like "opportunity" or "rights." In addition, presidents often associated equality with other sociopolitical terms like "freedom" and "liberty." Yet Truman, Eisenhower, Kennedy, and Johnson failed to articulate the tensions between concepts like freedom and equality; neither did they sufficiently distinguish the two concepts from each other. Moreover, modern presidents failed to offer a comprehensive definition of equality, one that acknowledged the tensions between different conceptions of equality, such as equality of opportunity and equality of condition. Public discourse that defined the notion of equality and discussed it in relation to freedom might have sounded confusing, since both concepts are part of the American ideology. But such rhetoric could have initiated a conversation to clarify the nation's ideology, its often vague and competing commitments between freedom, justice, equality, and rights. Modern presidents may have been reluctant to begin a broad discussion of equality during the Cold War, since Communism promised one kind of equality. But a president could have defined different concepts of equality and defended a particular concept against that proffered by Communist states.

In addition to focusing on equal rights and opportunities, modern presidential discussions of equality emphasized political equality rather than social equality between the races. Neither Truman nor Eisenhower mentioned social equality: their rhetoric seemed to reflect their personal attitudes on race, though Truman indicated in other speeches that bigotry was a product of a lack of education and interaction with African Americans. Kennedy hinted at social equality in his "moral issue" speech, claiming that Americans should treat one other as they would want to be treated. Johnson uttered a stronger remark on social equality than JFK, claiming that he wanted to help the nation overcome its bigotry, to reshape the attitudes and structures of American society, and to end hatred and promote love among the people of all races. Presidents' civil rights rhetoric was sensitive to the prevailing attitudes of their era: many Americans, especially in the 1940s and 1950s, opposed the idea that whites must interact with blacks in social settings or respect them as fully human, not viewing them inferiors. Presidents' focus on political equality presumably would allow them to improve African Americans' lives in a significant way without becoming bogged down by a tangential debate on social equality. In other words, presidential rhetoric implied that equal political rights were separate from issues of social equality. Modern presidential discourse on equality, then, reflected many African Americans' protest rhetoric. For example, in 1963, an excerpt used to promote James Baldwin's book *The Fire Next Time* became a familiar maxim: "I don't want to marry your daughter. I just want you to get off my back."

But is social equality separate from or unrelated to political equality? Or, perhaps as some presidents and protesters meant to imply, is political equality prior to social equality? Social acceptance of African Americans could create more stable political equality, but using discourse to encourage social equality would be a slow and difficult process that would prevent blacks from enjoying political rights in the meantime. Yet perhaps Eisenhower's maxim that you cannot change people's hearts (which many Americans still see as important for accomplishing racial progress) merely by changing laws has some validity. Still, laws can create habits that might eventually become habits of the heart. Modern presidential rhetoric on race points to the fact that the relationships between social equality and political equality are especially complicated. We should not expect any individual president's rhetoric to resolve the dilemmas of equality. At some moment, however, political rhetors must acknowledge and discuss that complex web of relationships in order to make further progress on racial issues.

Another complicated issue in presidential discourse on race is the relationship between civil rights as a domestic issue and civil rights as an international issue. Civil rights offenses and accomplishments at home clearly had implications abroad, and vice versa. Citizens of developing nations often criticized the United States, the self-proclaimed homeland of freedom, as hypocritical for its racist misdeeds. Communist countries also used those misdeeds to indict America in propaganda campaigns. In addition, many African Americans— who in increasing numbers had contact with people of color abroad—viewed civil rights within an international context. Many blacks leaders promoted civil rights as a global issue and often became outraged at the U.S. government when other nations afforded all races equal rights.

Presidents also were aware of the international dimensions of civil rights, especially the implications of racial problems on the Cold War. Unfortunately, some presidents talked as though civil rights was a significant issue only because it affected America's bargaining power in international political struggles. President Eisenhower, for example, seemed primarily concerned with racial issues as Cold War issues. His speech on September 24, 1957, emphasized that the violence at Little Rock had damaged the national reputation in the eyes of the world, that the violence had given our nation's enemies cause to gloat and use it to misrepresent the entire country. Ike suggested that, above all, compliance with federal court orders would restore the United States' good name and remove the stain from its international image. An alternative to Ike's rhetoric came in June of 1963. President Kennedy, who previously had followed Eisenhower's model of subordinating domestic civil rights to international concerns, claimed that civil rights was an important issue in its own right, not exclusively because of its impact on the nation's image abroad. JFK also suggested that civil rights was an international issue because the United States sent people of all races to fight in the worldwide struggle for freedom. Similarly, Lyndon Johnson observed in his voting rights address that men of every color fought to secure freedom in Vietnam.

Of the speeches I have analyzed in this book, President Truman's address to the NAACP had the highest potential for transforming civil rights into an issue of global concern and cooperation. Truman understood that racial discrimination damaged America's ethos in the struggle against Communism, yet his discourse did not subordinate civil rights to the Cold War. His NAACP address stated a positive case for a national-international civil rights connection instead of complaining that racial offenses tarnished the nation's image abroad. Moreover, Truman depicted the United States as poised to lead a worldwide movement for freedom rather than as a nation that only concerns itself with domestic freedom when shamed (or potentially shamed) into action. He suggested that an international code of human rights, crafted with American participation, would be a landmark in humanity's struggle for freedom. Yet the United States did not promote a binding international agreement on civil rights during the forties, fifties, or sixties, as government officials worried that the nation might find itself in the embarrassing situation of being indicted for offenses against African Americans—a situation that would tarnish the national image. No modern president developed or extended Truman's suggestion of extending the nation's struggle for civil rights outward, to make it an global issue of human dignity. Some African Americans, however, continued to petition the United Nations to forge a stronger connection between domestic and international civil rights and to provide a forum for international dialogue. Others, like Malcolm X, repeatedly urged blacks to consider their struggle within a worldwide struggle for freedom. External pressures and the potential of embarrassment might have made presidents fearful of locating civil rights in a global context, but an international conversation about civil rights could have informed all nations' understanding of racial issues and could have helped all nations move toward effective solutions to racial problems.

Instead of making arguments for international cooperation on civil rights, most presidents were consumed by responding to domestic racial crises, such as those in Little Rock, Tuscaloosa, and Selma. Each of these circumstances, which many Americans perceived as critical, posed serious challenges to presidential rhetoric. A critical situation demands that the president address the urgencies of the moment, yet Americans often want to hear that answers to timely exigencies are consistent with timeless principles. If a president identifies a situation as a crisis, he or she implies the failure of normal political institutions and principles: such an identification could lead to extraordinary solutions to overcome critical problems. Yet Presidents Kennedy and Johnson claimed that American democracy and a reinvigoration of traditional political principles would help the nation overcome its racial crises. Eisenhower acknowledged the failure of normal political agencies during the Little Rock disturbance but did not argue for action that would prevent future failures, such as civil rights legislation that included Title III. President Truman suggested new political principles and institutions that could prevent future problems but did not articulate a clear historical argument explaining why civil rights constituted a crisis in June of 1947.

Each president was forced to make difficult judgments about historical events, citizens' perceptions of those events, and the potential effects of identifying a situation as a crisis or speaking out about a situation that citizens have identified as a crisis. As critics and auditors, we should ask several critical questions about presidential rhetoric during times of stress. First, how and when does a situation become a crisis? A situation often becomes a crisis when normalized explanations no longer are compelling to a significant portion of the people. Second, do presidents construct crises rhetorically, or does the citizenry's understanding constitute a situation as a crisis? A situation often becomes understood as a crisis when rhetors and audiences are able to arrive jointly—though perhaps for different reasons—at a rhetoric that explains a situation's critical, extraordinary features. Third, can we distinguish between real and spurious crises? Identifying a situation as genuinely critical during its own historical moment is difficult, and perhaps a crisis is better understood as a phenomenon of cultural knowledge rather than one of fixed historical reality.

What constitutes a crisis and effective crisis rhetoric is complex. Truman identified civil rights as a crisis in his NAACP speech, but it is unclear how many citizens accepted his definition (or whether they should have), given the lack of immediate, extraordinary events: instances of racial terror in 1947 were no worse than in previous years. Truman might have argued, perhaps more effectively, that the cumulative effect of past instances of racism created a civil rights crisis. President Eisenhower never spoke out about the crisis of public school desegregation prior to September 24, 1957, despite prior circumstances similar to those at Little Rock. Neither did Kennedy label civil rights a "moral crisis" prior to June 11, 1963, though many Americans had become morally outraged by critical events that occurred months earlier, especially the violence in Birmingham. Instead, JFK waited until the desegregation of the University of Alabama, a moment of urgency and a moment of triumph for his administration. In response to the events in Selma, Lyndon Johnson attempted to trump Eisenhower's definition of civil rights as constitutional crisis and Kennedy's definition of civil rights as moral crisis by proclaiming that civil rights represented an American crisis. Yet LBJ did not speak until eight days after "Bloody Sunday," which had created intense public sentiments.

Since Truman, Eisenhower, Kennedy, and Johnson could have spoken out about civil rights at earlier, often equally or more critical moments, one could criticize their crisis rhetoric as late. And citizens and scholars have claimed that these presidents should have addressed racial problems sooner. But for a few presidents it seems that their sense of civil rights as critical had not matured until the moment they spoke. In some situations, especially in Lyndon Johnson's case, it seems that speaking before their actual moment of address could have rushed the political process or constrained legislative options. In evaluating presidential crisis rhetoric, especially in evaluating when crisis rhetoric seems to be appropriate or when critical events might constitute a crisis, we should keep in mind that the timing of discursive responses to racial problems is especially complex. Speech that seems timely to one audience might seem untimely to another. Speech that seems to respond in a timely fashion to one aspect of a critical situation might be untimely for another component of that situation. Speech that seems overdue might be superior for the process of developing a plan to resolve a critical situation or the process of passing legislation to address the underlying causes of a critical situation. Premature or inflated crisis rhetoric could undermine effective governance by raising expectations beyond what the government can accomplish. In addition, speaking out during perceived or constructed crises reinforces creating critical, potentially stormy moments as the means for protesters to receive attention.

Finding appropriate rhetoric for times of domestic tumult is difficult for a president. According to some communication scholars, chief executives have developed a fairly stable genre of discourse for addressing foreign policy crises, but U.S. presidents' means of addressing critical situations at home is not so immutable.[19] Rhetorical strategies that might defuse a crisis, such as denouncing enemies and promising severe retaliation, are difficult to use when the antagonists are American citizens. For example, Eisenhower indicted "extremists" but felt compelled to create identification with southerners, which undermined efforts to indict all citizens dedicated to obstructing school desegregation. Presidents often attempt to unify the nation behind a common goal or principle during foreign crises, but this strategy seems unlikely to be effective during a domestic crisis, when the division is caused by a national dispute over goals or principles. Although the speeches I have analyzed do share some common themes and strategies, each address is sufficiently distinct. Moreover, since each instance of presidential rhetoric centers around a civil rights crisis—as does the rhetoric examined in most other studies of presidential rhetoric during moments of domestic stress—it seems premature to draw conclusions about the nature of domestic crisis rhetoric.[20] Domestic crises may not have sufficiently common features that would lead to similar domestic crisis rhetoric by U.S. presidents. Understanding a president's general approach to political rhetoric and his or her previous speeches on particular political issues might tell us more about an episode of presidential rhetoric than knowing that a president happened to present that speech during a moment of domestic conflict.

Presidential rhetoric during civil rights crises has the potential to cultivate the complications described by critics of the rhetorical presidency. For example, overreliance on crisis rhetoric could undermine effective governance by making citizens and their public representatives lose sight of normal politics. Using vigorous, urgent rhetoric only during moments of racial conflict could condition the public to respond only to "crises." It seems uncertain whether civil rights has yet become part of normal politics or normal political discourse in the United States. Many Americans still do not have sustained discussions about racial problems. Often, only a particularly dramatic or critical event involving race will initiate civil rights conversations—such as the brutal murder of James Byrd, Jr., in Jasper, Texas, on June 7, 1998, by white supremacists who may have been inspired by the 1955 lynching of Emmett Till. Yet sustained, "normal" discussions about race, an absolute good for some critics of the rhetorical presidency, might fail to make racial problems seem sufficiently urgent. A chief problem for presidents and citizens involves how to engage in discourse about race that is neither dramatized to the extent that it encourages action peripheral to chronic racial problems, nor normalized to the extent that people become dulled to the magnitude of the nation's race problem. In Murray Edelman's words, how do we move civil rights out of the realm of merely "troubling conditions" into the realm of "social problems," while still making race seem a persistent and urgent issue?

Throughout the 1940s, 1950s, and 1960s, civil rights advocates urged presidents to speak out about civil rights more regularly. For example, many activists praised John Kennedy's "moral issue" address and demanded that the speech represent the first in a campaign of presidential rhetoric on race. Yet JFK's speech had been so eloquent and sweeping that the White House staff, especially speechwriters, may have wondered what else the president could say. Might some modern presidents have exhausted their eloquence, at least intermediately, through single, landmark speeches on civil rights? What would a sustained rhetorical campaign on civil rights look like? Bill Clinton's initiative on race, in part, aims at maintaining a national dialogue on race. President Clinton gave several speeches on racial issues and hosted town hall meeting on civil rights. Thus far, the governing function of this presidential rhetoric—its impact on national sentiments, discussions, and policies—is uncertain. Civil rights advocates who criticized Clinton as too concerned with rhetoric and not concerned enough with action should investigate how a president's words might affect national attitudes on race: contemporary civil rights activists should follow the lead of their predecessors and urge sustained presidential rhetoric that engages citizens on an individual and collective moral level, in addition to shaping public policy.

The "bully pulpit" afforded by the American presidency is important. Citizens often look to the president for meaningful rhetoric on civil rights. Citizens often are anxious to hear the commentary on a racial crisis by the nation's interpreter-in-chief. The persuasive powers of the office give the president an opportunity to provide leadership on civil rights, to induce the citizenry to move toward a greater good it might have ignored or resisted if not for powerful symbolic action. The president speaks with a single voice unmatched by the other branches of government. The president can reinforce and enliven the language of Supreme Court decisions, which often involve dissent, and help clarify the meaning of federal legislation and heal the divisions caused by congressional wrangling. For all the shortcomings of their rhetorical leadership on civil rights, modern presidents often moved the nation toward overcoming its racial problems through their discourse on race. Harry S. Truman helped make civil rights a part of the presidential vocabulary and challenged existing conceptions of civil rights. Dwight D. Eisenhower reestablished some sense of order during a period of crisis, confirmed the authority (if not the validity) of court rulings, and suggested that lawful desegregation was possible in the South. John F. Kennedy addressed the moral issues involved in civil rights and urged the passage of meaningful public accommodations legislation. Lyndon B. Johnson summoned the nation to leave behind its racist past, to treat every person equally, and to enact voting rights legislation. For the United States to make further achievements on civil rights, future presidents must understand the power of presidential rhetoric; the nature of the rhetorical presidency; and the problems, performance, and promise of civil rights rhetoric spoken by their modern predecessors.

Notes

Chapter One. Presidents, Race, and Rhetoric

1. Louis Martin to Robert F. Kennedy, May 13, 1963, White House Central Files, EX HU2/MC, Box 365A, John F. Kennedy Library.
2. Hugh Davis Graham, *The Civil Rights Era: Origins and Development of National Policy, 1960–1972* (New York: Oxford University Press, 1990), 7; Richard P. Longaker, *The President and Individual Liberties* (Ithaca: Cornell University Press, 1961), 3.
3. James MacGregor Burns, *Presidential Government: The Crucible of Leadership* (Boston: Houghton Mifflin, 1965), 281, 285–86.
4. Longaker, *President and Individual Liberties,* 18.
5. Donald R. McCoy and Richard T. Ruetten, *Quest and Response: Minority Rights and the Truman Administration* (Lawrence: University Press of Kansas, 1973), 54.
6. Roy Wilkins and Tom Matthews, *Standing Fast: The Autobiography of Roy Wilkins* (New York: Viking, 1982), 307.
7. Peter Baker, "Clinton Urges U.S. to Renounce Bigotry," *Washington Post,* June 15, 1997, A1+.
8. "Clinton Meets with Race Advisory Board," from *All Things Considered,* Narr. Mara Liasson and Linda Wertheimer, National Public Radio, WPSU, State College, Pa., Sept. 30, 1997.
9. Skip Thurman, "Even Supporters Grumble Over Clinton Panel on Race," *Christian Science Monitor,* Sept. 30, 1997, 3.
10. Michael A. Fletcher and Dan Balz, "Race Relations Initiative May Pose Risks for Clinton," *Washington Post,* June 12, 1997, A1+.
11. Thurman, "Even Supporters," 3.
12. Edward S. Corwin, *The President: Office and Powers,* 4th ed. (New York: New York University Press, 1957), 312.
13. Clinton Rossiter, *The American Presidency,* rev. ed. (New York: Harcourt Brace, 1960), 18, 34, 32, 33.
14. Richard E. Neustadt, *Presidential Power: The Politics of Leadership* (New York: Wiley, 1960), 10.
15. Craig Allen Smith and Kathy B. Smith, *The White House Speaks: Presidential Leadership and Persuasion* (Westport, Conn.: Praeger, 1994), 3; Jeffery K. Tulis, *The Rhetorical Presidency* (Princeton: Princeton University Press, 1987), 10; Samuel Kernell, *Going Public: New Strategies of Presidential Leadership* (Washington, D.C.: CQ Press, 1993), 3.
16. Neustadt, *Presidential Power,* 100.

17. George C. Edwards III, *The Public Presidency: The Pursuit of Popular Support* (New York: St. Martin's, 1983), 65.

18. George C. Edwards III, "Presidential Rhetoric: What Difference Does It Make?" in *Beyond the Rhetorical Presidency,* ed. Martin J. Medhurst (College Station: Texas A&M University Press, 1996), 216–17.

19. Kernell, *Going Public,* 3–4.

20. Tulis, *Rhetorical Presidency,* 147.

21. Ibid., 18, 178.

22. James W. Ceasar et al., "The Rise of the Rhetorical Presidency," in *Essays in Presidential Rhetoric,* 3rd ed., ed. Theodore Otto Windt, Jr., and Beth Ingold (Dubuque: Kendall/Hunt, 1992), 5, 19.

23. Roderick P. Hart, *The Sound of Leadership: Presidential Communication in the Modern Age* (Chicago: University of Chicago Press, 1987), 14.

24. Ibid., xxiii, 41, 47, 196.

25. Ibid., 40.

26. Theodore Otto Windt, Jr., *Presidential Rhetoric: 1961 to the Present,* 4th ed. (Dubuque: Kendall/Hunt, 1987), 3.

27. Tulis, *Rhetorical Presidency,* 179; Windt, *Presidential Rhetoric,* 4.

28. Tulis, *Rhetorical Presidency,* 179.

29. Theodore Otto Windt, Jr., *Presidents and Protestors: Political Rhetoric in the 1960s* (Tuscaloosa: University of Alabama Press, 1990), 5.

30. Murray Edelman, *Constructing the Political Spectacle* (Chicago: University of Chicago Press, 1988), 12.

31. Martin J. Medhurst and Thomas W. Benson, *Rhetorical Dimensions in Media: A Critical Casebook,* 2nd ed. (Dubuque: Kendall/Hunt, 1991), vii.

32. Stephen E. Lucas, "The Renaissance of American Public Address: Text and Context in Rhetorical Criticism," *Quarterly Journal of Speech* 74 (1988): 253.

33. Edwin Black, "The Second Persona," *Quarterly Journal of Speech* 56 (1970): 113.

34. Eugene E. White, *The Context of Human Discourse: A Configurational Criticism of Rhetoric* (Columbia: University of South Carolina Press, 1992), 12–20.

35. Langston Hughes, *The Collected Poems of Langston Hughes,* ed. Arnold Rampersad (New York: Knopf, 1994), 9; W. E. B. Du Bois, "An Estimate of FDR," in *W. E. B. Du Bois: A Reader,* ed. David Levering Lewis (New York: Henry Holt, 1995), 481; Wilkins and Matthews, *Standing Fast,* 127.

36. Arthur M. Schlesinger, *The Age of Roosevelt: The Political of Upheaval* (Boston: Houghton Mifflin, 1960), 434.

37. Anthony J. Badger, *The New Deal: The Depression Years, 1933–1940* (New York: Noonday, 1989), 254.

38. Raymond Wolters, "The New Deal and the Negro," in *The New Deal: The National Level,* ed. John Braeman, Robert H. Bremner, and David Brody (Columbus: Ohio State University Press, 1975), 186.

39. Harvard Sitkoff, *A New Deal for Blacks: 1954–1992,* rev. ed. (New York: Hill and Wang, 1993), 68.

40. Wolters, "New Deal and the Negro," 185.

41. "This Week," *Chicago Defender,* July 1, 1933, 11.

42. Jesse O. Thomas, "A 'New Deal' for the Negro," *Opportunity,* Apr., 1933, 108; John P. Davis, "A Black Inventory of the New Deal," *Crisis,* May, 1935, 141; Charles H. Houston and John P. Davis, "TVA: Lily-White Reconstruction," *Crisis,* Oct., 1934, 290.

43. Arthur Raper, *Preface to Peasantry: A Tale of Two Black Belt Counties* (Chapel Hill: University of North Carolina Press, 1936), 56.

44. Patricia Sullivan, *Days of Hope: Race and Democracy in the New Deal Era* (Chapel Hill: University of North Carolina Press, 1996), 57.

45. Ralph J. Bunche, "A Critique of New Deal Social Planning as it Affects Negroes," in *Ralph J. Bunche: Selected Speeches and Writings,* ed. Charles P. Henry (Ann Arbor: University of Michigan Press, 1995), 68–69.

46. Barton J. Bernstein, "The New Deal: The Conservative Achievements of Liberal Reform," in *Towards a New Past: Dissenting Essays in American History,* ed. Barton J. Bernstein (New York: Pantheon, 1968), 277; Sitkoff, *New Deal for Blacks,* 75; Wolters, "New Deal and the Negro," 170.

47. Robert C. Weaver, "The New Deal and the Negro: A Look at the Facts," *Opportunity,* July, 1935, 202.

48. Wolters, "New Deal and the Negro," 211.

49. "The Roosevelt Record," *Crisis,* Nov., 1940, 343.

50. Nancy J. Weiss, *Farewell to the Party of Lincoln: Black Politics in the Age of FDR* (Princeton: Princeton University Press, 1983), 227.

51. Kenneth O'Reilly, *Nixon's Piano: Presidents and Racial Politics from Washington to Clinton* (New York: Free Press, 1995), 122.

52. Lester B. Granger, "The President, the Negro, and Defense," *Opportunity,* July, 1941, 294.

53. "A Notable Victory," *Opportunity,* Jan., 1939, 2.

54. John B. Kirby, *Black Americans in the Roosevelt Era: Liberalism and Race* (Knoxville: University of Tennessee Press, 1980), 107.

55. "Roosevelt Record," 343.

56. Weiss, *Farewell to the Party of Lincoln,* 136.

57. Ibid., 41.

58. "At the White House," *Crisis,* July, 1933, 160.

59. Guido Van Rijn, *Roosevelt's Blues: African-American Blues and Gospel Songs on FDR* (Jackson: University of Mississippi Press, 1997), 39.

60. "The Democratic Convention," *Opportunity,* July, 1936, 197.

61. "200,000 Negroes Greet President Roosevelt," *New York Age,* Dec. 7, 1935, 1.

62. Weiss, *Farewell to the Party of Lincoln,* 210.

63. Ibid.

64. Franklin D. Roosevelt, "Presidential Statement on New Agriculture Building at Tuskegee Institute," in *The Public Papers and Addresses of Franklin D. Roosevelt,* ed. Samuel I. Rosenman (New York: Random House, 1936), 4:500.

65. "Roosevelt Talks to Alabama Student Group," *New York Times,* Mar. 31, 1939, A16.

66. Franklin D. Roosevelt, "Address at the Dedication of the New Chemistry Building, Howard University," in *The Public Papers and Addresses of Franklin D. Roosevelt,* ed. Samuel I. Rosenman (New York: Random House, 1937), 5:538.

67. Kirby, *Black Americans in the Roosevelt Era,* 20.

68. Stephen Early to Walter White, June 12, 1933, OF 2538 (NAACP), Box 1, Franklin D. Roosevelt Library.

69. Stephen Early to Charles Michelson, June 21, 1935, PPF 1336 (NAACP), Box 1, Franklin D. Roosevelt Library.

70. Marvin McIntyre to William Hassett, June 23, 1935, OF 2538 (NAACP), Box 2, Franklin D. Roosevelt Library.

71. William Hassett to David Niles, June 24, 1938, PPF 1336 (NAACP), Box 1, Franklin D. Roosevelt Library.

72. Allan Morrison, "The Secret Papers of FDR," in *The Negro in Depression and War: Prelude to Revolution, 1930–1945,* ed. Bernard Sternsher (Chicago: Quadrangle, 1964), 67.

73. Weiss, *Farewell to the Party of Lincoln,* 160.

74. Earl Ofari Hutchinson, *Betrayed: A History of Presidential Failure to Protect Black Lives* (Boulder: Westview, 1996), 30.

75. Writers League Against Lynching to Franklin D. Roosevelt, Dec. 4, 1933, OF 93a (Colored Matters), Box 7, Franklin D. Roosevelt Library.

76. "Mr. Roosevelt's Opportunity," *Chicago Defender,* Dec. 9, 1933, 14.

77. Franklin D. Roosevelt, "Address before the Federal Council of Church of Christ in America—'The Right to a More Abundant Life,'" in *The Public Papers and Addresses of Franklin D. Roosevelt,* ed. Samuel I. Rosenman (New York: Random House, 1937), 2:519.

78. W. E. B. Du Bois, "Postscript," *Crisis,* Jan., 1934, 20.

79. Weiss, *Farewell to the Party of Lincoln,* 101.

80. Hutchinson, *Betrayed,* 32.

81. Weiss, *Farewell to the Party of Lincoln,* 245.

82. Walker White, *A Man Called White: The Autobiography of Walter White* (New York: Viking, 1948), 170.

83. Press Conference #125, May 25, 1934, Presidential Press Conferences, Franklin D. Roosevelt Library.

84. Press Conference #198, Apr. 24, 1935, Presidential Press Conferences, Franklin D. Roosevelt Library.

85. Walter White, "Costigan-Wagner Bill," *Crisis,* Jan., 1935, 11.

86. Hutchinson, *Betrayed,* 43.

87. "Negro Vote Reported Still for Democrats," *New York Times,* Feb. 4, 1940, A8.

88. "The Race Riots," *New Republic,* July 5, 1943, 12; Mary McLeod Bethune to Franklin D. Roosevelt, June 22, 1943, PPF 1820 (Speeches), Box 7, Franklin D. Roosevelt Library; Walter White to Franklin D. Roosevelt, June 21, 1943, OF 93c (Colored Matters), Box 8, Franklin D. Roosevelt Library; Statement on a Program of Action on Nation-Wide Race Riots, Conference of National Organizations to Franklin D. Roosevelt, June 29, 1943, OF 93c (Colored Matters), Box 8, Franklin D. Roosevelt Library; "Defeat at Detroit," *Nation,* July 3, 1943, 4.

89. Jonathan Daniels to Franklin D. Roosevelt, June 22, 1943, PPF 1820 (Speeches), Box 7, Franklin D. Roosevelt Library; Franklin D. Roosevelt to Stephen Early, June 23, 1943, PPF 1820 (Speeches), Box 7, Franklin D. Roosevelt Library; Francis Biddle to Franklin D. Roosevelt, July 14, 1943, OF 93c (Colored Matters), Box 8, Franklin D. Roosevelt Library; Franklin D. Roosevelt to Jonathan Daniels, Aug. 17, 1943, OF 93c (Colored Matters), Box 8, Franklin D. Roosevelt Library.

90. William E. Leuchtenburg, "The Conversion of Harry Truman," *American Heritage,* Nov., 1991, 221.

91. Weiss, *Farewell to the Party of Lincoln,* 211.

92. Bernstein, "New Deal," 281; Weiss, *Farewell to the Party of Lincoln,* 296–99.

Chapter Two. Harry Truman and the NAACP

1. Van Rijn, *Roosevelt's Blues*, 204.
2. "Estimate of FDR," 481.
3. Herbert Aptheker, ed., *A Documentary History of the Negro People in the United States,* vol. 4 (New York: Carol Publishing, 1992), 568–69.
4. For studies of President Eisenhower's civil rights rhetoric, see Steven R. Goldzwig and George N. Dionisopoulos, "Crisis at Little Rock: Eisenhower, History, and Mediated Political Realities," in *Eisenhower's War of Words,* ed. Martin J. Medhurst (East Lansing: Michigan State University Press, 1994), 189–221; Martin J. Medhurst, "Eisenhower, Little Rock, and the Rhetoric of Crisis," in *The Modern Presidency and Crisis Rhetoric,* ed. Amos Kiewe (Westport: Praeger, 1994), 19–46. Kennedy's civil rights discourse is analyzed in Windt *Presidents and Protesters;* Steven R. Goldzwig and George N. Dionisopoulos, "John F. Kennedy's Civil Rights Discourse: The Evolution from 'Principled Bystander' to Public Advocate," *Communication Monographs* 56 (1989): 170–98. For rhetorical analyses of Lyndon Johnson's civil rights discourse, see David Zarefsky, "Subordinating the Civil Rights Issue: Lyndon Johnson in 1964," *Southern Speech Communication Journal* 48 (1983): 103–18; David Zarefsky, "Civil Rights and Civil Conflict: Presidential Communication in Crisis," *Central States Speech Journal* 31 (1980): 59–66; and David Zarefsky, "Lyndon Johnson Redefines 'Equal Opportunity': The Beginnings of Affirmative Action," *Central States Speech Journal* 31 (1980): 85–94. For a notable exception to the relative dearth of studies about Truman's civil rights discourse, see Steven R. Goldzwig, "Civil Rights and the Cold War: A Rhetorical History of the Truman Administration's Desegregation of the United States Army," in *Doing Rhetorical History: Concepts and Cases,* ed. Kathleen J. Turner (Tuscaloosa: University of Alabama Press, 1998), 143–69.
5. Truman's February 2, 1948, special message to the Congress on civil rights is treated briefly in Robert Underhill, *The Truman Persuasions* (Ames: Iowa State University Press, 1981), 254. Broader themes in Truman's civil rights discourse are discussed briefly in Celeste Michelle Condit and John Louis Lucaites, *Crafting Equality: America's Anglo-African Word* (Chicago: University of Chicago Press, 1993), 177–78.
6. It is unclear whether theater patrons watched the speech on newsreels or heard an audio broadcast. But one citizen, for example, informed the president that he had "just returned from the theater where I heard your speech on the equality of the races." Letter, Rufus R. Todd to Harry S. Truman, July 6, 1947, White House Central Files, PPF 200 (Speeches), Box 306, Harry S. Truman Library.
7. Letter, Walter White to Harry S. Truman, July 9, 1947, White House Central Files, PPF 200 (Speeches), Box 306, Harry S. Truman Library; Newspaper Clipping, Eleanor Roosevelt, "My Day," July 2, 1947, Papers of George M. Elsey, Speech File, Box 17, Harry S. Truman Library; David McCullough, *Truman* (New York: Simon & Schuster, 1992), 569.
8. William C. Berman, *The Politics of Civil Rights in the Truman Administration* (Columbus: Ohio State University Press, 1970), 9; Franklin D. Mitchell, *Embattled Democracy: Missouri Politics, 1919–1932* (Columbia: University of Missouri Press, 1968), 182; Alonzo L. Hamby, *Man of the People: A Life of Harry S. Truman* (New York: Oxford University Press, 1995), 114; McCoy and Ruetten, *Quest and Response,* 14.

9. McCullough, *Truman*, 588; William E. Leuchtenburg, "The Conversion of Harry Truman," *American Heritage*, Nov., 1991, 66.

10. Robert J. Donovan, *Conflict and Crisis: The Presidency of Harry S. Truman, 1945–1948* (New York: Norton, 1977), 322; McCullough, *Truman*, 247; Ronald D. Sylvia, "Presidential Decision Making and Leadership in the Civil Rights Era," *Presidential Studies Quarterly* 25 (1995): 398; John Egerton, *Speak Now Against the Day: The Generation Before the Civil Rights Movement in the South* (Chapel Hill: University of North Carolina Press, 1995), 411.

11. Barton J. Bernstein, "The Ambiguous Legacy: The Truman Administration and Civil Rights," in *Politics and Policies of the Truman Administration*, ed. Barton J. Bernstein (Chicago: Quadrangle, 1970), 272; Alonzo L. Hamby, *Beyond the New Deal: Harry S. Truman and American Liberalism* (New York: Columbia University Press, 1973), 64–65.

12. Berman, *Politics of Civil Rights in the Truman Administration*, 57; William E. Juhnke, "President Truman's Committee on Civil Rights: The Interaction of Politics, Protest and Presidential Advisory Committee," *Presidential Studies Quarterly* 19 (1989): 594; McCoy and Ruetten, *Quest and Response*, 43.

13. O'Reilly, *Nixon's Piano*, 146.

14. Donovan, *Conflict and Crisis*, 31.

15. Leuchtenburg, "Conversion of Harry Truman," 57; Egerton, *Speak Now Against the Day*, 413.

16. McCoy and Ruetten, *Quest and Response*, 16.

17. O'Reilly, *Nixon's Piano*, 145.

18. McCoy and Ruetten, *Quest and Response*, 15.

19. Donovan, *Conflict and Crisis*, 30; Berman, *Politics of Civil Rights in the Truman Administration*, 8; Lyle Dorsett, *The Pendergast Machine* (New York: Oxford University Press, 1968), 82.

20. Berman, *Politics of Civil Rights in the Truman Administration*, 29; Bernstein, "Ambiguous Legacy," 272; William H. Chafe, "Postwar American Society: Dissent and Social Reform," in *The Truman Presidency*, ed. Michael J. Lacey (Cambridge: Cambridge University Press, 1989), 167; Hamby, *Beyond the New Deal*, 65; O'Reilly, *Nixon's Piano*, 162.

21. Berman, *Politics of Civil Rights in the Truman Administration*, 51–52; McCoy and Ruetten, *Quest and Response*, 52; O'Reilly, *Nixon's Piano*, 153; "President Truman's Committee on Civil Rights," 594; *Speak Now Against the Day*, 414; Sylvia, "Presidential Decision Making and Leadership in the Civil Rights Era," 399; Hamby, *Man of the People*, 640; McCullough, *Truman*, 587.

22. John Hope Franklin, *Racial Equality in America* (Columbia: University of Mississippi Press, 1993), 102.

23. Bernstein, "Ambiguous Legacy," 303; *Politics of Civil Rights in the Truman Administration*, 52; John Hope Franklin, *From Slavery to Freedom: A History of African Americans*, 7th ed. (New York: Knopf, 1994), 461–62.

24. Oral History Interview (No. 398), George M. Elsey, Harry S. Truman Library.

25. Oral History Interview (No. 15), Jonathan Daniels, Harry S. Truman Library.

26. "The Permanent FEPC Drive Continues," *Pittsburgh Courier*, Sept. 22, 1945, 6.

27. McCoy and Ruetten, *Quest and Response*, 51.

28. Harry S. Truman, *Public Papers of the Presidents of the United States: Harry S. Truman, 1946* (Washington, D.C.: GPO, 1947), 423.

29. "Truman Lashes Discrimination," *Chicago Defender*, Sept. 14, 1946, 2.

30. "We Can Help," *Chicago Defender*, Oct. 5, 1946, 14.

31. McCoy and Ruetten, *Quest and Response*, 48.

32. Harry S. Truman, *Public Papers of the Presidents of the United States: Harry S. Truman, 1947* (Washington, D.C.: GPO, 1948), 9; "President Truman's Message," *Chicago Defender*, Jan. 18, 1947, 14; W. E. B. Du Bois, "The Winds of Time," *Chicago Defender*, Feb. 1, 1947, 15.

33. Channing H. Tobias to Harry S. Truman, July 9, 1947, White House Central Files, PPF 200 (Speeches), Box 306, Harry S. Truman Library.

34. "Growth of Political Troubles," *United States News,* May 23, 1947, 22.

35. Sullivan, *Days of Hope,* 243; Bernstein, "Ambiguous Legacy," 232.

36. McCoy and Ruetten, *Quest and Response*, 98; Harvard Sitkoff, "Harry Truman and the Election of 1948: The Coming of Age of Civil Rights in American Politics," *Journal of Southern History* 37 (1971): 597.

37. "Washington Trends," *Newsweek*, June 23, 1947, 12.

38. Sitkoff, "Harry Truman and the Election of 1948," 605.

39. Donovan, *Conflict and Crisis*, 173.

40. Clifford's memorandum recommended a "determined campaign to help the Negro" (and a public campaign to capitalize on its efforts) to win African American votes in the 1948 election. Clark Clifford to Harry S. Truman, Nov. 19, 1947, Papers of Clark M. Clifford, Box 23, Harry S. Truman Library.

41. C. P. Trussell, "Congress Is Split on Truman Report," *New York Times,* Jan. 9, 1947, 15.

42. Leuchtenburg, "Conversion," 60.

43. Walter L. Hixson, *Parting the Curtain: Propaganda, Culture, and the Cold War, 1945–1961* (New York: St. Martin's Griffin, 1997), 129.

44. McCoy and Ruetten, *Quest and Response,* 66.

45. O'Reilly, *Nixon's Piano,* 147.

46. "Largest Mass Meeting in Nation's History Planned by NAACP," in *Papers of the NAACP,* ed. Randolph Boehm (Frederick, Md.: University Publications of America, 1982).

47. McCoy and Ruetten, *Quest and Response,* 73; Berman, *Politics of Civil Rights in the Truman Administration,* 61; David Niles to Matthew Connelly, June 16, 1947, Clark M. Clifford Files, Box 3, Harry S. Truman Library.

48. Philleo Nash to David K. Niles, June 2, 1947, Papers of Philleo Nash, Box 58, Harry S. Truman Library.

49. Speech draft, Robert Carr and Milton Stewart, n.d., Papers of George M. Elsey, Speech File, Box 17, Harry S. Truman Library.

50. Speech draft, Second Draft, June 27, 1947, Papers of George M. Elsey, Speech File, Box 17, Harry S. Truman Library; Speech Draft, Third Draft, Papers of Clark M. Clifford, Presidential Speech File, Box 29, Harry S. Truman Library; Speech Draft, Fourth Draft, Papers of Clark M. Clifford, Presidential Speech File, Box 29, Harry S. Truman Library.

51. For example, Lamar Candle of the Justice Department submitted his comments on a draft of the speech, but his suggestions are marked "Arrived too late for us to use any of the changes he proposed." Speech Draft, Lamar Candle, June 29, 1947, Papers of George M. Elsey, Speech File, Box 17.

52. Eugene E. White and Clair R. Henderlider, "What Harry S. Truman Told Us about His Speaking," *Quarterly Journal of Speech* 40 (1954): 41.

53. All quotations from the speech are taken from the version printed in the *Public*

Papers, 1947, pp. 311–13, edited to include minor changes during the actual delivery (from an audio recording of the speech in the author's possession, available on *The Selected Speeches of Harry S. Truman, 1945–1947,* Harry S. Truman Library).

54. Truman, *Public Papers, 1947,* 98.

55. McCoy and Ruetten, *Quest and Response,* 55.

56. The definition of crisis rhetoric suggested here is taken from Amos Kiewe, ed., *The Modern Presidency and Crisis Rhetoric* (Westport: Praeger, 1994), xvii.

57. Murray Edelman, *Constructing the Political Spectacle* (Chicago: University of Chicago Press, 1988), 12.

58. Sacvan Bercovitch, *The American Jeremiad* (Madison: University of Wisconsin Press, 1978), 159.

59. "Democratic Elections—In Poland," *Crisis,* Mar., 1947, 75; "Foreign Policy and FEPC," *Crisis,* May, 1947, 137.

60. Sacvan Bercovitch, *Rites of Asset: Transformations in the Symbolic Construction of America* (New York: Routledge, 1993), 49.

61. Martin J. Medhurst, *Dwight D. Eisenhower: Strategic Communicator* (Westport: Greenwood, 1993), 110–19.

62. Theodore Sorensen to the President, Nov. 28, 1962, Theodore C. Sorensen Papers, Box 30, John F. Kennedy Library.

63. Proceedings of a Meeting of the President's Committee on Civil Rights, June 30, 1947, Records of the President's Committee on Civil Rights, Box 14, Harry S. Truman Library.

64. McCoy and Ruetten, *Quest and Response,* 74.

65. A search of the Periodicals Content Index (PCI), a computer database that indexes more than two thousand U.S. and international periodicals since their first date of publication, also revealed no international coverage of Truman's address.

66. The articles notes that "Truman delivered, last week, an address . . . intended to exhort all the people of the world . . . to adopt an international program for the defense of human rights" ("Truman Contra la Discriminación," 12). (Translated from the Spanish by the author.)

67. Newspaper Clipping, *Daily Service,* Oct. 1, 1947, White House Central Files, PPF 200 (Speeches), Box 306, Harry S. Truman Library.

68. "Mr. Truman on Civil Rights," *St. Louis Post-Dispatch,* June 30, 1947, 2C.

69. Berman, *Politics of Civil Rights in the Truman Administration,* 65.

70. Walter White to the President, July 9, 1947, White House Central Files, PPF 200 (Speeches), Box 306, Harry S. Truman Library; "Action Needed, NAACP Told," *Philadelphia Afro-American,* July 5, 1947, 1; "Civil Rights, Human Freedom," *Philadelphia Afro-American,* July 5, 1947, 4.

71. Berman, *Politics of Civil Rights in the Truman Administration,* 64.

72. "Harry Truman Speaks," *New York Age,* July 12, 1947, 6.

73. "Truman to the NAACP," *Crisis,* Aug., 1947, 233; "Calls on U.S. Government to Lead the Way," *Chicago Defender,* July 5, 1947, 1; Louis Lautier, "Nation's Capital," *Norfolk Journal and Guide,* July 12, 1947, 7; "Mr. Roosevelt and Mr. Truman," *Pittsburgh Courier,* July 12, 1947, 6; "Now for the Deeds," *Chicago Defender,* July 12, 1947, 14.

74. "Civil Rights, Human Freedom," 4; "Harry Truman Speaks," 6; "President Calls for Fair Play," *Norfolk Journal & Guide,* July 5, 1957, 1; "Calls on U.S. Government to Lead the Way," 1.

75. Brenda Gayle Plummer, *Rising Wind: Black Americans and U.S. Foreign Affairs, 1935–1960* (Chapel Hill: University of North Carolina Press, 1996), 77–80.

76. Channing H. Tobias to the President, July 9, 1947, White House Central Files, PPF 200 (Speeches) Box 306, Harry S. Truman Library; Raymond Pace Alexander to the President, July 15, 1947, Papers of David K. Niles, Box 27, Harry S. Truman Library.

Chapter Three. Dwight Eisenhower against the Extremists

1. Harvard Sitkoff, *The Struggle for Black Equality, 1954–1992*, rev. ed. (New York: Hill and Wang, 1993), 25.
2. Sherman Adams, *Firsthand Report: The Story of the Eisenhower Administration* (New York: Harper & Brothers, 1961), 355.
3. Medhurst, *Dwight D. Eisenhower*, 22.
4. Dwight D. Eisenhower, *Public Papers of the Presidents of the United States: Dwight D. Eisenhower, 1957* (Washington, D.C.: GPO, 1958), 546.
5. Michael S. Mayer, "Regardless of Station, Race or Calling: Eisenhower and Race," in *Dwight D. Eisenhower: Soldier, President, Statesman,* ed. Joann P. Krieg (New York: Greenwood, 1987), 34.
6. Chester J. Pach, Jr., and Elmo Richardson, *The Presidency of Dwight D. Eisenhower,* rev. ed. (Lawrence: University Press of Kansas, 1991), 139.
7. Congress, Senate, Armed Service Committee, *Hearing on Universal Military Training,* 80th Cong., 2nd sess., 1948.
8. Mayer, "Regardless of Station, Race or Calling," 38.
9. Dwight D. Eisenhower, *The White House Years: Waging Peace, 1956–1961* (Garden City: Doubleday, 1965), 148; Arthur Larson, *Eisenhower: The President Nobody Knew* (New York: Charles Scribner's Sons, 1968), 127; Roy Reed, *Faubus: The Life and Times of an American Prodigal* (Fayetteville: University of Arkansas Press, 1997), 209; Oral History Interview, James C. Hagerty (OH 91), Columbia Oral History Project, Dwight D. Eisenhower Library.
10. O'Reilly, *Nixon's Piano,* 165–66.
11. Pach and Richardson, *Presidency of Dwight D. Eisenhower,* 139.
12. Earl Warren, *The Memoirs of Earl Warren* (Garden City: Doubleday, 1977), 291–92; Robyn Duff Ladino, *Desegregating Texas Schools: Eisenhower, Shivers, and the Crisis at Mansfield High* (Austin: University of Texas Press, 1996), 37; Emmet John Hughes, *The Ordeal of Power: A Political Memoir of the Eisenhower Years* (New York: Atheneum, 1963), 201.
13. Larson, *Eisenhower: The President Nobody Knew,* 127, 126.
14. Allan Wolk, *The Presidency and Black Civil Rights: Eisenhower to Nixon* (Rutherford, N.J.: Fairleigh Dickinson University Press, 1971), 220–21.
15. Medhurst, "Eisenhower, Little Rock, and the Rhetoric of Crisis," 21–22.
16. Ladino, *Desegregating Texas Schools,* 55.
17. James C. Duram, *A Moderate among Extremists: Dwight D. Eisenhower and the School Desegregation Crisis* (Chicago: Nelson-Hall, 1981), 252; Robert Frederick Burk, *The Eisenhower Administration and Black Civil Rights* (Knoxville: University of Tennessee Press, 1984), 132.
18. Duram, *A Moderate among Extremists,* 250.
19. Tony Freyer, *The Little Rock Crisis: A Constitutional Interpretation* (Westport: Greenwood, 1984), 120.
20. Burk, *Eisenhower Administration and Black Civil Rights,* 159.

21. Robert F. Burk, "Dwight D. Eisenhower and Civil Rights Conservatism," in *Dwight D. Eisenhower: Soldier, President, Statesman,* ed. Joann P. Krieg (New York: Greenwood, 1987), 52.

22. Pach and Richardson, *Presidency of Dwight D. Eisenhower,* 137.

23. Oral History Interview, Herbert Brownell (OH 157), Columbia Oral History Project, Dwight D. Eisenhower Library.

24. Pach and Richardson, *Presidency of Dwight D. Eisenhower,* 156.

25. O'Reilly, *Nixon's Piano,* 168; Frederick E. Morrow, *Black Man in the White House* (New York: Macfadden, 1963), 11.

26. Wolk, *Presidency and Black Civil Rights,* 33; Pach and Richardson, *Presidency of Dwight D. Eisenhower,* 140.

27. Mayer, "Regardless of Station, Race, or Calling," 39.

28. E. Frederic Morrow to Sherman Adams, June 4, 1957, White House Central Files, OF 142-A (Negro Matters), Box 731, Dwight D. Eisenhower Library.

29. Hughes, *Ordeal of Power,* 347.

30. Herbert Brownell and John P. Burke, *Advising Ike: The Memoirs of Herbert Brownell* (Lawrence: University Press of Kansas, 1993), 197.

31. The White Citizens' Council claimed about 250,000 members at its height between 1956 and 1957 and exercised an influence far more pervasive than membership rolls would indicate. Councils often had a veneer of public respectability—though their rhetoric of white supremacy and racial segregation was scarcely different from that of the Ku Klux Klan—and often usurped the voice of the white community. See Numan V. Bartley, *The Rise of Massive Resistance: Race and Politics in the South during the 1950s* (Baton Rouge: Louisiana State University Press, 1969).

32. Dwight D. Eisenhower, *Public Papers of the Presidents of the United States: Dwight D. Eisenhower, 1956* (Washington, D.C.: GPO, 1958), 304.

33. Herbert Brownell, "Eisenhower's Civil Rights Program: A Personal Assessment," *Presidential Studies Quarterly* 21 (1991): 238.

34. James F. Byrnes to Dwight D. Eisenhower, Nov. 20, 1953, White House Central Files, OF 142-A-4 (Negro Matters), Box 731, Dwight D. Eisenhower Library; Dwight D. Eisenhower to James F. Byrnes, Dec. 1, 1953, Papers as President of the United States, Ann Whitman File, Name Series, Box 3, Dwight D. Eisenhower Library.

35. Eisenhower, *White House Years,* 150.

36. Eisenhower, *Public Papers, 1956,* 114, 115.

37. Dwight D. Eisenhower, *Public Papers of the Presidents of the United States: Dwight D. Eisenhower, 1953* (Washington, D.C.: GPO, 1954), 30.

38. Larson, *Eisenhower,* 14.

39. Pach and Richardson, *Presidency of Dwight D. Eisenhower,* 149.

40. Mar. 21, 1956, Papers as President of the United States, Ann Whitman File, Ann Whitman Diary Series, Box 8, Dwight D. Eisenhower Library.

41. O'Reilly, *Nixon's Piano,* 173.

42. Pach and Richardson, *Presidency of Dwight D. Eisenhower,* 149.

43. Williams Peters, *The Southern Temper* (New York: Doubleday, 1959), 242; Warren, *Memoirs of Earl Warren,* 289; Richard Kluger, *Simple Justice: The History of "Brown v. Board of Education" and Black America's Struggle for Racial Equality* (New York: Knopf, 1976), 753; George H. Gallup, *The Gallup Poll: Public Opinion, 1935–1971,* (New York: Random House, 1972), 2:1332–33; Harry S. Ashmore, *An Epitaph for Dixie* (New York: Norton, 1957), 182.

44. Eisenhower, *White House Years,* 150; Hughes, *Ordeal of Power,* 201, 242; Larson, *Eisenhower,* 124.
45. Hughes, *Ordeal of Power,* 200.
46. Burk, *Eisenhower Administration and Black Civil Rights,* 165.
47. Eisenhower, *Public Papers, 1956,* 734–35, 766.
48. Thurgood Marshall to Dwight D. Eisenhower, Sept. 6, 1956, White House Central Files, GF 124-A-1 (School Decision), Box 916, Dwight D. Eisenhower Library. Central Files, GF 124-A-1 (School Decision), Box 916, Dwight D. Eisenhower Library.
49. Attorney General Brownell believed that the law did not warrant federal intervention in the Mansfield case, believing that the government could only intervene after a desegregation plan had been submitted, approved, and defied—and after the district court had requested the administration to intervene. Other members of the Justice Department, however, argued that the administration should take the initiative and test the federal government's powers in the Mansfield case (Brownell and Burke, *Advising Ike,* 204–5). In the Clinton case, Brownell claimed that "the State of Tennessee is capable of handling any situation which now exists or may arise in Clinton in the future as a result of desegregation in the public schools," despite continued obstruction by local citizens and a request from the Anderson County school board for federal intervention. See: Letter, Herbert Brownell, Jr., to the Chairman and Members of the Anderson County Board of Education, Dec. 4, 1956, White House Office: Staff Research Group, Box 12, Dwight D. Eisenhower Library.
50. Burk, *Eisenhower Administration and Black Civil Rights,* 186.
51. Reed, *Faubus,* 184–85.
52. Burk, *Eisenhower Administration and Black Civil Rights,* 176.
53. Eisenhower, *Public Papers, 1957,* 640–41. Ironically, Eisenhower's language was remarkably similar to that of Faubus's legislative secretary, J. L. (Bex) Shaver. During the gubernatorial campaign of 1956, Faubus directed Shaver and two other officials to formulate a stand on interposition. Contrary to more defiant Arkansans, Shaver tried to develop a conception of interposition that could facilitate change from a segregated to a desegregated school system. In testimony before Congress, Shaver claimed that social justice would take a long time and cannot be legislated: It has "to come from the hearts of people. . . . Real progress wells from the people and is not handed down from above" (Freyer, *Little Rock Crisis,* 79). Given this rhetoric from one of Faubus's key aides and the governor's ultimate obstruction at Little Rock (however related to or incongruous with Shaver's intentions), perhaps it is not surprising that some Arkansas segregationists were shocked by Ike's intervention.
54. Eisenhower, *Public Papers, 1957,* 641.
55. Notes of Telephone Calls, Sept. 11, 1957, Papers as President of the United States, Ann Whitman File, DDE Diary Series, Box 27, Dwight D. Eisenhower Library.
56. Sherman Adams called Eisenhower on September 11 to inform him that Faubus wanted to "find a way out of the situation in which he has gotten and . . . would like to ask for a meeting with the President." Adams also noted that negotiations had begun over a telegram asking for an appointment and that Attorney General Brownell opposed a meeting, believing that Faubus had "soiled himself badly." Eisenhower then called Brownell to discuss the content of a meeting with the governor. Ike also directed Brownell to prepare a telegram that included a state-

ment by the governor that he "would be guided by Federal court orders." Notes of Telephone Calls, Sept. 11, 1957, Papers as President of the United States, Ann Whitman File, DDE Diary Series, Box 27, Dwight D. Eisenhower Library.

57. Oct. 8, 1957, Papers as President of the United States, Ann Whitman File, Administration Series, Box 23, Dwight D. Eisenhower Library.

58. Sept. 14, 1957, Papers as President of the United States, Ann Whitman File, Ann Whitman Diary Series, Box 9, Dwight D. Eisenhower Library.

59. Medhurst, "Eisenhower, Little Rock, and the Rhetoric of Crisis," 31.

60. Andrew Goodpaster to James Hagerty, Sept. 19, 1957, James C. Hagerty Papers, Box 6, Dwight D. Eisenhower Library.

61. Oral History Interview, Allan Shivers (OH 238), Dec. 23, 1969, Columbia Oral History Project, Dwight D. Eisenhower Library.

62. Eisenhower's reluctance to intervene went beyond concern with federal authority. Rather his stand demonstrated extreme loath to intervene in what he perceived to be a state's affair even when federal authority was clear. By September 20, the White House had agreed that there was "no doubt whatever about the authority of the President to call out the troops." Notes of Telephone Calls, Sept. 20, 1957, Papers as President of the United States, Ann Whitman File, DDE Diary Series, Box 27, Dwight D. Eisenhower Library.

63. "Eisenhower Urged to Speak to Nation on Integration," *Norfolk Journal & Guide,* Sept. 21, 1957, 13.

64. "What About It, Ike?" *New York Age,* Sept. 21, 1957, 11.

65. Eisenhower, *Public Papers, 1957,* 679.

66. "Arkansas," *New Republic,* Sept. 16, 1957, 4.

67. Reed, *Faubus,* 224.

68. Woodrow Wilson Mann to Dwight D. Eisenhower, Sept. 23, 1957, James C. Hagerty Papers, Box 6, Dwight D. Eisenhower Library; Eisenhower, *Public Papers, 1957,* 198; Freyer, *Little Rock Crisis,* 108.

69. In a letter to his friend Alfred Gruenther on the morning of September 24, Ike claimed, "I do not want to exaggerate the significance of the admittedly serious situation in Little Rock. I do not want to give the picture of a Cabinet in constant session, or fretting and worrying about the actions of a misguided governor." Dwight D. Eisenhower to General Alfred M. Gruenther, Sept. 24, 1957, Papers as President of the United States, Ann Whitman File, Whitman Diary Series, Box 9, Dwight D. Eisenhower Library.

70. Notes of Telephone Calls, Sept. 24, 1957, Papers as President of the United States, Ann Whitman File, DDE Diary Series, Box 27, Dwight D. Eisenhower Library.

71. Woodrow Wilson Mann to Dwight D. Eisenhower, Sept. 24, 1957, James C. Hagerty Papers, Box 6, Dwight D. Eisenhower Library.

72. Eisenhower, *Public Papers, 1956,* 766; Eisenhower, *Public Papers, 1957,* 546.

73. See, for example, Benjamin Fine, "Little Rock Gets State Police Aid at School Today," *New York Times,* Sept. 23, 1957, A1; and Benjamin Fine, "Little Rock Negro Students to Seek Entry This Week," *New York Times,* Sept. 22, 1957, A1.

74. Proposed Statement, Herbert Brownell, Jr., Sept. 23, 1957, James C. Hagerty Papers, Box 6, Dwight D. Eisenhower Library.

75. Notes of Telephone Calls, Sept. 24, 1957, Papers as President of the United States, Ann Whitman File, DDE Diary Series, Box 27, Dwight D. Eisenhower Library.

76. Three speech drafts are located in the Papers as President of the United States, Ann Whitman File, Speech Series, Box 22; three drafts are in the James C. Hagerty

Papers, Box 6; and one draft is located in the Papers of John Foster Dulles, White House Memoranda Series, Box 5. These collections are held at the Dwight D. Eisenhower Library.

77. Notes of a Telephone Call, Sept. 24, 1957, Papers of John Foster Dulles, Telephone Call Series, Box 7, Dwight D. Eisenhower Library. Dulles also apparently wrote six sentences about the international implications of the resistance in Little Rock, which, with editing, ultimately became the close of the president's speech. Speech Suggestions, White House Office, Office of the Staff Secretary, Subject Series, Alphabetical Subseries, Box 17, Dwight D. Eisenhower Library.

78. Kenneth Burke, *A Grammar of Motives* (Berkeley and Los Angeles: University of California Press, 1969), 7–9.

79. All quotations are from the speech text printed in Eisenhower, *Public Papers, 1957,* 689–94.

80. The abolition of segregation had not produced a truly integrated system in the District of Columbia, but it was a productive start. The American Friends Service Committee and the Anti-Defamation League, for example, applauded the racial progress made in the district's school system (see Burk, *Eisenhower,* 54–60).

81. Burke, *Grammar of Motives,* 9–10.

82. Title III, as originally conceived, would have broadened the definition of federal conspiracy to deprive civil rights to encompass the actions of individuals, increased the penalties for civil rights violations that included loss of life, and authorized the attorney general to file injunctions against obstructions of civil rights. It would have given the attorney general direct authority to intervene in the obstruction of school desegregation plans. Title III was eliminated from the Civil Rights Act of 1957 in large part because of the claims by southern legislators that it would produce federal military intervention in the South.

83. Stephen E. Ambrose, *Eisenhower: The President* (New York: Simon & Shuster, 1984), 420.

84. Reed, *Faubus,* 184.

85. Freyer, *Little Rock Crisis,* 11, 56–57.

86. Medhurst, *Dwight D. Eisenhower,* 111.

87. In the months preceding the Little Rock crisis, the United States had criticized the U.S.S.R. for its human rights violations in Hungary. The Little Rock situation afforded the Soviets an opportunity to turn the tables.

88. Burk, *Eisenhower Administration and Black Civil Rights,* 186.

89. Walter L. Hixon, *Parting the Curtain: Propaganda, Culture, and the Cold War, 1945–1961* (New York: St. Martin's Griffin, 1997), 131.

90. "As Others See Us: U.S. and Little Rock," *Newsweek,* Oct. 7, 1957, 34.

91. "Faubus Rebellion Damages U.S. Prestige in Africa," *Philadelphia Afro-American,* Sept. 28, 1957, 6.

92. Daily Report: Foreign Radio Broadcasts Supplement, Foreign Broadcast Information Service, Sept. 27, 1957, Records of Bryce N. Harlow, Box 11, Dwight D. Eisenhower Library.

93. Medhurst, *Dwight D. Eisenhower,* 110.

94. Jackie Robinson to Dwight D. Eisenhower, Sept. 13, 1957, White House Central Files, GF 124-A-1 (School–Arkansas), Box 920, Dwight D. Eisenhower Library; Roy Wilkins to Dwight D. Eisenhower, Sept. 18, 1957, James C. Hagerty Papers, Box 6, Dwight D. Eisenhower Library; Anita L. Ehrman, "Integration Issue in South Gives Reds Ammunition," *Norfolk Journal & Guide,* Sept. 21, 1957,

1. The *Pittsburgh Courier* also reported that the administration needed to assert its authority so that the nation can "hold its head up with dignity throughout the world as the champion of the underprivileged," Harold L. Keith, "Dixie Governors Plot to Block Intergration," *Pittsburgh Courier,* Sept. 14, 1957, 4.

95. Plummer, *Rising Wind,* 252.

96. For a discussion of this critique, see John Lewis Gaddis, *Strategies of Containment: A Critical Appraisal of Postwar American National Security Policy* (New York: Oxford University Press, 1982), 175–76.

97. Gallup, *Gallup Poll,* 2:1517.

98. Sept. 14–30, 1957, Papers as President of the United States, Ann Whitman File, Ann Whitman Diary Series, Box 9, Dwight. D. Eisenhower Library.

99. "Senators, Governors Comment," *Congressional Quarterly Weekly Report,* Sept. 27, 1957, 1147.

100. Richard B. Russell to Dwight D. Eisenhower, Sept. 26, 1957, Papers as President of the United States, Ann Whitman File, Administration Series, Box 23, Dwight D. Eisenhower Library.

101. Armisted Selden, Jr., to Dwight D. Eisenhower, Sept. 24, 1957, White House Central Files, GF 124-A-1 (School–Arkansas), Box 920, Dwight D. Eisenhower Library.

102. Ambrose, *Eisenhower,* 421.

103. Price Daniel to Dwight D. Eisenhower, Sept. 24, 1957, White House Central Files, OF 142-A-5 (Little Rock, Arkansas, School Integration), Box 732, Dwight D. Eisenhower Library; Dwight D. Eisenhower to Price Daniel, Oct. 3, 1957, White House Central Files, OF 142-A-5 (Little Rock, Arkansas, School Integration), Box 732, Dwight D. Eisenhower Library; Dwight D. Eisenhower to John Stennis, Oct. 7, 1957, White House Central Files, OF 142-A-5 (Little Rock, Arkansas, School Integration), Box 733, Dwight D. Eisenhower Library.

104. Eisenhower's claim that he came to the White House to speak, however, seems to have resonated with at least one southerner. Ft. Worth resident Monty Moncrief wrote to the president on September 25 to commend him on the address: "Your return to White House from your much needed vacation to address the nation on the disgraceful situation in Little Rock is high indicative of your sterling character as president." Telegram, Monty Moncrief to Dwight D. Eisenhower, Sept. 15, 1957, White House Central Files, OF 142-A-5 (Little Rock, Arkansas, School Integration), Box 732, Dwight D. Eisenhower Library.

105. Harry Ashmore to Dwight D. Eisenhower, Sept. 24, 1957, White House Central Files, GF 124-A-1 (School–Arkansas), Box 920, Dwight D. Eisenhower Library; Harry Bullis to Dwight D. Eisenhower, Sept. 25, 1957, White House Central Files, OF 142-A-5 (Little Rock, Arkansas, School Integration), Box 732, Dwight D. Eisenhower Library; Nelson Rockefeller to Dwight D. Eisenhower, Sept. 25, 1957, White House Central Files, PPF 20-X-91 (Little Rock Situation), Box 644, Dwight D. Eisenhower Library.

106. Anthony Lewis, "Eisenhower on Air," *New York Times,* Sept. 25, 1957, 1; "To Preserve the Constitution," *Washington Post,* Sept. 25, 1957, A 13; Ronnie Donnie, "They Like Faubus," *New Republic,* Oct. 14, 1957, 11; "Eisenhower, Faubus, and the Court," *New Republic,* Sept. 30, 1957, 5.

107. "What About It, Ike," *New York Age,* Sept. 21, 1957, 11; "Smashing a Conspiracy," *Pittsburgh Courier,* Oct. 5, 1957, 8; "Salute to the President," *Pittsburgh Courier,* Oct. 12, 1957, 8; "Faubus Still on Spot in Arkansas," *Pittsburgh Courier,* Sept. 28,

1957, 3; "Praises Ike for Action in Arkansas," *Pittsburgh Courier,* Oct. 5, 1957, 5; John B. Henderson, "Do Politicians Want Law or Lawlessness?" *Norfolk Journal & Guide,* Oct. 5, 1957, 8.

108. "Ike Underestimated the South," *Philadelphia Afro-American,* Oct. 5, 1957, 4.

109. Medhurst, "Eisenhower, Little Rock, and the Rhetorical Crisis," 37.

110. Daily Report: Foreign Radio Broadcasts Supplement, Foreign Broadcast Information Service, Sept. 27, 1957, Records of Bryce N. Harlow, Box 11, Dwight D. Eisenhower Library.

111. Alistair Cooke, "The Trouble at Little Rock," *Listener,* Sept. 26, 1957, 462.

112. Foreign Radio Broadcasts Supplement, Foreign Broadcast Information Service, Sept. 27, 1957, Records of Bryce N. Harlow, Box 11, Dwight D. Eisenhower Library.

113. "As Others See Us," *Newsweek,* 34.

114. "Red Press Gloats Over Little Rock," *New York Times,* Sept. 26, 1957, 14.

115. Eisenhower, *Public Papers, 1957,* 704.

116. Freyer, *Little Rock Crisis,* 142–43.

117. Ibid., 18, 73, 172.

Chapter Four. John F. Kennedy and the Moral Crisis of 1963

1. Victor Lasky, *J.F.K.: The Man and the Myth* (New York: Macmillan, 1963), 200–201.

2. Bicknell Eubanks, "Dixie Ponders Kennedy Role," *Christian Science Monitor,* Dec. 3, 1957, 8.

3. Lasky, *J.F.K.,* 202.

4. "Though the Heavens Fall," *Time,* Oct. 12, 1962, 20.

5. John F. Kennedy, *Public Papers of the Presidents of the United States: John F. Kennedy, 1962* (Washington, D.C.: GPO, 1962), 727.

6. Nicholas Katzenbach, "Origin of Kennedy's Civil Rights," in *The Kennedy Presidency: Seventeen Intimate Perspectives of John F. Kennedy,* ed. Kenneth W. Thompson (Lanham: University Press of America, 1985), 52.

7. Manning Marable, *Race, Reform, and Rebellion: The Second Reconstruction in Black America, 1945–1990,* 2nd ed. (Jackson: University Press of Mississippi, 1991), 73.

8. See, for example: Carl M. Brauer, *John F. Kennedy and the Second Reconstruction* (New York: Columbia University Press, 1977), 259–63; Harold C. Fleming, "The Federal Executive and Civil Rights: 1961–1965," *Daedalus* 94 (1965): 941–42; Robert E. Gilbert, "John F. Kennedy and Civil Rights for Black Americans," *Presidential Studies Quarterly* 12 (1982): 395–96; Bruce Miroff, *Pragmatic Illusions: The Presidential Politics of John F. Kennedy* (New York: David McKay, 1976), 256–57; Mark Stern, *Calculating Visions: Kennedy, Johnson, and Civil Rights* (New Brunswick: Rutgers University Press, 1992), 87–88; and Harris Wofford, *Of Kennedys and Kings: Making Sense of the Sixties* (Pittsburgh: University of Pittsburgh Press, 1980), 172–73.

9. Windt, *Presidents and Protestors,* 81–84; Goldzwig and Dionisopoulos, "John F. Kennedy's Civil Rights Discourse," 190–92; Smith and Smith, *White House Speaks,* 148–51.

10. James MacGregor Burns, *John Kennedy: A Political Profile* (New York: Harcourt, Brace, 1960), 148.

11. Richard Reeves, *President Kennedy: Profile of Power* (New York: Simon & Shuster, 1993), 467; Stephen B. Oates, *Let the Trumpet Sound: A Life of Martin Luther King, Jr.* (New York: Harper Collins, 1994), 158; Harry S. Ashmore, *Civil Rights and Wrongs: A Memoir of Race and Politics, 1944–1994* (New York: Pantheon, 1994), 140; Oral History Interview, Harris Wofford, Nov. 29, 1965, John F. Kennedy Library.

12. Brauer, *John F. Kennedy and the Second Reconstruction,* 14.

13. Arthur M. Schlesinger, Jr., *A Thousand Days: John F. Kennedy in the White House* (New York: Fawcett Premier, 1965), 848.

14. Theodore C. Sorensen, *Kennedy* (New York: Harper & Row, 1965), 471.

15. Schlesinger, *Robert Kennedy and His Times* (New York: Ballantine, 1978), 340.

16. Oral History Interview, Harris Wofford, May 22, 1968, John F. Kennedy Library.

17. Clayborne Carson, *In Struggle: SNCC and the Black Awakening of the 1960s* (Cambridge: Harvard University Press, 1995), 88.

18. David Halberstam, *The Children* (New York: Random House, 1998), 253.

19. Sorensen, *Kennedy,* 471.

20. Sitkoff, *Struggle for Black Equality,* 115, 96.

21. Halberstam, *Children,* 253; Reeves, *President Kennedy,* 62.

22. Kennedy did vote for Title III, however, which would have given the attorney general broad powers to intervene in civil rights cases—and likely would have prevented the desegregation crisis at Little Rock and, perhaps, the desegregation crisis at the University of Mississippi.

23. Many blacks also interpreted Kennedy's negotiations during the desegregation crisis at the University of Mississippi to be mere political maneuvering. Martin Luther King, Jr., later claimed that the performance by Governor Ross Barnett and President Kennedy "made Negroes feel like pawns in a white man's political game." See: "It's a Difficult Thing to Teach a President," *Look,* Nov. 17, 1964, 64.

24. Reeves, *President Kennedy,* 60.

25. Brauer, *John F. Kennedy and the Second Reconstruction,* 28.

26. Miroff, *Pragmatic Illusions,* 226.

27. Schlesinger, *Robert Kennedy and His Times,* 883; O'Reilly, *Nixon's Piano,* 190.

28. Hutchinson, *Betrayed,* 115–16.

29. Fleming, "Federal Executive and Civil Rights," 943.

30. The plank favored the enactment of FEPC legislation and promised "effective moral and political leadership" by the president "to make equal opportunity a living reality for all Americans." "Party Platforms of 1960: Democratic Platform," in *History of American Presidential Elections, 1789–1968,* ed. Arthur M. Schlesinger, Jr., and Fred L. Israel (New York: Chelsea House, 1971), 4:3509.

31. Sorensen, *Kennedy,* 471. Taylor Branch, *Parting the Waters: America in the King Years, 1954–1963* (New York: Simon & Schuster, 1993), 918–19. In a recent article for the *New York Times,* Anthony Lewis recalls Kennedy's speech with fondness and longs for moral leadership on the social problems confronting the nation; Anthony Lewis, "Because It Is Right," *New York Times,* Apr. 28, 1997, A15. John F. Kennedy, "Speech by Senator John F. Kennedy, Washington, January 14, 1960," in *History of American Presidential Elections, 1789–1968,* ed. Arthur M. Schlesinger, Jr., and Fred L. Israel (New York: Chelsea House, 1971), 4:3539.

32. Kennedy, "Speech by Senator John F. Kennedy, Washington, January 14, 1960," 4:3540.

33. United States Congress, Senate Committee on Commerce, *Freedom of Communications: Final Report of the Committee on Commerce* (Washington, D.C.: GPO, 1961), 1:635, 1055.

34. Leo Egan, "Kennedy Assures Liberals He Seeks No Support in South," *New York Times,* June 24, 1960, 1.

35. United States, *Freedom of Communications,* 1:191–92, 1:1083, 3:150–51.

36. Ibid., 1:432, 1075.

37. Henry Hampton and Steve Fayer, eds., with Sarah Flynn, *Voices of Freedom: An Oral History of the Civil Rights Movement from the 1950s through the 1980s,* (New York: Bantam, 1990), 69–71.

38. Campaign biographer Theodore White claimed, "The entire episode received only casual notice from the generality of American citizens in the heat of the last three weeks of the presidential campaign. But in the Negro community the Kennedy intervention rang like a carillon." Theodore H. White, *The Making of the President, 1960* (New York: Atheneum, 1961), 323.

39. Wofford, *Of Kennedys and Kings,* 175.

40. David J. Garrow, *Bearing the Cross: Martin Luther King Jr. and the Southern Christian Leadership Conference* (New York: William Morrow, 1986), 128; Wofford, *Of Kennedys and Kings,* 24.

41. John F. Kennedy, *Profiles in Courage,* rev. ed. (New York: Harper & Row, 1964), 258.

42. Wofford, *Of Kennedys and Kings,* 31; Kathleen Hall Jamieson, *Packaging the Presidency: A History and Criticism of Presidential Campaign Advertising,* 3rd ed. (New York: Oxford University Press, 1996), 143.

43. *J.F.K. Remembered: A Special Look Back at John F. Kennedy's 1000 Days as President,* Prod. ABC News, 1988, videocassette. Farmer claims that his decision to undertake the Freedom Rides, which caused the administration grief, was inspired in part by Kennedy's words about change and freedom. Reeves, *President Kennedy,* 123.

44. Gerald S. Strober and Deborah H. Strober, eds., *"Let Us Begin Anew": An Oral History of the Kennedy Presidency* (New York: Harper Collins, 1993), 273.

45. Simeon Booker, "What Negroes Can Expect from Kennedy," *Ebony* Jan., 1961, 33; Civil rights leaders had also helped create the feeling that President Kennedy should provide the moral leadership he promised. In an article for the *Nation* on February 4, 1961, King claimed, "A second area in which the president can make a significant contribution toward the elimination of racial discrimination is that of moral persuasion." Martin Luther King, Jr., *A Testament of Hope: The Essential Writings and Speeches of Martin Luther King, Jr.,* ed. James M. Washington (New York: Harper Collins, 1986), 154.

46. Victor S. Navasky, *Kennedy Justice* (New York: Atheneum, 1971), 97.

47. Garrow, *Bearing the Cross,* 162.

48. "What the Negro American Wants," *Crisis,* June/July 1963, 343.

49. King, *Testament of Hope,* 112; "Dr. King Denounces President on Civil Rights," *New York Times,* June, 10 1963, 1.

50. "Races: The Long March," *Time,* June 21, 1963, 16.

51. Leonard Ingalls, "North Cautioned by Urban League," *New York Times,* June 10, 1963, 1.

52. "J.F.K. Called on to Show Some Guts," *Philadelphia Afro-American,* June 22, 1963, 26.

53. "Terribly Dangerous," *Newsweek,* June 10, 1963, 27.

54. Schlesinger, *Thousand Days,* 852–53.

55. John F. Kennedy, *Public Papers of the Presidents of the United States: John F. Kennedy, 1960* (Washington, D.C.: GPO, 1961), 1, 2.

56. John F. Kennedy, *Public Papers of the Presidents of the United States: John F. Kennedy, 1961* (Washington, D.C.: GPO, 1962), 22, 75.

57. Kennedy, *Public Papers, 1961,* 397.

58. David Halberstam, *The Best and the Brightest* (New York: Random House, 1969), 41.

59. Stern, *Calculating Visions,* 4.

60. Kennedy, *Public Papers, 1961,* 22.

61. Schlesinger, *Thousand Days,* 538.

62. Halberstam, *Children,* 254.

63. Robert Kennedy telephoned King personally and asked him to avoid further demonstrations, which would alienate support and embarrass the president. Oral History Interview, Martin Luther King, Jr., Mar. 9, 1964, John F. Kennedy Library.

64. Wofford, *Of Kennedys and Kings,* 156.

65. Herbert S. Parmet, *J.F.K.: The Presidency of John F. Kennedy* (New York: Dial, 1983), 255.

66. Sorensen, *Kennedy,* 484; Kennedy, *Public Papers, 1962,* 728.

67. King, *Testament of Hope,* 522.

68. Garrow, *Bearing the Cross,* 232.

69. Milton Viorst, *Fire in the Streets: America in the 1960s* (New York: Touchstone, 1981), 215.

70. Garrow, *Bearing the Cross,* 248.

71. White, *Making of the President,* 170.

72. News reports about and images of the racial violence in Birmingham circulated internationally. Radio Moscow—broadcasting in more than thirty languages—claimed, "We have the impression that American authorities both cannot and do not wish to stop outrages by racists" (Reeves, *President Kennedy,* 488). *Pravda* ran a story titled, "Monstrous Crimes Among Racists in the United States." The Soviets broadcast 1,420 anti-American commentaries in the two weeks following the settlement at Birmingham. And the *New York Times* reported that Birmingham was competing with an insurrection in Haiti for top billing in news media across non-Communist Asia. See Branch, *Parting the Waters,* 786, 807.

73. John F. Kennedy, *Public Papers of the Presidents of the United States: John F. Kennedy, 1963* (Washington, D.C.: GPO, 1964), 372.

74. Branch, *Parting the Waters,* 791.

75. Ingalls, "North Cautioned by Urban League," 1.

76. Branch, *Parting the Waters,* 787.

77. Proposed Statement, no date, President's Office Files, Subject File, Box 96, John F. Kennedy Library.

78. Kennedy, *Public Papers, 1963,* 408.

79. Stern, *Calculating Visions,* 86.

80. Oral History Interview, Burke Marshall, June 14, 1964, John F. Kennedy Library.

81. John W. Bowers, Donovan J. Ochs, and Richard J. Jensen, *The Rhetoric of Agitation and Control,* 2nd ed. (Prospect Heights, Ill.: Waveland, 1993), 119.

82. Transcript of a Conversation between Robert F. Kennedy and George Wallace, Apr. 25, 1963, Robert F. Kennedy Papers, John F. Kennedy Library.

83. E. Culpepper Clark, *The Schoolhouse Door: Segregation's Last Stand at the University of Alabama* (New York: Oxford University Press, 1993), 205.

84. The events of the final two days of the desegregation of the University of Alabama are captured on Robert Drew Associates' 1963 documentary film *Crisis: Behind a Presidential Commitment.* My account is drawn primarily from this film, and the quotations from the participants in the desegregation are taken from my transcription of Drew's documentary.

85. Clark, *Schoolhouse Door,* 215.

86. The attorney general had called his brother early on the morning of June 11, recommending that he federalize the Guard before Katzenbach's attempt to gain entry for the students. JFK said the administration should wait and let Wallace make the first move. Oral History Interview, Robert F. Kennedy, Dec. 6, 1964, John F. Kennedy Library.

87. Gilbert, "John F. Kennedy and Civil Rights for Black Americans," 396; Fleming, "Federal Executive and Civil Rights," 942.

88. Stern, *Calculating Visions,* 87–88.

89. "Art of the Necessary," *Commonweal,* June 14, 1963, 317; Richard L. Strout, "Kennedys Feel Civil-Rights Heat," *Christian Science Monitor,* June 1, 1963, 1.

90. Sorensen, *Kennedy,* 495; Notes ["RFK Notes"], Robert F. Kennedy, Dec. 11, 1963, President's Office Files, Box 45, John F. Kennedy Library. The final paragraphs do not appear in the second draft contained in Sorensen's papers at the Kennedy Library. Speech Draft ["TCS–2nd draft"], Theodore Sorensen, June 11, 1963, Theodore C. Sorensen Papers, Box 73, John F. Kennedy Library.

91. Louis Martin to Robert F. Kennedy, May 13, 1963, White House Central Files, EX HU2/MC, Box 365A, John F. Kennedy Library.

92. George Reedy to Lyndon Johnson, May 24, 1963, Vice Presidential Civil Rights File, Box 6, Lyndon B. Johnson Library.

93. Edison Dictaphone Recording of a Conversation between Lyndon Johnson and Theodore Sorensen, June 3, 1963, Lyndon B. Johnson Library.

94. For a discussion of the suggestions made by Johnson that found their way into Kennedy's speech, see Roderick P. Hart and Kathleen E. Kendall, "Lyndon Johnson and The Problem of Politics: A Study in Conversation," in *Beyond The Rhetorical Presidency,* ed. Martin J. Medhurst (College Sation: Texas A&M University Press, 1996), 77–103. Table 2 of their chapter is titled "Rhetorical Suggestions Offered and Accepted in the Johnson-Sorensen Conversation." It illustrates the inclusion of five of Johnson's rhetorical suggestions into the president's June 11 speech.

95. Norbert A. Schlei to Robert F. Kennedy, June 4, 1963, Robert F. Kennedy Papers, Attorney General's General Correspondence, Box 11, John F. Kennedy Library.

96. Michael P. Riccards, "Rare Counsel: Kennedy, Johnson, and the Civil Rights Bill of 1963," *Presidential Studies Quarterly* 11 (1981): 397.

97. Schlessinger, *Robert Kennedy and His Times,* 343; Sorensen, *Kennedy,* 495.

98. Burke Marshall claims: "Every single person who spoke about it in the White House—every one of them—was against . . . his speech in June, against making it a moral issue, against the March on Washington. The conclusive voice within the government at that time, there's not question about it at all, that Robert

Kennedy was the one. He urged it, he felt it, he understood it." Oral History Interview, Burke Marshall, June 14, 1964, John F. Kennedy Library.

99. Schlessinger, *Robert Kennedy and His Times,* 348.
100. See Alasdair MacIntyre, *After Virtue: A Study in Moral Theory* (Notre Dame: Notre Dame University Press, 1981); Walter R. Fisher, "Narration as Human Communication Paradigm: The Case of Public Moral Argument," *Communication Monographs* 51 (1984): 1–22; Thomas S. Frentz, "Rhetorical Conversation, Time, and Moral Argument," *Quarterly Journal of Speech* 71 (1985): 1–18.
101. Robert N. Bellah, "Civil Religion in America," *Daedalus* 96 (1967): 2–3.
102. Roderick P. Hart, *The Political Pulpit* (West Layfayette, Ind.: Purdue University Press, 1977), 12.
103. Russell B. Nye, *This Almost Chosen People: Essays in the History of American Ideas* (East Lansing: Michigan State University Press, 1966), 165.
104. Mircea Eliade, *The Sacred and the Profound: The Nature of Religion,* trans. Willard R. Trask (New York: Harper and Row, 1959), 68.
105. Kenneth Burke, *Attitudes Toward History,* 3rd ed. (Berkeley and Los Angeles: University of California Press, 1984), 129.
106. George Washington, *The Writings of George Washington,* ed. John C. Fitzpatrick, vol. 30 (Washington, D.C.: GPO, 1939), 294–95; Herman Melville, *Redburn, White-Jacket, and Moby Dick,* ed. G. Thomas Tanselle (New York: Library of America, 1982), 506.
107. Bellah, "Civil Religion in America," 5.
108. John 8:7; Matthew 7:3–5, *New Revised Standard Version Bible.* Lyndon Johnson had made a similar appeal in a civil rights address at Tufts University the previous day. Johnson claimed that civil rights "is not a sectional problem . . . no part of our country is so without sin that it can cast the first stone."
109. Graham, *Civil Rights Era,* 75.
110. Louis Martin, "Organizing Civil Rights," in *The Kennedy Presidency: Seventeen Intimate Perspectives of John F. Kennedy,* ed. Kenneth W. Thompson (Lanham, Md.: University Press of America, 1985), 93.
111. Telephone Conversation between the President and James H. Davis, June 14, 1963, President's Office Files, Presidential Recordings and Transcripts, Dictabelt 22A, Item 3, John F. Kennedy Library.
112. Ingalls, "North Cautioned by Urban League," 22.
113. Kennedy's argument that civil rights was a national issue, not merely a southern problem, was prescient; yet, it received almost no attention during his time. In July, 1963, the *Progressive* commended Kennedy for his reference to civil rights problems in the North but noted that "his words did not command the attention they deserved." See: "The North Is Next," *Progressive,* July, 1963, 3–4. The president's words about northern racial problems have commanded little attention from scholars since 1963.
114. Matthew 7:12, *New Revised Standard Version Bible.*
115. Celeste Michelle Condit, "Crafting Virtue: The Rhetorical Construction of Public Morality," *Quarterly Journal of Speech* 73 (1987): 84.
116. Chaim Perelman and Lucie Olbrechts-Tyteca, *The New Rhetoric: A Treatise on Argumentation,* trans. John Wilkinson and Purcell Weaver (Notre Dame, Ind.: Notre Dame University Press, 1969), 221–22.
117. Kennedy appeals here to what seems to have been a common *topos* in public discourse about race in the early 1960s. For example, in 1961, John Howard Griffin

published *Black Like Me*, a book that describes the author's attempt to take the perspective of blacks in the South. In 1962, ABC-TV aired *Walk in My Shoes*, Nicholas Webster's sixty-minute documentary that invited its audience to see the world from a black point of view.

118. Kennedy had used this same passage, almost verbatim, during his second televised debate with Richard Nixon in 1960. Louis Martin had given these statistics to Harris Wofford, who then forwarded them to Senator Kennedy.

119. Condit, "Crafting Virtue," 89.

120. Immanuel Kant, *On the Foundation of Morality,* trans. Brendan E. A. Liddell (Bloomington: Indiana University Press, 1970), 140.

121. Perelman and Olbrechts-Tyteca, *New Rhetoric,* 222; Condit, "Crafting Virtue," 83.

122. "The South States Its Case," *U.S. News & World Report,* June 24, 1963, 78.

123. Phillip S. Foner and George E. Walker, eds., *Proceedings of the Black National and State Conventions, 1840–1865,* vol. 1 (Philadelphia: Temple University Press, 1979), 310.

124. Du Bois, *Crisis,* Nov., 1910, 10.

125. Hughes, *Collected Poems,* 191.

126. Frederick Douglass, "What to the Slave Is the Fourth of July?" in *The Frederick Douglass Papers,* vol. 2., ed. John W. Brassingame, et al. (New Haven: Yale University Press, 1979), 359–88.

127. James Weldon Johnson, *The Selected Writings of James Weldon Johnson,* vol. 1, ed. Sondra Kathryn Wilson (New York: Oxford University Press, 1995), 182.

128. King, *Testament of Hope,* 301, 302.

129. Even opponents of the address recognized its importance: former Mississippi Governor J. P. Coleman called Kennedy's speech "the greatest challenge to the South in 100 years." Bill Simpson, "Ex-Gov. Coleman Flays President," *Jackson Clarion-Ledger,* June 12, 1963, 1.

130. Richard H. Rovere, "Letters from Washington," *New Yorker,* June 22, 1963, 90.

131. Anthony Lewis, "A New Racial Era," *New York Times,* June 13, 1963, 14; "Gone with the Wind," *St. Petersburg Times,* June 12, 1963, 14A; "Address by President Gives Calm Appraisal," *Nashville Tennessean,* June 12, 1963, 14; "Appeal to Conscience," *St. Louis Post-Dispatch,* June 12, 1963, President's Office Files, Speech Files, Box 45, John F. Kennedy Library; "Races: The Long March," *Time* June 21, 1963, 17.

132. "J.F.K. in the 'Bully Pulpit,'" *Newsweek,* June 24, 1963, 27; "We Face a Moral Crisis," *Milwaukee Journal,* June 12, 1963, President's Office Files, Speech Files, Box 45, John F. Kennedy Library; Rovere, "Letters from Washington," 90; Ted Lewis, "Capitol Stuff," *New York Daily News,* June 14, 1963; "JFK: The Leader Is Led," *Daily Standard,* June 12, 1963. The last two articles are located in President's Office Files, Speech Files, Box 45, John F. Kennedy Library.

133. "Law and Justice," *New Republic,* June 22, 1963, 3; Loren Miller, "Freedom Now— But What Then?" *Nation,* June 29, 1963, 539; "North Is Next," 3.

134. Martin Luther King, Jr., to John F. Kennedy, June 12, 1963, White House Central Files, Box 1478, John F. Kennedy Library; Roy Wilkins to John F. Kennedy, June 12, 1963, NAACP Papers, Transfile 2 ("Government–National, Kennedy, John F., General, 1961–1963"), Library of Congress; Jackie Robinson, "A Salute to Kennedy," *Norfolk Journal & Guide,* June 22, 1963, 6; "JK's Right Plea Seen Greatest Since Lincoln: Will Nation Heed It?" *Norfolk Journal and Guide,* June 15,

1963, 1; "The President's Great Speech," *Philadelphia Afro-American,* June 22, 1963, 4.

135. Garrow, *Bearing the Cross,* 269, 265, 274.

136. Branch, *Parting the Waters,* 828.

137. "South States Its Case," 78.

138. Karl E. Meyer, "The Kennedy Revolution," *New Statesman,* June 14, 1963, 889–90, 890; Murray Kempton, "Speech Day," *Spectator,* June 14, 1963, 766; "Comment," *Manchester Guardian Weekly,* June 27, 1963, 8; an editorial in the June 14 issue of *Life* magazine, for instance, urged the president to "cancel his European trip and tend to these compelling matters at home." "More Law—Plus Leadership," *Life,* June 14, 1963, 4.

139. Gallup, *Gallup Poll,* 2:1869, 1789, 1828.

140. The *Christian Science Monitor* reported on this kind of anxiety on May 31: "The question being asked is whether the Kennedy administration's efforts are sufficient. Will they stave off violence? Will they assure that the Negro, in his sudden impatience after long years of waiting, does not now 'lose faith in the American dream?'" William H. Stringer, "State of the Nations: Administration's Race Policy," *Christian Science Monitor,* May 31, 1963, 1.

141. Walter Lippman, "Point of No Return," *Washington Post,* June 11, 1963, A15.

142. "An End and a Beginning," *Newsweek,* June 24, 1963, 29.

143. "President's Great Speech," 4.

144. John Lewis, "Text of Speech to be Delivered at Lincoln Memorial, August 28, 1963," *Student Nonviolent Coordinating Committee Papers, 1959–1972* (Sanford, N.C.: Microfilming Corporation of America, 1982).

145. John Lewis, with Michael D'Orso, *Walking with the Wind: A Memoir of the Movement* (New York: Simon & Schuster, 1998), 198.

146. "Many Citizens Request Copies of Speech That Shook Nation," *Norfolk Journal & Guide,* June 22, 1963, 9; Chalmers M. Roberts, "Kennedy Speaks Out: Moment Well Chosen to Push Rights Drive," *Washington Post,* June 12, 1963, A6.

147. Condit and Lucaites, *Crafting Equality,* 1.

148. Sorensen, *Kennedy,* 470, 494, 495.

149. Schlesinger, *Thousand Days,* 881.

150. Goldzwig and Dionisopoulos, "John F. Kennedy's Civil Rights Discourse," 190; Brauer, *John F. Kennedy and the Second Reconstruction,* 259; Stern, *Calculating Visions,* 88; Miroff, *Pragmatic Illusions,* 257.

151. Lyndon B. Johnson, *Vantage Point: Perspectives of the Presidency, 1963–1969* (New York, Holt, Rinehart and Winston, 1971), 18.

152. Lyndon B. Johnson, *Public Papers of the Presidents of the United States: Lyndon B. Johnson, 1963–1964* (Washington, D.C.: GPO, 1965).

Chapter Five. Lyndon Johnson Overcomes

1. Hart, *Sound of Leadership,* 210.

2. David Zarefsky, "Lyndon B. Johnson," *American Orators of the Twentieth Century: Critical Studies and Sources,* ed. Bernard K. Duffy and Harold R. Ryan (Westport, Conn.: Greenwood, 1987), 224.

3. E. W. Kenworthy, "Congress Ready to Move Swiftly on Voting Rights," *New York Times,* Mar. 17, 1965, 29.

4. Merle Miller, *Lyndon: An Oral Biography* (New York: Putnam's, 1980), 56.

5. Stern, *Calculating Visions,* 116.

6. Hugh Sidney, *A Very Personal Presidency: Lyndon Johnson in the White House* (New York: Antheneum, 1968), 109.

7. Leonard Baker, *The Johnson Eclipse: A Presidency's Vice Presidency* (New York: Macmillan, 1966), 198.

8. Monroe Billington, "Lyndon B. Johnson and Blacks: The Early Years," *Journal of Negro History* 62 (1977): 28.

9. Ibid., 29.

10. Stern, *Calculating Visions,* 118.

11. Billington, "Lyndon B. Johnson and Blacks," 31.

12. Williams overwhelmingly approved of Johnson's job as Texas director and claimed that LBJ "was running the best NYA program in all of the states." Bethune held Johnson in far greater esteem than the other southern youth administrators. Robert Dallek, *Lone Star Rising: Lyndon Johnson and His Times, 1908–1960* (New York: Oxford University Press, 1991), 143.

13. Paul K. Conkin, *Big Daddy from the Pedernales: Lyndon Baines Johnson* (Boston: Twayne, 1986), 79.

14. Booth Mooney, *The Lyndon Johnson Story* (New York: Farrar Straus, 1956), 35.

15. Stern, *Calculating Visions,* 119.

16. Robert Mann, *The Walls of Jericho: Lyndon Johnson, Hubert Humphrey, Richard Russell, and the Struggle for Civil Rights* (New York: Harcourt Brace, 1996), 66.

17. Johnson, *Vantage Point,* 155.

18. Billington, "Lyndon B. Johnson and Blacks," 33.

19. Mann, *Walls of Jericho,* 65.

20. Ibid., 84.

21. Dallek, *Lone Star Rising,* 369.

22. Billington, "Lyndon B. Johnson and Blacks," 28.

23. Mann, *Walls of Jericho,* 155.

24. Billington, "Lyndon B. Johnson and Blacks," 41.

25. Stern, *Calculating Visions,* 144.

26. Conkin, *Big Daddy from the Pedernales,* 139.

27. Mann, *Walls of Jericho,* 230.

28. Stern, *Calculating Visions,* 143.

29. Georgia Democrat Herman Talmadge developed a new filibuster strategy to ensure a southern victory. By organizing their opposition into platoons, southerners were able to drain their opponents and filibuster successfully.

30. Tom Wicker, *JFK and LBJ: The Influence of Personality upon Politics* (New York: Morrow, 1968), 173; "Lyndon Johnson and the Civil Rights Revolution: A Panel Discussion," in *Lyndon Baines Johnson and the Uses of Power,* ed. Bernard J. Firestone and Robert C. Vogt (New York: Greenwood, 1988), 182.

31. Wofford, *Of Kennedys and Kings,* 47.

32. Mann, *Walls of Jericho,* 272.

33. Oral History Interview, James Farmer, Oct., 1969, Oral History Collection, Lyndon B. Johnson Library; Conkin, *Big Daddy from the Pedernales,* 143.

34. "Lyndon Johnson and the Civil Rights Revolution," 174.

35. Mann, *Walls of Jericho,* 318.

36. Conkin, *Big Daddy from the Pedernales,* 164.

37. For example, in a conversation with Mississippi senator John Stennis, Johnson

conveyed the experience of two of his employees, Gene and Helen Williams: "Well you know, John, the other day a sad thing happened. Helen Williams and her husband, Gene . . . drove my official car from Washington down to Texas. . . . They drove through your state, and when they got hungry, they stopped at the grocery stores on the edge of town in colored areas and bought Vienna sausages and beans and ate them with a plastic spoon. And when they had to go to the bathroom, they would stop, pull off on a side road, and Helen Williams, an employee of the vice-president of the United States, would squat in the road to pee. And you know, John, that's just bad. That's wrong. And there ought to be something to change that. And it seems to me that if people in Mississippi don't change it voluntarily, that it's just going to be necessary to change it by law." Miller, *Lyndon,* 367.

38. Baker, *Johnson Eclipse,* 227–29.
39. Steven F. Lawson, "Civil Rights," in *Exploring the Johnson Years,* ed. Robert A. Divine (Austin: University of Texas Press, 1981), 97.
40. Mann, *Walls of Jericho,* 384.
41. Soon after the assassination on November 22, 1963, Johnson spoke with Farmer, King, Young, NAACP lobbyist Clarence Mitchell, and A. Philip Randolph, president of the Brotherhood of Sleeping Car Porters.
42. "Negro Leaders Meet LBJ—Here are the Results They See," *U.S. News and World Report,* Dec. 16, 1963, 49; "Man of the Year: Never Again Where He Was," *Time,* Jan. 3, 1964, 27; E. W. Kenworthy, "Joint Chiefs See President; Hear Demand for Economy," *New York Times,* Nov. 30, 1963, 1.
43. Eric F. Goldman, *The Tragedy of Lyndon Johnson* (New York: Knopf, 1969,) 64–65.
44. Bruce Altschuler, *LBJ and the Polls* (Gainesville: University of Florida Press, 1990), 21.
45. Robert Dallek, "Lyndon B. Johnson, 1963–1969," in *Character Above All: Ten Presidents from FDR to George Bush,* ed. Robert A. Wilson (New York: Simon & Schuster, 1995), 115.
46. Ibid., 181.
47. Carl T. Rowan, "Was LBJ the Greatest Civil Rights President Ever?" *Ebony,* Dec., 1990, 76; Hutchinson, *Betrayed,* 142.
48. Robert Dallek, *Flawed Giant: Lyndon Johnson and His Times, 1961–1973* (New York: Oxford University Press, 1998), 111.
49. Graham, *Civil Rights Era,* 23.
50. Robert A. Caro, *The Years of Lyndon Johnson: Means of Ascent* (New York: Knopf, 1990), xviii.
51. See, for example: George Reedy, *Lyndon Johnson: A Memoir* (New York: Andrews & McMeel, 1982), 52; Tulis, *Rhetorical Presidency,* 161; Windt, *Presidential Rhetoric,* 52; David Zarefsky, "The Great Society as a Rhetorical Proposition," *Quarterly Journal of Speech* 65 (1979): 366.
52. See, for example, Doris Kearns, *Lyndon Johnson and the American Dream* (New York: Harper & Row, 1976), 217–18; Lawson, "Civil Rights," 116.
53. David J. Garrow, *Protest at Selma: Martin Luther King Jr. and the Voting Rights Act of 1965* (New Haven: Yale University Press, 1978), 36; Johnson, *Vantage Point,* 161; Goldman, *Tragedy of Lyndon Johnson,* 318, 228.
54. A report on voting registration and participation presented to the president in mid-December emphasized the continuing problem of racial discrimination in

voting and suggested that only rigid safeguards established by the federal government would eradicate the discrimination discovered by the U.S. Commission on Civil Rights. Report of the President's Commission on Registration and Voting Participation, Nov. 26, 1963, Lyndon B. Johnson Library.

55. Lee White to Bill Moyers, Dec. 30, 1964, Lee White Papers, Box 3, Lyndon B. Johnson Library.

56. Task Force Issue Paper on Civil Rights [authored by Louis Martin, Roy Wilkins, Jeanne Noble, Whitney Young, Berl Bernhard, D'Jaris Watson, Lee White, and Cliff Alexander], July 17, 1964, Legislative Background: Voting Rights Act of 1965, Box 1, Lyndon B. Johnson Library.

57. Matthew Reese to Lyndon Johnson, Dec., 1964, Office Files of Lee White, Box 3, Lyndon B. Johnson Library.

58. Nicholas Katzenbach to Lyndon Johnson, Dec. 28, 1964, Justice Department Administrative History, Volume 7, Part Xa, Lyndon B. Johnson Library.

59. Lyndon B. Johnson, *Public Papers of the Presidents of the United States: Lyndon B. Johnson, 1965* (Washington, D.C.: GPO, 1966), 5.

60. In a press conference just prior to the State of the Union message, Bill Moyers told reporters that LBJ soon would make proposals to end voting rights restrictions. He added: "Now whether these will take the form of a Constitutional Amendment or legislation has not been decided finally." News Conference, Jan. 4, 1965, Legislative Background: Voting Rights Act of 1965, Box 1, Lyndon B. Johnson Library.

61. Garrow, *Protest at Selma*, 42.

62. Constitutional Amendment, Draft, Jan. 8, 1965, Justice Department Administrative History, Volume 7, Part Xa, Lyndon B. Johnson Library.

63. John D. Morris, "President to Ask Law to End Curbs of Negro Voting," *New York Times,* Feb. 7, 1965, 1.

64. Steven F. Lawson, *Black Ballots: Voting Rights in the South, 1944–1969* (New York: Columbia University Press, 1976), 309.

65. John D. Pomfret, "President Promises Dr. King Vote Move," *New York Times,* Feb. 10, 1965, 1.

66. Lee White to Lyndon Johnson, Mar. 4, 1965, White House Central Files, LE HU2/2-7, Box 66, Lyndon B. Johnson Library.

67. Horace Busby to Bill Moyers and Lee White, Nov. 27, 1965, Office Files of Bill Moyers, Box 6, Lyndon B. Johnson Library.

68. Graham, *Civil Rights Era,* 92.

69. United States Congress, *Congressional Record,* vol. 3, part 2 (Washington, D.C.: GPO, 1965), 1913.

70. Telegram to Lyndon Johnson [from a bipartisan group of eleven House members who traveled to Selma], Feb. 19, 1965, Legislative Background: Voting Rights Act of 1965, Box 1, Lyndon B. Johnson Library.

71. "GOP Group Demands Action on Voting Rights," *Washington Post,* Feb. 24, 1965, A5.

72. Johnson, *Vantage Point,* 162.

73. Lloyd F. Bitzer, "The Rhetorical Situation," *Philosophy & Rhetoric* 1 (1968): 6.

74. In conversations with Vice President Hubert Humphrey, Johnson emphasized his strong desire for voting rights legislation. Humphrey claims: "He used to tell me, 'Yes, yes, Hubert, I want all those other things—buses, restaurants, all of that—but the right to vote with no ifs, ands, or buts, that's the key. When the

Negroes get that, they'll have every politician, north and south, east and west, kissing their ass, begging for their support.'" Miller, *Lyndon,* 371. In an oral history interview, White House aide Jack Valenti claimed, "It was his judgment . . . that the key to all the Negroes' future free movement and power in the United States had to do with the vote." Oral History Interview, Jack Valenti, Oct. 18, 1969, Oral History Collection, Lyndon B. Johnson Library.

75. See President Johnson's press conference of Saturday, Mar. 13, 1965. Johnson, *Public Papers, 1965,* 279.

76. Johnson, *Vantage Point,* 162.

77. Busby's draft was a revision and substantial expansion of a preliminary draft message prepared by the Justice Department. Memorandum, Horace Busby to Bill Moyers and Lee White, Feb. 27, 1965, Horace Busby Papers, Box 3, Lyndon B. Johnson Library.

78. Harry McPherson to Lyndon Johnson, Mar. 12, 1965, Appointment File (Diary Backup), Box 15, Lyndon B. Johnson Library.

79. Both McPherson's draft and White's draft are undated (though they include suggestions that McPherson had made in a memorandum dated March 12) and are located in the Office Files of Horace Busby, Box 3, Lyndon B. Johnson Library.

80. White House aide Jack Valenti took thorough notes at this meeting. All subsequent references and quotations from this meeting are taken from these notes. Notes of an Oval Office Meeting, Jack Valenti, Mar. 14, 1965, Appointment File (Diary Backup), Box 15, Lyndon B. Johnson Library.

81. Johnson, *Vantage Point,* 164.

82. The administration went to great lengths to convince the public that LBJ had written the speech. In a White House report on March 16, Jack Valenti noted: "There is considerable speculation and interest in the President's speech of Monday night: Who was the principal writer? How was it written, the method and the timing, etc? I have responded . . . with the following: The President wrote the speech. He talked out what he wanted to say—and as drafts were prepared in response to his dictation, the President personally edited and revised. . . . I mention this to pointup the interest—and to caution our people NOT to mention the names of anyone who had anything to do with the speech else they will take that as evidence of someone doing the principal creative effort." Report to the President, Jack Valenti, Mar. 16, 1965, Legislative Background: Voting Rights Act of 1965, Box 1, Lyndon B. Johnson Library.

83. Stern, *Calculating Visions,* 218.

84. Johnson *Vantage Point,* 162.

85. All quotations from the speech are taken from the version printed in the *Public Papers, 1965,* 281–87, edited to include changes made during the actual delivery (from a videotape of the speech in the author's possession).

86. Congress, House, Committee on the Judiciary, *Voting Rights: Hearings before Subcommittee No. 5 of the Committee on the Judiciary.* 1965.

87. Notes of an Oval Office Meeting, Jack Valenti, Mar. 14, 1965, Appointment File (Diary Backup), Box 15, Lyndon B. Johnson Library.

88. Bellah, *Broken Covenant,* 3.

89. Irving Bernstein, *Guns or Butter: The Presidency of Lyndon Johnson* (New York: Oxford University Press, 1996), 235.

90. George Meany to Lyndon Johnson, Mar. 16, 1965, EX SP2-3/1965/HU2-7, Box 68, Lyndon B. Johnson Library.

91. Earl Warren to Lyndon Johnson, Mar. 15, 1965, EX SP2-3/1965/HU2-7, Box 68, Lyndon B. Johnson Library.

92. Richard L. Strout, "Johnson Gives His Pledge," *Christian Science Monitor,* Mar. 17, 1965, 1; "The Starry Heavens—The Moral Law," *Newsweek,* Mar. 29, 1965, 19; "Civil Rights," *Time,* Mar. 26, 1965, 20; "A Continuing Battle," *New Republic,* Mar. 27, 1965, 5; "LBJ's Best," *New Republic,* Mar. 27, 1965, 4; "The Nation Aroused," *Nation,* Mar. 29, 1965, 321.

93. Tom Wicker, "Johnson Urges Congress at Joint Session to Pass Law Insuring Negro Vote," *New York Times,* Mar. 16, 1965, 31.

94. "America's Conscience," *Christian Science Monitor,* Mar. 17, 1965, 14.

95. "Nation Aroused," 321; "A Continuing Battle," *New Republic,* Mar. 27, 1965, 5.

96. Wicker, "Johnson Urges Congress," 1; "Starry Heavens," 20.

97. "We Shall Overcome," *New York Times,* Mar. 16, 1965, 44.

98. "LBJ's Best," 4.

99. Carl Rowan to Lyndon Johnson, Aug. 6, 1965, EX SP2-3/1965/HE, Box 67, Lyndon B. Johnson Library.

100. "The Road from Selma," *New Statesman,* Mar. 19, 1965, 429; Murray Kempton, "President Johnson's Challenge," *Spectator,* Mar. 19, 1965, 348; Richard Scott, "President Calls for Equal Rights," *Manchester Guardian Weekly,* Mar. 18, 1965, 3.

101. Robert M. Sayre to Juanita Roberts, Apr. 6, 1965, EX SP2-3/1965/HE, Box 67, Lyndon B. Johnson Library.

102. Plummer, *Rising Wind,* 322.

103. Martin Luther King, Jr., to Lyndon Johnson, Mar. 16, 1965, EX SP2-3/1965/HU2-7, Box 68, Lyndon B. Johnson Library; King, *Testament of Hope,* 228; "Rights Aides Hail Johnson Address," *New York Times,* Mar. 17, 1965, 27; John Lewis to Lyndon Johnson, Apr. 20, 1965, White House Central Files, SP2-3/1965, Box 67, Lyndon B. Johnson Library; A. Philip Randolph to Lyndon Johnson, Mar. 17, 1965, EX SP2-3/1965/HU2-7, Box 68, Lyndon B. Johnson Library.

104. Helen Thomas, "LBJ's Speech Grasps Heartbreaks and Hopes," *Kansas City Call,* Mar. 19, 1965, 4,1.

105. "We Shall Overcome," *Kansas City Call,* Mar. 19, 1965, 19.

106. "President Johnson's Message," *Norfolk Journal & Guide,* Mar. 27, 1965, 8.

107. "What Selma Crusade Means," *Philadelphia Afro-American,* Mar. 27, 1965, 4.

108. "President Johnson's Message," 8.

109. Jackie Robinson, "3 Cheers for LBJ," *Norfolk Journal & Guide,* Mar. 27, 1965, 8.

110. "It Took a Hundred Years," *Pittsburgh Courier,* Apr. 3, 1965, 10.

111. "That Speech—LBJ Goes All the Way!" *Amsterdam News,* Mar. 20, 1965, 1; "We Are Overcoming," *Amsterdam News,* Mar. 20, 1965, 1.

112. Alvin Spivak, "We Shall Overcome, Says the President," *Norfolk Journal & Guide,* Mar. 20, 1965, 1.

113. "We Shall Overcome," 19.

114. "President Johnson's Message," 8.

115. Hampton and Fayer, *Voices of Freedom,* 236.

116. King, *Testament of Hope,* 217–18.

117. John Lewis with Michael D'Orso, *Walking with the Wind: A Memoir of the Movement* (New York: Simon & Schuster, 1998), 340.

118. Carson, *In Struggle,* 161.

119. James Forman, *The Making of Black Revolutionaries: A Personal Account* (New York: Macmillan, 1972), 336.

120. Mary King, *Freedom Song: A Personal Story of the 1960s Civil Rights Movement* (New York: William Morrow, 1987), 480.

121. Hampton and Fayer, *Voices of Freedom,* 238.

122. Viorst, *Fire in the Streets,* 321.

123. Ibid., 330.

124. Joseph A. Califano, Jr., *The Triumph and Tragedy of Lyndon Johnson: The White House Years* (New York: Simon & Schuster, 1991), 56; Conkin, *Big Daddy from the Pedernales,* 216.

125. "We Shall Overcome," 19; Spivak, "We Shall Overcome, Says the President," 1; Stern, *Calculating Visions,* 228.

126. "Dissoi Logoi," in *Older Sophists,* ed. Rosamond Kent Sprague (Columbia: University of South Carolina Press, 1972), 283, 279.

127. Miller, *Lyndon,* 435.

128. An April 11, 1965, Gallup poll reported that 34 percent of respondents claimed that President Johnson was pushing too fast on civil rights; 38 percent claimed that the administration was moving at about the right pace; and 17 percent claimed that LBJ was not moving fast enough. Gallup, *Gallup Poll,* 3:1933.

129. Viorst, *Fire in the Streets,* 341.

Chapter Six. Presidential Rhetoric and the Civil Rights Era

1. Mann, *Walls of Jericho,* 481.

2. Garry Wills, *Nixon Agonistes* (New York: New American Library, 1971), 272–73.

3. Rowland Evans, Jr., and Robert D. Novak, *Nixon in the White House* (New York: Random House, 1971), 136–37.

4. Condit and Lucaites, *Crafting Equality,* xii–xiii.

5. Edelman, *Constructing the Political Spectacle,* 73.

6. O'Reilly, *Nixon's Piano,* 290.

7. Recent revisionist histories of Nixon's presidency underscore that he did take some positive measures on civil rights, such as supporting the Philadelphia Plan and signing voting rights amendments and equal opportunity legislation. See: Hugh Davis Graham, "Richard Nixon and Civil Rights: Explaining an Enigma," *Presidential Studies Quarterly* 26 (1996): 93–106; Joan Hoff, *Nixon Reconsidered* (New York: Basic Books, 1994), 89–113. Yet Congress forced Nixon's hand on most of these issues, and his civil rights policies were, at best, ideologically inconsistent—or motivated purely by political calculations at worst. In any case, Nixon's civil rights rhetoric itself was inconsistent, and his rhetoric also was incongruous with his policies.

8. Richard M. Nixon, *Public Papers of the Presidents of the United States: Richard M. Nixon, 1970* (Washington, D.C.: GPO, 1971), 312, 318.

9. In speeches soon after the March 24, 1970, statement, Nixon began using the "quality education" terminology. For representative examples, see the desegregation portions of his 1970 speeches in St. Petersburg, Florida, and Longview, Texas.

10. O'Reilly, *Nixon's Piano,* 304.

11. John D. Ehrlichman, *Witness to Power* (New York: Simon & Schuster, 1982), 223; Stephen E. Ambrose, *Nixon: The Triumph of a Politician* (New York: Simon & Schuster, 1989), 407.

12. Richard M. Nixon, *Public Papers of the Presidents of the United States: Richard M. Nixon, 1973* (Washington, D.C.: GPO, 1974), 129.

13. O'Reilly, *Nixon's Piano,* 304.

14. Burke, *Grammar of Motives,* 362.

15. Civil religious language repelled some civil rights activists who were on the margins of the movement. Some members of SNCC, for example, decried moderate civil rights leaders as "preachers" and were searching for an areligious protest rhetoric.

16. Bercovitch, *Rites of Asset,* 49.

17. Ike's implicit message that obstructionists should obey the Court's ruling because it is national law was inadequate, since many southerners were unwilling to obey a law that they perceived as unjust. Segregationists could use the rhetoric of the civil rights movement itself to justify their actions, since many civil rights activists advocated resisting unjust Jim Crow laws.

18. This understanding of equality is consonant with that of the Founding Fathers, who did not believe the phrase "all men are created equal" to mean that all people possess equal endowments or are entitled to equal conditions. Stephen E. Lucas, "Justifying America: The Declaration of Independence as a Rhetorical Document," in *American Rhetoric: Context and Criticism,* ed. Thomas W. Benson (Carbondale: Southern Illinois University Press, 1989), 86.

19. For discussions of common features of foreign crisis rhetoric, see: Bonnie J. Dow, "The Function of Epideictic and Deliberative Strategies in Presidential Crisis Rhetoric," *Western Journal of Speech Communication* 53 (1989): 294–310; Richard A. Cherwitz and Kenneth S. Zagacki, "Consummatory Versus Justificatory Crisis Rhetoric," *Western Journal of Speech Communication* 50 (1986): 307–24; Theodore Otto Windt, Jr., "The Presidency and Speeches on International Crisis: Repeating the Rhetorical Past," in *Essays in Presidential Rhetoric,* 3rd ed., ed. Theodore Otto Windt, Jr., and Beth Ingold (Dubuque: Kendall/Hunt, 1992), 125–34.

20. Other studies of presidential rhetoric during moments of domestic crises include: Medhurst, "Eisenhower, Little Rock, and the Rhetoric of Crisis"; Goldzwig and Dionisopoulos, "Crisis at Little Rock"; Goldzwig and Dionisopoulos, "John F. Kennedy's Civil Rights Discourse"; and Zarefsky, "Civil Rights and Civil Conflict."

Index

Bullis, Harry, 98
"bully pulpit," 7–8, 9, 59, 66, 71, 103, 114, 136, 220
Bunche, Ralph, 21, 23
Burk, Robert, 73
Burke, Kenneth, 83, 85, 139, 210
Burns, James MacGregor, 3
Busby, Horace, 179
busing, 202
Byrd, Harry, 165, 167
Byrd, James, Jr., 219
Byrnes, James, 41, 62, 67

Caldwell, Arthur, 74
Califano, Joseph, Jr., 195
Carmichael, Stokely, 193
Caro, Robert, 171
Carr, Robert, 42
Carter, Jimmy, 136
categorical imperative, 142
Celler, Emmanuel, 182
Center for New Black Leadership, 5
Central High School. *See* Little Rock, Ark.
Chafe, William H., 35
Chicago Defender, 20, 23, 26, 31, 38, 39, 40, 54, 55, 99, 148, 169
Christian morality, 134, 145, 207
Christian Science Monitor, 105, 132, 187
Christian virtue, 139, 143, 145–46
Churchill, Winston, 44
civic virtue, 107, 136, 154, 207
Civilian Conservation Corps, 163
civil liberties, 38
civil religion, 137–38, 139, 184–86, 198, 211
civil rights: broadening conceptions of, 46–47, 57; as crisis, 208; as equal opportunity, 52; and international affairs, 49–50, 52, 93–95, 111, 120–22, 215; as moral issue, 104, 106, 135–36, 154, 157; and presidential leadership, 8; as southern problem, 197–98
Civil Rights Act (1957), 64, 74, 85, 110, 113, 126, 167, 176
Civil Rights Act (1960), 64–65, 176
Civil Rights Act (1964), 158, 159, 172–73, 176
Clark, Culpepper, 128

Clark, Jim, 176
Clark, Ramsey, 197
Clay, Lucius, 61
Clement, Frank, 72
Clifford, Clark, 41, 42, 108
climate, 91
Clinton, Bill, 4–5, 12, 13, 219–20
Clinton, Tenn., 67, 72–73, 102
Cloud, John, 176–77
Cold War, 94, 120–22, 205, 215; and civil rights, 3, 100–101; shaping Kennedy's rhetoric, 113; and Truman, 41–42, 44, 49, 52
Collier's, 53
Collins, LeRoy, 192
Columbia, Tenn., 44
Commonweal, 132
Communism, 93, 215
Condit, Celeste, 141, 142, 155, 202
Conference on National Organizations, 28
Congress, 8–9, 10, 11, 149
Congress of Industrial Organizations, 28
Congress of Racial Equality (CORE), 39, 117, 168
Conkin, Paul, 163, 167, 168–69, 195
Connelly, Matthew, 42
Connor, Eugene "Bull," 123
Constitution, 11, 45, 46, 141, 144, 209–10
context, 17, 204
Cooke, Alistair, 100
Coolidge, Calvin, 32
Corwin, Edward, 7, 8
Costigan-Wagner Bill, 27
Council on African Affairs, 93
courage, 134, 157
credibility, 16, 83, 84
crises, 17; domestic, 218–19; real v. spurious, 11, 14, 217; rhetoric of, 11, 107, 136, 154, 160, 217
Crisis (film), 132
Crisis (NAACP periodical), 18, 20, 22, 23, 24, 26, 27, 37, 49–50, 53, 54, 145, 148
Cuban Missile crisis, 121

Daily Standard, 147
Dallek, Robert, 165

public opinion, 57; rhetoric, 4, 6, 10; symbolic power, 7–8, 14
President's Committee on Civil Rights, 35, 38, 44, 51, 56
President's Committee on Equal Employment Opportunity, 169
President's Committee on Government Contracts, 65
President's Initiative on Race and Reconciliation, 4, 12
Profiles in Courage, 116, 118
Progressive, 148
Progressive Citizens of America, 40
protest rhetoric, 146
public discourse. *See* rhetoric
public opinion, 7–8, 11, 14, 51, 57, 96, 151, 181, 198, 201
public personae, 16
Public Works Administration, 19–20
Pullum, Joe, 18

Rabb, Maxwell, 79–80
race riots, 28–29
racial code words, 201–202
racial violence, 26, 28–29, 34, 38, 45, 48, 52, 65, 120–21, 200–201. *See also* lynching
racism, 120, 132, 200
Radio Moscow, 100
Radio Warsaw, 100
Randolph, A. Philip, 22, 149
Raper, Arthur, 21
Rayburn, Sam, 165
Reconstruction, 83
Reed, Roy, 62
Reedy, George, 133–34, 174
Reese, Matthew, 173
Reeves, Richard, 108, 110
Republican Party, 40
Reynolds, Gerald, 5
Rhein-Neckar-Zeitung, 100
rhetoric: and action, 5, 11; and crises, 209; and courage, 154; as governance, 11, 12; and moral theory, 138; and policy, 30, 180; and presidential power, 7–8; as sermonic, 136; symbolic force, 9, 13; timing, 152–53, 155–57, 161
rhetorical criticism, 6, 15–18, 56

rhetorical leadership, 5–6, 8, 11, 132, 203–204
Richardson, Elmo, 64, 68
riots, 199
"ritual of consensus," 211
Roberts, Chalmers, 153
Robeson, Paul, 38
Robinson, Jackie, 94, 148, 189
Robinson, Joseph, 27
Rockefeller, Nelson, 98, 125
Rolph, James, 26
Roosevelt, Eleanor, 33, 116–17
Roosevelt, Franklin D., 7; action on civil rights, 18–23, 29–30; death, 31–32; "four freedoms" vocabulary, 211; rhetoric, 4, 24–27, 29–30, 104; and rise of civil rights movement, 6; silence on civil rights, 25–26, 28–29, 36–37, 56, 203–204; symbolic action, 23–24, 29–30
Roosevelt, Theodore, 114
Ross, Malcolm, 41
Rossiter, Clinton, 7–8
Ruetten, Richard, 34, 44, 52
Rusk, Dean, 130
Russell, Richard, 96–97, 144, 150, 165, 166, 167
Rustin, Bayard, 149

St. Louis Post-Dispatch, 53, 147
St. Petersburg Times, 147
scapegoating rhetoric, 136
scene-act ratio, 85
scene-agent ratio, 83
Schlei, Norbert, 134
Schlesinger, Arthur M., Jr., 112, 120, 135, 155, 156
school desegregation, 166
scriptures, 141
"second constitution," 11
"Second Reconstruction," 106
secular and sacred, 141
secular prayer, 139
secular time, 185
segregation, 20, 125, 140, 157; de facto, 202–203. *See also Brown v. Board of Education*
Selden, Armisted, Jr., 96
Sellers, Cleveland, 193

PROPERTY OF THE LIBRARY
YORK COUNTY COMMUNITY COLLEGE
112 COLLEGE DRIVE
WELLS, MAINE 04090
(207) 646-9282

Presidential Rhetoric Series
Martin J. Medhurst, General Editor

Medhurst, Martin J., ed. *Beyond the Rhetorical Presidency.*
   1996.
Medhurst, Martin J. and H.W. Brands, eds. *Critical Reflections
   on the Cold War: Linking Rhetoric and History.* 2000.

PROPERTY OF THE LIBRARY
YORK COUNTY COMMUNITY COLLEGE
112 COLLEGE DRIVE
WELLS, MAINE 04090
(207) 646-9282